HD 9000 6 F5

Er
lif

Date Due

ENDING HUNGER IN OUR LIFETIME

THE JOHNS HOPKINS UNIVERSITY PRESS

Other Books Published
in Cooperation with the
International Food Policy
IFPRI Research Institute

Intrahousehold Resource Allocation in Developing Countries: Models, Methods, and Policy / Edited by Lawrence Haddad, John Hoddinott, and Harold Alderman

Sustainability, Growth, and Poverty Alleviation: A Policy and Agroecological Perspective / Edited by Steven A. Vosti and Thomas Reardon

Famine in Africa: Causes, Responses, and Prevention / By Joachim von Braun, Tesfaye Teklu, and Patrick Webb

Paying for Agricultural Productivity / Edited by Julian M. Alston, Philip G. Pardey, and Vincent H. Smith

Out of the Shadow of Famine: Evolving Food Markets and Food Policy in Bangladesh / Edited by Raisuddin Ahmed, Steven Haggblade, and Tawfiq-e-Elahi Chowdhury

Agricultural Science Policy: Changing Global Agendas / Edited by Julian M. Alston, Philip G. Pardey, and Michael J. Taylor

The Politics of Precaution: Genetically Modified Crops in Developing Countries / By Robert L. Paarlberg

Land Tenure and Natural Resource Management: A Comparative Study of Agrarian Communities in Asia and Africa / Edited by Keijiro Otsuka and Frank Place

Seeds of Contention: World Hunger and the Global Controversy over GM Crops / By Per Pinstrup-Andersen and Ebbe Schiøler

Innovation in Natural Resource Management: The Role of Property Rights and Collective Action in Developing Countries / Edited by Ruth Meinzen-Dick, Anna Knox, Frank Place, and Brent Swallow

Reforming Agricultural Markets in Africa / By Mylène Kherallah, Christopher Delgado, Eleni Gabre-Madhin, Nicholas Minot, and Michael Johnson

The Triangle of Microfinance: Financial Sustainability, Outreach, and Impact / Edited by Manfred Zeller and Richard L. Meyer

ENDING HUNGER IN OUR LIFETIME
FOOD SECURITY AND GLOBALIZATION

by C. Ford Runge, Benjamin Senauer,
Philip G. Pardey, *and* Mark W. Rosegrant

SOUTH PLAINS COLLEGE LIBRARY

Published for the International Food
Policy Research Institute

The Johns Hopkins University Press
Baltimore and London

© 2003 The International Food Policy Research Institute
All rights reserved. Published 2003

Photographs © Sebastião Salgado (Contact Press Images)

The generous support of the Ford Foundation has made this book possible.

Printed in the United States of America on acid-free paper
9 8 7 6 5 4 3 2 1

The Johns Hopkins University Press
2715 North Charles Street
Baltimore, Maryland 21218-4363
www.press.jhu.edu

International Food Policy Research Institute
2033 K Street, N.W.
Washington, D.C. 20006
(202) 862-5600
www.ifpri.org

SOUTH PLAINS COLLEGE LIBRARY

LIBRARY OF CONGRESS CATALOGING-IN-PUBLICATION DATA

Ending hunger in our lifetime : food security and globalization / by C. Ford Runge . . . [et al.].
    p.   cm.
    "Published for the International Food Policy Research Institute."
    Includes bibliographical references and index.
    ISBN 0-8018-7725-3 (alk. paper) — ISBN 0-8018-7726-1 (pbk. : alk paper)
    1. Produce trade—Government policy—International cooperation. 2. Food industry and trade—Government policy—International cooperation. 3. Food supply—Government policy—International cooperation. 4. Globalization—Moral and ethical aspects. I. Runge, C. Ford (Carlisle Ford)
    HD9000.6.E53 2003
    338.1′9—dc21   2003044709

A catalog record for this book is available from the British Library.

This book is dedicated to our children—
Elizabeth, Carl, Alicia, Neil, Katie, Toby, Sydney,
Melissa, and Michael—and to all the world's children.

Expose thyself to feel what wretches feel,
That thou may'st shake the superflux to them,
And show the heavens more just.

KING LEAR (3.4.38–41)

Hunger will not take a day to end. It is not going to
end tomorrow or the day after. And it is certainly not going
to end suddenly by itself, for nothing good comes easy.

BABA A. ISABELLA

16 years old, Nalerigu, Ghana
From *A Better World in 2020:*
Wake-Up Calls from the Next Generation,
IFPRI/2020 Vision booklet, 2001

CONTENTS

FIGURES

TABLES

FOREWORD

Hunger, and the misery that accompanies it, have been scourges for millennia. Some people may always go hungry some of the time. But in a global society, increasingly interconnected communities can no longer conjure excuses for failing to banish the chronic, recurring, hunger-related crises afflicting their neighbors. In fact, the global community stands indicted for knowing much about how to reduce hunger, but not doing so. In this context, "business as usual" takes on a distinctly unethical meaning, describing as it does a global effort falling far short of ending hunger anytime soon, even by 2050. To transform business as usual into a just, economically viable, and sustainable process, rich and poor countries alike will have to make a concerted effort to increase investments, produce technological innovations, create more effective and new institutions at the local, national, and international levels, and strengthen or establish viable social safety nets for the poor. Only then can we end hunger and thereby realize the most basic of human rights.

This book presents a wide-ranging array of ideas, arguments, facts, and figures on ending hunger, drawing on new insights and research by the authors and others. It complements the work of the International Food Policy Research Institute's 2020 Vision initiative, extending and deepening themes from the recently published action plan, *Reaching Sustainable Food Security for All by 2020: Getting the Priorities and Responsibilities Right.*

Despite its breadth and complexity, the book argues clearly and readably that we know a lot about how to reduce hunger. This is not just wishful thinking. It is a hard assessment of what we know and what we can expect in the decades ahead. The authors detail the main actions required to make it happen in ways that sustain future food production while protecting the natural environment. At the core of this strategy are the basic concepts of social justice, public goods, and human capital. Throughout, the authors also highlight the ethical and moral dimensions of hunger.

No one can pretend that ending hunger will be easy, but it *must* and *can* be done. This book brings us closer to a shared sense of a partnership that spans civil organizations, government agencies, and private firms in pursuit of this goal. We hope it will bring efforts to end hunger to the attention of a wide audience and help to galvanize them to seek a world free, once and for all, from hunger's pangs.

Joachim von Braun
Director General, IFPRI

David Beckmann
President, Bread for the World

PREFACE

This book was written at a hinge in history. It began with generous support from the Ford Foundation in the late 1990s, during a period of unparalleled prosperity in the rich countries but persistent poverty and hunger in many poor ones. It was completed in the wake of growing economic and political instability, civil society discontent, and the terrorist attacks in New York and Washington, all of which contributed to the growing unease over the relationship between the world's rich and poor. This book provides a vision for a multilateral approach to addressing global hunger problems.

While these dramatic shifts made writing this book more difficult, they reinforced one of its main themes: that global peace and stability can only be achieved by ending the deprivation of the world's poor. Our goal in writing this book is to reach a wide audience with the message that widespread world hunger can be ended. The book is not meant to be a technical, academic study, although we did distill key findings from a large amount of research the International Food Policy Research Institute (IFPRI) and many others have done on this topic. Many colleges and universities offer courses on world food and agriculture or global nutrition, poverty, population, and environmental issues for which this book could serve as the main or a supplemental text. In addition, the book is written for anyone with a direct interest in the topic whether they be in an international or government agency, the NGO (nongovernmental organization) community, or elsewhere. Above all, we hope to reach people who are generally concerned about world hunger and poverty and who want to better understand the issue.

To underscore the reality and urgency of the issues involved, we have included the photographs of Sebastião Salgado, the famous Brazilian photographer. We believe they contribute significantly to the overall message of this book because they provide compelling visual evidence of both the suffering and the individual dignity of the world's poor, hungry, and dispossessed people.

In the writing, the book was a broadly collaborative effort. Bernard Wasow, then at the Ford Foundation, challenged us to write what it would take, in specific and rigorous terms, to end hunger in our lifetimes. Each of us assumed responsibility for developing forward-looking proposals in areas where we felt most qualified. Ford Runge worked mainly on trade, development, and institutional questions. Ben Senauer analyzed the relationship between hunger, poverty, and income growth. Phil Pardey focused on science, technology, and agricultural research. And Mark Rosegrant considered the sustainability of the environment, water, and food supply.

The institutional basis of this collaborative effort had three parts. First, the grant from the Ford Foundation supported the International Food Policy Research Institute (IFPRI), in Washington, D.C., where Pardey was and Rosegrant is a senior research fellow. Second, IFPRI supported Runge and Senauer at the University of Minnesota. Third, a share of the Ford grant went to Bread for the World, a nondenominational church-based organization headquartered in Washington, D.C., which focuses on hunger issues around the world. Bread for the World engaged Michael Kuchinsky, a political scientist and ordained minister, to coordinate studies of food security, especially in Africa. Michael's participation in the overall project was important and valued, continually emphasizing ethical and moral aspects of food security.

Behind these contributions were numerous other researchers and assistants at all three institutions, including Nienke Beintema, Connie Chan-Kang, Siet Meijer, Cai Ximing, and Patricia Zambrano at IFPRI; Louise Letnes, Mona Sur, and LeeAnn Jackson at Minnesota; and Bob Hoehn at Bread for the World. We also received skillful and able assistance from Uday Mohan, Heidi Van Schooten, Elaine Reber, Mary Jane Banks, Phyllis Skillman, and Kathleen Flaherty. Finally, we benefited enormously from the thought-provoking and extensive review comments by Marc Cohen at IFPRI, Vernon Ruttan at the University of Minnesota, Bernard Wasow of the Century Fund, and Brian Wright at the University of California, Berkeley, as well as David Beckmann at Bread for the World.

We began and ended our work on this book with two international meetings. In April 1999, 30 individuals from academic, aid, government, and civil organizations from around the world gathered at a workshop held at IFPRI to identify action strategies to end hunger. Precisely three years later, in a meeting postponed for several months due to the events of September 11, a group of 25 experts came together at Airlie House in Virginia, for a dialogue on ending hunger. This volume is much the better for the information, ideas, and insights we gleaned from those gatherings.

This book attempts to capture and synthesize what we know about poverty and hunger and how to end it. But it also reports new and important findings and projections by the authors for the purposes of writing this book. It thus builds on the work of others, while also drawing together disparate trends on food security to make a fresh and new argument in favor of ending hunger forever. For any errors or omissions, we remain fully responsible.

THE HASSANS—A PORTRAIT OF HUNGER

Meet the Hassans.[1] The Hassans live in Bangladesh, a country of some 128 million people about the size of the state of Wisconsin, which is one of the poorest countries outside of Africa. Eighty percent of Bangladeshis live, like the Hassans, in small agricultural villages. Much of the country is a vast rainfed delta where rice is the major staple. The monsoon rains of summer are the source of life, but too much rainfall and runoff, accelerated by deforestation in the mountains, can mean excessive flooding, killing young rice plants. Too little rain means drought and death for animals and people, especially the old and very young. The vagaries of nature, especially water, spell life or death for the Hassans and people like them who live on the edge. The Hassans' days are filled with hard physical work, and they are frequently sick. Their lives are defined by a daily struggle to eat. Millions more in Bangladesh and hundreds of millions throughout the developing world live like them.

The Hassan household includes a husband of 59, a wife of 44, two sons ages 14 and 11, and a 7-year-old granddaughter. An elderly invalid aunt also lives with them. The couple also has two older sons who have gone off to find work. The sons are not currently sending any money home, although such remittances are common. The parents have no formal education, but their 14-year-old has completed the eighth grade and their 11-year-old the fifth grade. Like many such families, they have lost children to early death. One, a boy, died at two from tetanus, a terrible infection for which vaccination is common elsewhere in the world. A baby girl died after only seven days.

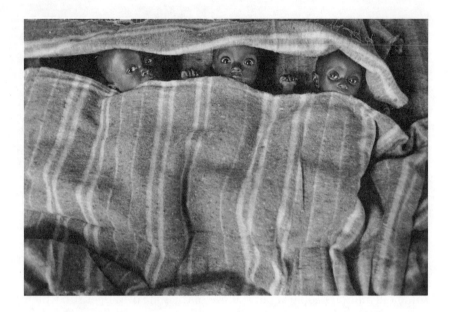

The family has three small plots of land, all owned by Mr. Hassan, who inherited them from his family. One, where their home sits, is a plot of about 2,500 square feet. The second is located a short distance away and is about the same size. The third, and largest, is half a mile away and is about 40 yards on a side, the size of a large garden plot for many suburban households in Europe, the United States, and other rich countries. The three plots total less than half an acre (0.45 acres) or 0.18 hectares. They depend on these parcels for enough rice, wheat, and vegetables to meet most of their daily food needs. During the monsoon season, the plots are subject to flooding. Their home has a floor of packed earth and a thatched roof. It is divided into a kitchen, a bedroom, and a shed for farm animals. The poultry owned by the family are kept in the kitchen at night. Mrs. Hassan cooks on the kitchen floor on a stove made of clay. Drinking water comes from a village well. Baths are taken in a nearby pond. Their toilet is an open pit.

Mr. Hassan pulls a rickshaw in a nearby village market (a job for only the poorest and most uneducated men in Bangladesh). This is the family's main source of income; there is no surplus from the farm. Mr. Hassan works an average of nine hours a day, 25 days a month, and earns the equivalent of about US$20 for a month's work. Despite his nine-hour days pulling human and other cargo, he and the family spend much time tending their plots. Mrs. Hassan divides her time between working as a manual earth digger and household activities and farming. As an earth digger she makes a little less than 50 cents a day, usually on public road improvement projects. Such projects come only periodically. The two sons attend school and help with chores. Throughout the year, the Hassans spend much of their time farming. At harvest, Mr. Hassan takes time away from his rickshaw, spending 14 hours a day harvesting and threshing (separating the grain from the straw). Mrs. Hassan will spend 13 hours threshing in addition to time spent on household chores.

The Hassan family grows rice, wheat, jute, and some vegetables. They are normally able to raise two crops a year on each plot. Their largest harvests during the year were 269 pounds of rice grain and 352 pounds of rice straw from the rice crop planted during the monsoon season, which runs from June to September, plus 528 pounds of wheat and 396 pounds of by-products raised during the dryer winter season (October–April), and 88 pounds of rice and 220 pounds of straw during the spring (April–June). The cropping seasons overlap somewhat, thus involving different plots. They used a small amount of urea fertilizer to improve their yields. The family picks and eats some 100 mangoes off a tree on their property each year. They own a goat and a chicken. They once owned a bullock, but it died.

Mr. Hassan is primarily responsible for farming tasks. Mrs. Hassan helps with the harvesting and does the winnowing (separating the grain from the husks) and drying of the rice. The jute is dried and sold for cheap cloth and burlap. All the rice is stored by the family for future consumption, but they must also buy additional rice with the money they earn from rickshaw pulling and earth digging. There are other cash outlays: Mr. Hassan hires the services of a power tiller operator for cultivation and purchases seed and fertilizer.

All told, the family's yearly cash income is a little less than $400, mostly from the rickshaw, which accounts for nearly three-quarters. Their major asset is the land, valued at about $917. Other assets include metal utensils ($10), a radio ($31), jewelry ($6), a wall clock ($5), the rickshaw ($42), and a large tree ($10). They have no bank account; household earnings are kept at home. Sometimes they have to borrow. One time they borrowed from a microcredit bank for farm expenses of $125, which they paid back with 15 percent interest.[2] Another time they borrowed $83 to buy their rickshaw from a community bank set up by a Western nongovernmental organization (NGO). The family also borrows smaller amounts from relatives, neighbors, and the local money lender.

In one month, household costs were $39. Food accounted for just over half these costs—rice accounted for 64 percent of food expenses, fish for 11 percent, and vegetables for 12 percent. No meat or dairy products were purchased. Over six months, 12 percent of their nonfood costs went to medical services, 24 percent to clothing, 22 percent to gifts for a wedding and other occasions, 18 percent to their sons' education and transportation, and 13 percent to house repairs and personal care. The seven-year-old granddaughter will someday need a dowry to be able to marry.

The Hassans eat twice a day. In the morning the family has *panta bhat,* a dish made with leftover rice, water, and salt, with green chilies and onions. At night they eat rice and *bharta,* a dish of crushed green chilies, garlic, and salt. Children are sometimes given a snack of *muri,* a puffed rice. In a typical 24-hour day, Mr. Hassan consumes 1,708 calories, Mrs. Hassan 1,491 calories, the older son 1,419 calories, the younger son 1,489 calories, their granddaughter 1,063 calories, and the elderly aunt who is sick eats almost nothing, only 288 calories. Mr. Hassan is about 5 feet, 4 inches tall and weighs 104 pounds. Mrs. Hassan is 4 feet, 10 inches tall and weighs 78 pounds. Mr. Hassan's body mass index (BMI)—a widely used measure of adult nutrition—is 17.5. BMI is determined by dividing a person's weight in kilograms by their height in meters squared. A BMI of 18.5–25 is considered normal. Anything below 18.5 indicates chronic undernutrition. Mrs. Hassan's BMI was 16.8. The sons suffer from both reduced height and extremely low weight, as does the granddaughter.

Based on nutrient recommendations for India, Mr. Hassan's recommended daily allowance (RDA) would be 2,800 calories for moderate work and 3,900 for heavy work, such as rickshaw pulling and farming. Mrs. Hassan's RDA is 2,200 calories for moderate work and 3,000 for heavy work, such as earth digging. The older son's RDA is 2,500 calories and the younger son's 2,100 calories. The granddaughter's is 1,800 calories (Gopalan, Sastri, and Balasubramian 1971). The Hassan family are so far below their RDAs that they suffer from chronic energy deficiency. Their diet is also deficient in many essential vitamins, minerals, and proteins. The Food and Agriculture Organization's (FAO's) minimum energy requirement for South Asia is 1,780 calories, assuming only light physical activity. Mr. and Mrs. Hassan are below this minimum.

The average price of rice means that it costs 40 cents a day to satisfy the total of 7,458 calories for the family, assuming rice is all they eat. An adequate calorie intake, using FAO measures, would cost 70 cents a day, nearly all of the 72 cents Mr. Hassan makes pulling the rickshaw, leaving only 2 cents for their other household needs. Economists talk about the "subsistence margin": for the Hassans there is no margin left.

Mr. Hassan recently suffered a fever, leaving him unable to work for five days. Now, the family must borrow money or sell assets, perhaps even their land, to make ends meet. Poor nutrition makes them easily sickened, reduces their ability to work, and affects the children's physical development. We cannot measure what hunger does to their mental state.

For most Americans and citizens of other developed countries who have not traveled in developing countries this portrait of the Hassans may be shocking. We are wealthy compared with much of the rest of the world. Someone in the upper-middle class with an annual household income of $75,000 or more is richer than 95 percent of the rest of the world's people—richer than 99.9 percent of all the humans who have ever lived (Brooks 2002). Those of us in this minority live in a world that may seem far removed from the Hassan family. We have the privilege of planning for a future many poor families may never know. This book is about that future.

GLOBAL VILLAGE

The struggles of one family, lost in the sea of humanity that is South Asia, are far-removed from global debates over trade, environment, and agriculture. But it is families like the Hassans who are the names and faces of world hunger, and it is because they must also be part of the solution that this book was written. In the chapters to follow, we will take a new look at what globalization means for food security, and what food security means for globalization. Both terms are suited more to rhetoric than to the reality faced daily by millions of poor families. An academic exercise listed fully 32 possible definitions of food security (Maxwell 1996). Globalization has become a cliché meaning that international forces are influential everywhere and sometimes destructive.[3]

It is difficult to imagine the Hassans spending much effort debating the many definitions of food security or globalization. Yet we believe that understanding and confronting hunger as it is experienced by hundreds of millions daily requires a new perspective in which the human dimensions of food insecurity are seen as global problems, requiring global as well as national and local actions. We accept globalization as a reality that will shape our responses to hunger at every level, including the local one. To deny both its creative and destructive possibilities is like denying the coming of the monsoon.

This perspective sets us clearly apart from two other camps of activists and academics. First are those who believe that local self-reliance will ultimately prove the key to unlocking the shackles of the world's 800 million poor and hungry. This group is hostile to the global institutions, corporations, and governments that dominate the international scene. (These advocates of local self-reliance are also hostile to mainstream economists, who have extolled the virtues of decentralized decision making since Adam Smith.) While we applaud the idea of self-reliance to a point, we believe that international institutions, the private sector, and governments must all take some responsibility toward ending poverty and hunger, and interdependence is often more rewarding than self-reliance. Without international cooperation to end hunger, local self-reliance will remain an unattainable ideal for many of the world's poorest.

The second group encompasses those who are so enthralled with private markets that they fail to grasp the essentially civic nature of international food security, environment, and health. All involve issues of "public goods," which Adam Smith's "invisible hand" (what Joseph Stiglitz calls the "palsied hand") of markets cannot provide without organized collective action. Food security is linked to environment and health in many ways. Here again there is a role for international institutions—both public and private—in guaranteeing that these linkages are seen and supported. This includes adequate agricultural research directed to those most in need, environmental protection, education, nutrition, and health care.

Markets also cannot assure social justice and the needs of civil society. Hunger and poverty are related to social justice at a number of levels. At the global level, social justice concerns the rights and duties of nations, especially the relationship between wealthy developed countries, frequently referred to as the North, and poorer developing countries, the South.[4] At the national level, it relates to the distribution of income and the humane treatment of a nation's poorest citizens. At the household level, it relates to those whose claims on meager resources are often weakest— women, children, and the elderly.

HUNGER AND FOOD SECURITY

The global, national, and local connections between food, the environment, and civil society are the major themes of this book. In the chapters to follow, we shall argue that in the wake of the Cold War, globalization has divided those who see it as a force for expanded economic opportunity and those who believe that it will widen the gap between rich and poor. As the debate over globalization rages in international fora and among governments and NGOs, families like the Hassans remain caught in a cycle of poverty and hunger. Powerful forces continue to lock them and millions of others out of the benefits globalization can bring. Among these forces is population growth, which while slowing worldwide, remains highest where the worst levels of hunger and malnutrition exist. Another force driving the persistence of hunger is obvious yet profound: people are simply too poor to get beyond the margin of subsistence. Their poverty is founded in an absence of "human capital"—education, health, nutrition, and the social and physical infrastructures to support them.[5]

Because food security is linked to poverty, and poverty is founded in underinvestment in human capital, expanding food security will require investments in people as part of a larger process of globalization. Some investments can take the form of aid, via NGOs like Oxfam and CARE, or by governments and international agencies such as the World Bank. But the majority of global investment resources remain in private hands, suggesting that the private sector has a central role to play—including poor farmers like the Hassans. Part of this role involves trade and trade policies allowing poorer farmers access to the rich markets of the developed world. A second, and largely unrealized, opportunity is through *private aid*—tapping major new sources of wealth resulting from globalization itself. The work of the Gates Foundation, for example, in funding developing world vaccination programs, could be extended to include programs of nutrition and agricultural productivity, perhaps involving many other foundations working in concert.

Additional forces confronting the ability of the world's poorest to feed themselves relate to natural resources and the environment. Water shortages, pollution, and soil loss all threaten agricultural productivity, most seriously in many of the poorest countries of the world. Establishing national and international policies for environmental protection are nowhere more important than in agriculture because it accounts for so large a proportion of global land use and because it represents some of humankind's most aggressive uses of nature. Here a different kind of infrastructure investment is required: research into the links between natural resources and agricultural productivity, especially in ecologically fragile areas, as well as investments in physical infrastructure (such as more efficient irrigation systems) to conserve scarce water resources.

Related to these investment needs is the shortfall in agricultural research in the poorest countries, where the scientists and laboratories that have powered so much of the agricultural productivity growth in the rich countries remain in short supply. Most of the important breakthroughs in food production in the past century have been scientifically based, including the key genetic innovations that led in the 1960s and 1970s to semi-dwarf (short-statured) rice and wheat varieties resulting in the Green Revolution. While the full impact of this revolution on the poorest farmers remains controversial, there is little question that it helped to stave off the Malthusian specter in countries such as India. Today, a new generation of genetic research holds further promise for reducing vulnerability to a variety of plant pests and diseases, reducing (among other things) the reliance on herbicides and pesticides for which the Green Revolution is criticized. Yet the controversy surrounding genetically engineered plants, especially in some developed countries, threatens to undermine support for agricultural research across a much wider front, slowing the adaptation of scientific methods to the needs of the world's poorest farmers. The difficulty of adapting such research to poor countries is also related to the expanding intellectual property framework that applies to plants and animals and their genetic material.

THE WAY FORWARD

Despite these daunting challenges, we believe there is now an opportunity to confront the forces that have caused upward of 800 million poor people to remain hungry and malnourished. While the 1996 World Food Summit goal of cutting this number in half by 2015 will almost certainly not be reached, our analysis shows that global hunger could be substantially reduced by 2025 and chronic mass hunger ended by 2050. This goal is no more ambitious than the near-elimination of the many infectious diseases that stalked the planet only a century ago. Unlike vaccination for disease, however, food insecurity requires a larger set of changes if it is to be eradicated. As we shall argue, these include institutional reforms in trade policies, the rehabilitation and renewal of commitments to multinational aid, significant reforms in natural resource management, and major new investments in agricultural science and technology. While national governments will play a central role in facilitating these changes, we believe that part of the burden will fall to the private sector, both as investment and as foundation-based private aid, and to NGOs and civil society broadly construed. We believe that broad international cooperation among rich and poor nations is essential, if the fight against hunger, misery, and discontent is to succeed.

PART ONE
THE CHALLENGE

2 • HUNGER IN A PROSPEROUS WORLD

As the twenty-first century begins, it is generally estimated that more than 800 million people are chronically undernourished and food insecure and that some 1.2 billion live on the equivalent of less than a dollar per day (FAO 2000f; World Bank 2000b). Like the Hassans, they eat too little to work and remain healthy, and they are hungry because they are too poor to afford enough to eat. At least until the nineteenth century, their plight was commonplace in most societies. Even the United States in 1900 had an average life expectancy of only 47 years, lower than the developing countries today (Maddison 2001). Today, in much of the world, the hungry are rarely seen, hidden by the growing prosperity furnished by global economic expansion and increases in agricultural productivity. They are hidden, like the Hassans, in hamlets and slums in regions barely touched by the glitter of modernity. But they exist—living and dying in a state of want.

They need not endure this bleak existence: chronic hunger can be banished. To do so, we must understand its root causes. In particular, since hunger is linked to poverty, the focus must be on how to attack poverty. A second and rather widely misinterpreted factor is population growth. While global rates of population growth have slowed dramatically, virtually all future population growth will occur in the countries least equipped to absorb it. Growth will be fastest in countries with the most hunger, and in many of them it would grow even faster if the AIDS virus was not killing their young adults.

Even the role of poverty is less obvious than it appears. Most of those who face hunger are poor in an *absolute* sense. They lack the income to buy enough food—even if the cost of living is cheap. Moreover, the causation works in both directions. While absolute poverty causes hunger, hunger itself causes absolute poverty. It contributes to illness, crippling people's capacity for work and thwarting children's ability to grow and learn. Robert Fogel, the Nobel Prize–winning economic historian, found that even in nineteenth-century Europe, the amount of work that could be performed was limited by calorie intake. Fogel's research found that about 30 percent of British economic growth over the past two centuries was accounted for by absolute improvements in nutrition (Fogel 1994, 386). For people such as the Hassans, poverty and hunger are a vise that squeezes vitality and well-being from their lives.

The Hassans, and the countries in which they and people like them live, also face *relative* poverty. Many believe they are poorer now in comparison to their own people, and other nations, than they used to be. This is one of the major themes of the antiglobalization movement: that global economic expansion has aggravated relative poverty in countries with rapid growth, such as China (Mazur 2000). Both absolute and relative poverty are serious problems, but they are different. In order to understand these causes of hunger, we will consider different levels and types of development and poverty reduction, gaining insight into how key changes can ultimately end widespread hunger.

Before proceeding, it may be useful to clarify some key terms (Table 2.1). Throughout this book hunger, food insecurity, and undernourishment will be used somewhat interchangeably, as they are in the major annual report on the subject by the Food and Agriculture Organization of the United Nations (FAO 2000f). The basic definition implied is a chronic lack of sufficient food, in terms of calories, such as the Hassans experience.

WHY ARE PEOPLE HUNGRY?

Today's supply of food, compared with the basic requirements of the world's population, is more than enough for everyone, equal to about 2,700 calories per person per day (Evans 1998, 184; FAO 1996b, 9). Yet, to say that hunger is strictly a distribution problem is akin to saying that if rain fell evenly over the earth there would be no droughts. It may be true, but reality is unchanged, and wishing will not make it so. No mechanism exists—or is ever likely to—to massively redistribute food worldwide on the basis of need alone. Short-term food assistance can only act as a stopgap, albeit an expensive one.[1] Long-term solutions to hunger require that

TABLE 2.1 • Definitions of key terms

Term	Definition
Hunger	A general term related to not getting enough to eat. Chronic hunger is a persistent state; transitory hunger a more temporary one
Food security	The most widely used definition is access by all people at all times to enough food for an active healthy life, but there are many other uses of the term
Undernourished	Used by the Food and Agriculture Organization (FAO) for diets with inadequate calories and as a specific indicator of hunger and food insecurity
Malnutrition	Refers to poor nutrition, which may include undernourishment, over consumption (obesity), or specific nutrient inadequacies
Child malnutrition	Typically is specifically used for children who are underweight (wasted) or too short (stunted) for their age

SOURCES: FAO 1999a, 2000b; World Bank 1986.

families, except in times of crisis, have the economic wherewithal to meet their own food needs. As we discuss elsewhere, this is not an argument for complete self-sufficiency, but for orderly markets and adequate incomes to assure that food is available and affordable. Indeed if we all had to provide for our own food needs, rather than specializing, it is questionable whether the world could produce sufficient food.

Even when food is relatively cheap, hunger can persist. Throughout the 1980s and 1990s substantial agricultural surpluses came from many countries, including the United States. Resulting low world prices created severe problems for farmers, but failed to eliminate chronic undernourishment in poor countries. India achieved its national goal of food self-sufficiency and even exported food in the 1990s, yet continued to have more undernourished people than any other country on earth (Hopper 1999; Measham and Chatterjee 1999). The lesson is that increased food production and low food prices are not sufficient to end hunger. Hunger today is less a problem of general food availability than of access.

People lack access to food because of inadequate income, political disadvantage, or war (Sen 1981, 1999). The denial of access hits home in the household, which is the basic unit for acquiring and sharing food the world over. Households such as the Hassans' acquire food by growing it, buying it, or receiving it as a gift or loan from a relative or neighbor, or through a government food program. At any point in this chain access may be blocked. A household's access to food is affected by both its income and wealth (assets). Income flows from the family's productive resources (labor, land, and capital). For most poor households, such as the Hassans, labor and skill are the main resources. Available technology, such as fertilizer and farm equipment, also affects the productivity of labor. Wages—the major source of income for most poor families are largely set by markets that also determine rents, borrowing costs, and food prices. The relationship between wages and food prices is particularly important. In short, if a household has the necessary income, or the wealth to spend or borrow against, it can always buy food. But if incomes are inadequate, because economic conditions are poor or political discrimination or hostilities have cut off income flows, and there are no assets to borrow against or sell, the household's access to food is lost.

Access to food also extends to its *distribution* within the household. In some societies, certain family members have access to more food than others. Patterns in South Asia, for example, show that males are clearly favored over females, and adults are often favored over children. Age and gender bias combine to favor the male head of household most and young female children least. This distribution clearly contributes to the malnourishment of women and children in many settings.[2]

If hunger and poverty are closely linked, one must ask who and where are the world's poor? The hungry are poor both absolutely and relatively. By any standard, including that of their own society, their capacity to purchase food is severely limited. Consider the number of people living, like the Hassans, on the equivalent of less than one 1993 U.S. dollar per day (Table 2.2). While the average person in a developed country lives on more than $50 per day, 265 million in East and Southeast Asia, 505 million in South Asia, and 289 million in Sub-Saharan Africa live on the equivalent of less than a dollar.[3] These numbers closely match estimates of the hungry in much of Asia and Latin America, but the estimates for South Asia (including Bangladesh) and Sub-Saharan Africa suggest that hunger may be substantially more widespread than estimated by FAO (Hopper 1999; Measham and Chatterjee 1999).

Although most of these poor people are found in rural areas in the poorest countries, the number in urban areas has been accelerating. This trend will continue. The rural poor continue to rely on agriculture as a primary livelihood as peasant farmers, tenants, or laborers, although the pat-

TABLE 2.2 • Number of hungry and poor people

Region	Undernourished people		Numbers
	Average number	Change	of poor
	1969–71 1996–98	from 1969	people, 1996[a]
	(millions/year)	to 1998 (%)	(millions)
East and Southeast Asia	506 221	−56.3	265
Latin America	55 55	0.0	76
Middle East/North Africa	51 36	−29.4	21
South Asia	238 294	+23.5	505
Sub-Saharan Africa	108 186	+72.2	289
All developing regions	959 792	−17.5	1,156

SOURCE: FAO 1999a, 2000b; World Bank 1999.
[a] World Bank estimate of the number of people living on the equivalent of less than one U.S. dollar per day after adjusting for differences in the purchasing power of currencies among countries.

tern varies by region. Many of the poor in South Asia are landless or near landless farm laborers. In Latin America, smallholder farmers predominate, but many who lack the land on which to subsist must work off-farm at part-time jobs. In Africa and Southeast Asia, large numbers of poor are peasant farmers living in environmentally fragile areas with low agricultural productivity and few natural resources, such as the Sahel (Conway 1997).

A distinction must also be made between chronic and transitory hunger (World Bank 1986). Most households that are susceptible to transitory hunger are poor or near poor, getting just enough nourishment under normal circumstances but facing periods of hunger that come and go. They lack the assets to cushion a sharp decline in income or a spike in food prices. Many cultures have a term that translates as the "hungry season"— the period just before the next harvest when food stocks are lowest. It is during these times that transitory hunger is most widespread. Severe transitory hunger leads to famine; an acute food shortage frequently exacerbated by political campaigns or wars (von Braun, Teklu, and Webb 1998). One of the most recent risks of widespread famine occurred in 2002 in several countries in southern Africa as the result of years of drought. However, the situation in Zimbabwe was made worse by a campaign against white farmers that disrupted food production (*New York Times* 2002). Historically, the potato blight was only partly to blame for the Irish potato famine, which was made far worse by policies of the English government designed to weaken and subdue the Irish people (Sen 1981).

Chronic hunger, by contrast, results either from persistent and absolute poverty so great that sufficient food is simply unaffordable (von Braun et al. 1992). Poverty is due not only to a lack of income but a lack of physical and financial assets and human capital resulting from inadequate education, training, health, and nutrition. Studies of rural households have found that differences in living standards are primarily related to a lack of human capital and resources such as land and livestock (World Bank 1990, 33). Rates of pay for the hungry poor are low because they typically have few skills and little education (and also low levels of health and nutrition), and are therefore less productive. Another study found that among smallholder farmers, education was more important than land ownership in determining their welfare (World Bank 1990, 33). Frequently, what land the rural poor own, if any, is less productive, more prone to drought and flooding, and more susceptible to environmental degradation. Above all, the poor lack human capital.

HOW MANY POOR ARE HUNGRY?

Hunger and food insecurity are subject to various definitions, but we need some indicator to gauge whether we are gaining or losing ground in the struggle to end hunger. The FAO measure of chronic undernourishment and food insecurity—typically referred to as hunger—is an estimate of the number of people who, like the Hassans, consume too few calories to meet a minimum daily energy requirement. The measure relies on food balance sheets that compare national average estimates of per capita food supply (based on production and trade) and estimates the total distribution of calories in the population. Some countries use household data, but many use regional averages to determine how many fall below the minimum requirements (FAO 1996b; Smith 1999). FAO's measure often serves as a benchmark for estimating progress toward reducing hunger.[4] The 1996 Rome Declaration's call to reduce the number of undernourished people by half no later than 2015, for example, was made in reference to FAO's estimates (FAO 1996a).

During 1969–71, FAO estimated that there were 959 million undernourished people, equal to 25.9 percent of the world's population (Table 2.2). In 1996–98, the total number of hungry people, estimated to be 826 million— 792 million in developing countries and 34 million in developed countries, primarily in central and eastern Europe and the former Soviet Union—was equal to 13.6 percent of the world's population. This 20-year reduction in the share of the world's population affected by chronic hunger was substantial given global population increases of 2.36 billion over the same period (from 3.70 billion in 1970 to 6.06 billion in 2000). Most of the increase was in the developing countries.

The number of hungry is greatest in East and Southeast Asia (primarily China), in South Asia (mainly India), and increasingly in Sub-Saharan Africa, as shown in Table 2.2. Between 1969–71 and 1996–98, East and Southeast Asia saw a decline of 285 million in the number of undernourished, as rapid economic growth translated into a dramatic reduction in poverty and hunger. Undernourishment dropped sharply in China as well, with high economic growth rates. By contrast, in Sub-Saharan Africa, the number of hungry increased by 72 percent from 1969–71 to 1996–98 as population grew and economic performance worsened.

An alternative measure of hunger and malnutrition is the number of children less than five years old who are wasted, that is, underweight for their age. Data on weight is gathered by the United Nations (UN) based on country surveys. In 2000, 26.7 percent of preschool children in developing countries were underweight by UN measures—a decline from 37.4 percent in 1980; yet malnutrition still affected 150 million children, with serious consequences for their health and development. Some 40 percent of children were underweight in South Asia (78 million) and 36 percent in Sub-Saharan Africa (32 million). The number of underweight children is declining in South Asia, but in Sub-Saharan Africa both the number and proportion of underweight children are rising. In 2000, 8.2 million more children were suffering from malnutrition (underweight) than in 1990 (UN, ACC/SCN 2000).[5]

Yet another measure of malnutrition relates to micronutrients in the diet. Data on micronutrients collected by the United Nations in 2000 indicated that 56 percent of pregnant women, 44 percent of nonpregnant women, and 53 percent of school-age children suffered from anemia (iron deficiency) in developing countries, affecting their productivity and cognitive ability. Goiter (a disease of the thyroid gland caused by iodine deficiency) affects about 740 million people globally. It is estimated that more than 2 billion people have diets deficient in iodine. Vitamin A deficiency afflicts an estimated 225–250 million preschool children, damaging their sight, stunting their growth, and weakening their immune systems; it can also lead to blindness and death in severe cases. Mortality rates for young children with a deficiency dropped by 23 percent with an improvement in their Vitamin A status (UN, ACC/SCN 2000).

DEFUSING THE POPULATION BOMB

The intuition that hunger results from too many people is an old and strong one. The two Chinese characters that together mean "population" are the symbols for a person and an open mouth (Dyson 1998). In 200 A.D., when the world's population was around 300 million people, the Roman Quintus Septimus Florens Tertullianus wrote that "we are burdensome to the world, the resources are scarcely adequate to us and complaints are everywhere while already nature does not sustain us. Truly, pestilence and hunger and war and flood must be considered as a remedy for nations, like a pruning back of the human race becoming excessive in numbers" (translated from Latin by Bart K. Holland, quoted in Johnson 1998, 8).

Just over 200 years ago in 1798, Thomas Malthus famously predicted that population would outrun food production, resulting in mass starvation (Malthus 1992, reprinted from 1817). His grim logic stands like a specter over modern discussions of resources and the environment, suggesting that we will soon outrun the ecological "carrying capacity" of the earth. In 1964, Lester Brown wrote "the less developed world is losing the capacity to feed itself" (quoted in Johnson 1975, 12). He echoed those sentiments a decade later at a time of exceptionally high—but as it turned out short-lived—spikes in world food prices, observing, "The soaring demand for food, spurred by continuing population growth and rising affluence has begun to outrun the productive capacity of the world's farmers and fishermen" (Brown 1973, 3). The eminent ecologist Paul Ehrlich predicted in *The Population Bomb* that in the 1970s "the world will undergo famines—hundreds of millions of people are going to starve to death in spite of any crash programs embarked upon now" (1968, xi). The biologist Garrett Hardin published *The Limits of Altruism* in 1977, which advocated a triage approach to foreign aid: many nations had no hope of feeding their burgeoning populations, so aiding them, he argued, was a waste of resources better spent on countries with some prospect of success.

Yet the Malthusian and neo-Malthusian specter, while fearsome, has yet to fully materialize. Malthus himself was less pessimistic in his later writings on the subject (Malthus 1992, reprinted from 1817; Smil 2000). In addition, he could not have known in 1798 that the world stood at the dawn of a scientific revolution that would transform both industry and agriculture, helping to support global populations nearly six times those of his own age. Nor could he have known that growing incomes and wealth would eventually cause population growth rates to decline. Still, in many parts of the world the Malthusian threat remains real, primarily because people are numerous, poor, and isolated. When poverty is tied to rapid population growth rates (as it generally is), the risk of widespread hunger is ever present. And in those parts of the world where HIV/AIDS and other diseases appear to bear Malthus out, their effect is to sap the productivity from their people, deepening poverty and susceptibility to hunger.

A sharp reduction in infant mortality rates resulting from improved health and sanitation in developing countries led to the rapid growth of world population starting about 1950, causing it to double from 3 billion to more than 6 billion between 1960 and 2000 (Figure 2.1). Although the

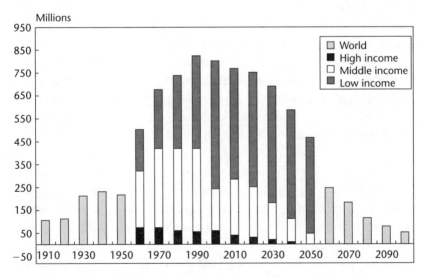

FIGURE 2.1   •   Additions by decade to the world's population, 1910–2100

SOURCES: Data for 1910–40 are from the UN Population Division 1998a, for 1950–2050 from FAO 2001b, and for 2055–2100 from the UN, Population Division 2000, Table 17.

NOTES: Country-level population data were aggregated to high-, middle-, and low-income levels following the World Bank's country income-level classification. Low-income economies are those with a 1999 per capita gross national income (GNI) less than $755; middle-income, a 1999 per capita GNI between $755 and $9,265; and high-income, a 1999 per capita GNI more than $9,266.

rate of population growth slowed considerably from 1990 onward, the world is still expected to reach 8 billion people by 2025, an increase of one-third from 2000. As incomes expand in developing countries, food demand will increase even more.

The United Nations (UN) has projected global population using various assumptions of fertility, reflecting age-distribution and the impact of family planning among other factors. Population is projected for 2050 at 10.9 billion under the United Nation's high-fertility scenario, 7.9 billion under its low-fertility scenario, and 9.3 billion under the medium-fertility scenario. Even the medium-fertility variant represents more than a 50 percent increase from 2000 (UN, Population Division 2001). The most important point is that literally *all* of this increase will occur in the developing world (UN, Population Division 2001). Just six countries (Bangladesh, China, India, Indonesia, Nigeria, and Pakistan) account for half this growth.

Population growth will be highest in the poorest countries. By 2050, today's developed countries will have 1.18 billion people and the developing countries 8.14 billion, with 1.86 billion in the very poorest developing world nations (UNFPA 2001). As a group, the 49 countries with today's lowest per capita incomes will triple in size from 668 million in 2000 to 1.86 billion in 2050. The trend is most pronounced in Africa, which has nearly tripled its numbers since 1960. In Gambia, for example, population grew at a phenomenal rate of 3.8 percent annually between 1980 and 2000, meaning that the country's population almost doubled over this period. The population of Tanzania and Honduras also grew faster than 3 percent per year, while all developing countries grew at an annual rate of 1.9 percent or more over the same period (FAO 2001c). If population grows at a rate of 2 percent per year it will double in 30 years; growing by 3 percent annually it will have doubled in just 25 years. Malthus still haunts these countries, where food production has generally failed to keep up with population growth and they are too poor to import sufficient food to make up the shortfall.

Notwithstanding these alarming numbers, global population growth appears to be slowing and by the end of the twenty-first century may be in decline. World population grew at only 1.33 percent annually between 1995 and 2000, down significantly from a peak of 2.04 percent in 1965–70. The annual rate of population gain is expected to fall to 0.34 percent in 2045–50 under the UN's medium-fertility projection. This means that the average annual addition to world population has fallen from a peak in 1986–90 of 86 million to 77 million in 2000 and is expected to decline to 64 million in 2015–20 and to drop sharply to 30 million in 2045–50 (UNFPA 2001). Under the low-fertility projection the rate of population growth could actually be negative by 2050. Even under the high-fertility forecast, population will grow at less than 1 percent annually by 2045–50. If these trends continue over the next 25–50 years, by 2050 the period of major population growth will be over (see Figure 2.1).

The reasons for this slowdown are complex, but relate crucially to expanded economic opportunity. As incomes expand, families around the world choose to have fewer children, opting instead to invest more in the children they already have, since the likelihood that each child will survive to adulthood has risen. The average number of live births per woman over her lifetime globally was 5.0 in the early 1950s, but it fell to 2.7 in 1998. In the past 25 years, the number has fallen from 5.1 to 2.6 in Asia and from 5.0 to 2.7 in Latin America, but only from 6.6 to 5.1 in Africa. Currently, 40 percent of the world's people live in China or India, so what happens in those two countries is crucial. China, where population growth has slowed dramatically, is expected to grow at only 0.7 percent annually from 1997 to 2015. India has had less but still considerable success at slowing population growth; it is expected to grow by 1.2 percent annually from 1997 to 2015 (UN, Population Division 1998). Fertility is already below the replacement rate in many (especially high-income) countries, although momentum from earlier high rates will keep population growth positive for several decades.

Three additional demographic trends—increasing urbanization, an aging population, and HIV/AIDS—also have significant implications for food security. In the past, the vast majority of the world's poor and undernourished lived in rural areas. In the twenty-first century, food insecurity will increasingly become an urban problem. The proportion of people in developing countries who live in cities has nearly doubled since 1960, from 22 percent to over 40 percent. More than 57 percent is expected to be urban by 2030 (UN, Population Division 1998). Many of these urban areas are "megacities" with 10 million or more people. In 1999, 13 of the world's 17 megacities were in developing countries; by 2015, an estimated 22 megacities will be in the South. These developing-country megacities are already surrounded by rapidly growing slums and shantytowns. Huge public investments in water, sanitation, and transportation infrastructure, as well as in food supplies, will be required to avoid ever larger concentrations of poverty.

The world's population is also growing older as a result of the decrease in birth rates and an increase in life expectancy, resulting from improvements in health care and nutrition. Currently, there is one 60-year-old in the world for every three children less than 15 years old. There will be twice as many older people as children in the developed countries by 2050, and policymakers will face the challenge of caring for them. In the developing countries, by contrast, the ratio of the working-age population to the nonworking-age will remain about the same in 2050 as today. However, the nonworking group, predominantly children now, will be composed about equally of children and retired persons.

The tragic impact of HIV/AIDS in developing countries—especially in Sub-Saharan Africa—has been consistently underestimated. Over 34 million people worldwide were estimated to be infected with HIV/AIDS in 2000, 71 percent in Sub-Saharan Africa (UNAIDS 2000). Some 2.8 million died of AIDS in 1999, 85 percent of them in Africa. The impact that HIV/AIDS will have in Africa is now likened to that of the bubonic plague in Europe in the Middle Ages, when populations in whole villages and regions were reduced by two-thirds. In some African countries, one-quarter or more of the adult population is infected (UNAIDS 2000). Eighty percent of the people dying from AIDS are between the ages of 20 and 50. They are young and middle-aged adults in their most productive working years, frequently leaving orphaned children and abandoned elders.

The effects on the economy and society are particularly devastating. In Africa, 12 million children have lost their parents to AIDS, and this number is expected to reach 28 million by 2010 (UNAIDS 2000). The population of Sub-Saharan Africa will be an estimated 84 million lower in 2015 as a result (UN, Population Division 2001). In South Africa, for example, AIDS deaths will cause life expectancy to fall below 45 years by 2010–15; without HIV/AIDS it would have been 70. The impact of HIV/AIDS may be so overwhelming that any hope of economic growth and development will end. However, prevention campaigns can reduce the spread of HIV/AIDS significantly. In Uganda, for example, the infection rate was cut from 14 to 8 percent. In Senegal the rate has remained below 2 percent (UNAIDS 2000).

All told, population pressures remain a significant problem in the poorest countries facing the greatest food insecurity, despite a global slowdown in population growth. Although HIV/AIDS will exact a high toll in many of these same countries, the result will be to rob them of their most productive citizens.

GLOBALIZATION, RELATIVE POVERTY, AND FOOD SECURITY

The impact of globalization on poverty and economic inequality is hotly debated. Antiglobalization forces maintain that rapidly increasing economic, social, and technological interaction between countries is further impoverishing the poor, enriching multinational corporations, and harming the environment (Korten 1995).

At base, these opponents of global economic expansion believe that social justice and civil society will be its victims. Ironically, two manifestations and causes of globalization, cable and satellite television and the Internet, have fueled the sense that the dispossessed are not being heard, even as much clearer images of far-away desperation are brought home to us (Bhagwati 2002, 3). In economic terms, the fate of have-nots is tied to global economic forces, even in the face of evidence to the contrary. That trade and economic expansion may sometimes be exploitative does not prove the general thesis of the anti-globalists.

In general, the anti-globalization argument revolves more around relative than absolute poverty. Basic comparative data provide a mixed message, at least at the national level. The average gross domestic product (GDP) in the 20 richest countries, which was 15 times greater than that in the poorest 20 countries in 1960, had widened to 30 times greater by the late 1990s (World Bank 2000b). Between 1965 and 1997 the richest 10 percent of the world's population increased their share of the total global economy from 50.6 to 59.6 percent (Wasow 2000). The fifth of the world's population in the highest-income countries had 86 percent of total world GDP, 74 percent of world telephone lines, and 93 percent of Internet users in 1997 (UNDP 1999a). Per capita incomes have actually declined in several of the poorest 20 countries since 1960 and barely improved in the others. However, if population sizes are factored into the country comparisons, the perspective changes. Most of the 20 poorest nations have relatively small populations, whereas per capita incomes in some poor countries with very large populations, such as China, have grown rapidly.

In the 15 richest countries, per capita incomes grew by an average of 2.1 percent per year between 1965 and 1997. However, per capita income grew faster in 20 mainly developing countries during this period, of which the 9 most populous included Brazil, China, Egypt, India, Indonesia, Korea, Malaysia, Pakistan, and Thailand, with a combined population of over 2.8 billion (Wasow 2000). There were marked regional differences among developing countries. Incomes in Asia, especially East Asia, grew rapidly, dramatically reducing poverty. Between 1978, when China began to liberalize its policies, and the mid-1990s, some 170 million Chinese were lifted from absolute poverty, and the poverty rate fell 60 percent (World Bank 2000b). Per capita incomes, however, stagnated or fell between 1990 and 1999 in 70 countries, with a total population of 800 million.

Even if the absolute economic status of many poor people in developing world countries has improved, recent trends have generated intense debate. Studies by the World Bank using household data, representing 85 percent of the world's population for the years 1988 and 1993, concluded that global income inequality rose dramatically.[6] However, a detailed analysis by Bhalla (2002) reached very different and provocative conclusions, finding that a measure of inequality among individuals on a global basis declined by about 6 percent since 1980 and about 10 percent since peaking in 1968, so the global distribution of income has become more equal. Bhalla also estimated the number of people living in absolute poverty in 1998 at about 600 million, about half the 1.2 billion estimated by the World Bank.[7]

Regardless of the exact numbers, the pattern that emerges is that the "haves" have benefited enormously from globalization, which has generously rewarded those with higher education levels and better workplace skills. While many poor people in the developing world have also benefited, and poverty rates have fallen in many developing countries, many of the poorest are being left further behind. Globalization has by-passed and increasingly marginalized them.

In general, it is the people at the margins of globalization who are hungry. What does this imply for food security? First, it suggests that those by-passed by the global economy are much more likely to remain poor in an absolute sense and to fall further behind in relative terms. Since hunger and poverty are so closely joined, it is in these poor countries that hunger is most prevalent. Second, developing countries with rising incomes have not tended to reject globalization but to embrace it. If openness to the global economy is measured in terms of trade (exports plus imports) as a share of GDP, then an increase in the ratio of trade to GDP of 1 percent has raised per capita income by 0.9 to 2 percent, according to two studies

(Ades and Glaeser 1999; Frankel and Romer 1999). Between 1960 and 1995, the economies of developing countries more open to trade grew at slightly more than 2 percent annually, whereas the growth rate was just over 1 percent for more closed economies (World Bank 2000b). The share of trade in the economies of the poorest countries actually declined (World Bank 2000b). Hence, trade appears to increase growth, which can reduce country-level poverty and help break the cycle of poverty and hunger. Moreover, although growth alone is not a panacea, faster economic growth from more open trade does not necessarily increase inequality. When a large number of countries are examined over several decades, increased trade led inequality to rise in some countries and fall in others. Overall, the incomes of the poorest 20 percent of the population rose at roughly the same rate as GDP (Dollar and Kraay 2002, 128).

In sum, the greatest reductions in poverty have occurred in regions with the fastest rates of economic growth (Figure 2.2). In East Asia, for example, high rates of export-led growth reduced the number of people living on less than $1 per day by 185 million between 1990 and 1998 (World Bank 2001b, 42). Most of this improvement occurred in China. In Sub-Saharan Africa, however, there were almost 50 million more people living in poverty in 1998 than 1990. The economic transition from Communism has also brought increased hardship to parts of Eastern Europe and Central Asia.

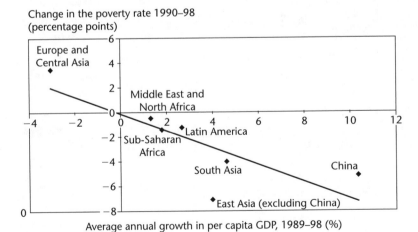

FIGURE 2.2 • Poverty reduction and growth

SOURCE: World Bank 2000a.

NOTE: Poverty reduction relates to the percentage change in the proportion of the population estimated to be living on less than one U.S. dollar per day.

The picture that emerges is that global economic forces by-pass those with low levels of skill and education, almost all of whom are already poor, and lift up those households and countries that have invested in them. To participate in the benefits of global economic growth requires policies of economic openness, which have reduced poverty in most countries that have embraced them. A failure to open a country to the global economy is an invitation to be sidelined, especially in those countries that have failed to invest in education and other forms of social and economic infrastructure. It is in these countries that pockets of food insecurity are likely to persist. It is also, regrettably, where the scourge of HIV/AIDS and other health problems have often been most prevalent, robbing the productivity of young adults in whom educational investments have been made.

There is a final, and critical, aspect of globalization and income distribution that relates to food security. As we argue in the chapters to follow, the sense that the fruits of global economic growth have been unequally distributed tends to undermine faith and confidence in the global trading system in the poorer developing countries. The result is to drive these countries toward policies of isolation, self-sufficiency, and protectionism—an invitation to be by-passed—reconfirming and reinforcing their fears. For this reason, the elimination of poverty and hunger, and a more equitable division of the spoils of prosperity, is not only a moral imperative but a practical means of enlisting developing countries' support for a program of trade liberalization with a human face. Basic attention should therefore be given, both within and among countries, to the plight of the poorest and most vulnerable groups (Bread for the World Institute 1997). Indifference to inequality, as Marie Antoinette learned in the French Revolution, leads the poor to question the very legitimacy of the existing order. Market capitalism is a powerful mechanism for human betterment, but not necessarily for ensuring equity (Rawls 1971). A larger set of institutions and policies is needed, both nationally and internationally, to reflect principles of social justice and fairness.

ENDING HUNGER: THE TASK

We have maintained that ending global hunger is possible in our lifetimes. What would it take? A number of scenarios for major regions of the world help us to gauge the magnitude of the task (Senauer and Sur 2001). These regions are Sub-Saharan Africa, East and Southeast Asia excluding China, China, South Asia, Latin America and the Caribbean, the Middle East,

North Africa, and the Newly Independent States (NIS) of the former Soviet Union and Eastern Europe. The time frames are 2025 and 2050. The hunger estimates are based on a methodology described in Appendix A and in Senauer and Sur (2001).

First, we estimated the number of chronically hungry people, specifically defined here as those consuming fewer calories than the minimum energy requirement in 2025, based on current forecasts of population and economic growth. Alternative scenarios were then developed by changing the assumptions of the distribution of income to reflect policies that were explicitly designed to meet the needs of the poorest people ("pro-poor growth"). We also considered policies that were explicitly anti-poor. In addition, we changed the level of food prices to reflect either advances in agricultural technology or shortfalls in production. Together, these scenarios tell us about the role of growth and poverty reduction, the role of technology in production, and the level of food prices, all of which will determine the fate of the world's hungry in this century.

Business as Usual . . . The first thing to determine is what will happen to the number of hungry people by 2025 if population and income grow as currently projected. Population growth rates from the United Nations and economic growth projections by the World Bank, which are shown in Table 2.3, were used.

TABLE 2.3 • Assumptions for annual growth in population and gross domestic product (GDP), 1997–2025

| | Annual growth rates, 1997–2025 | | |
| | GDP | Population | GDP/capita |
Region	(% rounded to the nearest tenth)		
Sub-Saharan Africa	3.6	2.3	1.2
East Asia (excluding China)	5.0	0.7	4.3
China	6.0	0.6	5.2
South Asia (excluding India)	4.6	1.8	2.7
India	5.8	1.2	4.6
Latin America	3.8	1.2	2.5
Middle East/North Africa	3.8	1.7	2.1
Newly Independent States	2.1	0.0	2.1

SOURCE: Authors, IMPACT projections, June 2001.
NOTE: The Newly Independent States include countries of the former Soviet Union and Eastern Europe.

Economic growth is highest in China, followed by South Asia and East Asia (excluding China). Growth is lowest in the NIS (the former Soviet Union and Eastern Europe). Population growth declines in all regions: it averages 0.6 percent in China and is negative in the NIS. It is highest in Sub-Saharan Africa, notwithstanding the impact of HIV/AIDS. Although economic growth is 3.6 percent in Sub-Saharan Africa, rapid population growth means per capita incomes increase only 1.2 percent annually. If the latest impact assessments of HIV/AIDS are used, African population growth may be lower, but the effects on productivity will be so devastating that economic growth will fall even further (Altman 2000).

Given these growth rates the number of chronically hungry is estimated to decline globally by 23 percent, as shown in Table 2.4 in column (1)—about 636 million people if FAO's 1996–98 estimate of 826 million is used as the baseline. This is not even close to the 1996 World Food Summit goal of cutting the current number of hungry people in half by 2015, but it does suggest that even modest income expansion, combined with decelerating populations, can cut the numbers of food insecure. The number of undernourished falls in some regions but rises in others. By 2025, the number of food insecure falls substantially in East Asia, South Asia, China, and the NIS and only modestly in Latin America. There is no change in the Middle East/North Africa. However, largely because of slow economic growth, the food insecure total in Sub-Saharan Africa rises by more than 50 percent.[8]

If Food Prices Change . . . Now consider the effect of food price changes, assuming income and population growth rates remain the same. First, suppose that real food prices fall so that at every income level, 10 percent more calories might be consumed. This could be the result of expanded production from improved agricultural technology, discussed in later chapters. The important impact of the price changes here is on those who consume less than the minimum energy requirement. The effect of this real price change, combined with the current economic and population growth forecasts, reduces the world's chronically hungry by 47 percent. Regional declines are proportionally largest in China and South Asia, and with the price decrease, hunger increases by only 8 percent in Sub-Saharan Africa.

The significance of declining food prices is that for poor families such as the Hassans, food spending usually accounts for at least 50 percent and as much as 80 percent of total household purchases. Rural landless laborers,

TABLE 2.4 • Estimates of the change in the number of hungry people by 2025 (percent)

Country/region	Current trends (1)	Lower food prices[a] (2)	Higher food prices[b] (3)	Pro-poor growth[c] (4)	Anti-poor growth[d] (5)	Lower prices and pro-poor growth[e] (6)	Slow growth[f] (7)
Sub-Saharan Africa	+52	+8	+120	+22	+71	−26	+136
East Asia	−42	−63	−5	−63	−27	−76	+16
China	−71	−81	−52	−80	−63	−88	−31
South Asia	−56	−71	−28	−71	−44	−81	0
Latin America	−8	−40	+43	−40	+14	−61	+52
Middle East/North Africa	0	−36	+62	−33	+21	−59	+72
Newly Independent States	−47	−66	−15	−66	+33	−78	−27
Total	−23	−47	+18	−43	−8	−65	+36

SOURCE: Senauer and Sur 2001.

NOTE: The Newly Independent States include countries of the former Soviet Union and Eastern Europe.

[a]Ten percent increase in calories consumed resulting from lower real food prices.

[b]Ten percent decrease in calories consumed resulting from higher real food prices.

[c]Increase income share of lowest quintile by 50 percent and share of second lowest by 25 percent; adjust from highest quintile.

[d]Decrease income share of lowest two quintiles by 20 percent.

[e]Ten percent increase in calories consumed, plus increase in income share of lowest quintile by 50 percent and second-lowest by 25 percent.

[f]Economic growth (GDP) at half the rates in Table 2.2.

subsistence farmers who must purchase some food, or the urban poor therefore benefit directly from lower food prices (Pinstrup-Andersen, Pandya-Lorch, and Rosegrant 1999). The 10 percent shift in calorie consumption discussed here would require about a 20 percent fall in the price of staple food.[9] Food price declines of such magnitude would only occur with a substantial increase in investment and technological change, especially in agricultural research focused on the needs of poor farmers.

If, on the other hand, food prices *rise* substantially given factors such as environmental degradation, global warming, or declining increases in crop yields due to lack of investment in agricultural research and technology, these results are turned upside down (Brown 1995). If a 10 percent decline in calories consumed results, assuming economic and population growth rates are unchanged, the estimated number of hungry would increase by 18 percent worldwide by 2025. Even the assumed levels of economic growth would not be enough to offset the effects of a substantial increase in food prices. An appalling 120 percent rise in undernourished people in Sub-Saharan Africa would result

If the Distribution of Income Changes . . .   Finally, consider changes in income distribution, combined with the currently forecast rates of economic and population growth. One such change would redistribute income gains from economic growth so that the poorest people would receive a larger share of these gains. A policy that led to higher rates of growth in the incomes for the poor has been pursued, for example, in Asian countries like South Korea, Taiwan, and Thailand (Sen 1999; Rosegrant and Hazell 2000). Such policy places high priority on basic education and health care, income-earning opportunities for the poor, and agricultural growth focused on smallholder farmers (World Bank 2000a, 2000c). The elements of such a pro-poor growth strategy are discussed in detail in Chapter 6.

Consider a shift in the share of increased income, so that the poorest one-fifth increase their share of total national income by 50 percent and the second poorest one-fifth by 25 percent. The result of such pro-poor policy would be to reduce the global number of hungry by 43 percent by 2025 as shown in Table 2.3. The most marked reductions would occur in East Asia, China, and South Asia. Hunger would still increase in Sub-Saharan Africa but only by 22 percent.

Unfortunately, an increase in relative income inequality has often accompanied rapid economic growth. To test the effect of such increasing inequality, or "anti-poor" growth, what would happen if the relative shares of income of the lowest two quintiles declined by 20 percent? In this case, the number of chronically undernourished persons would decline by only 8 percent and basic hunger would climb by 71 percent in Sub-Saharan Africa. The lesson is that if the gains from economic growth are broadly shared, food security improvements from economic growth can be further enhanced.

A final set of estimates combined the effect of declines in real food prices with a pro-poor economic growth strategy. A 10 percent increase in calories consumed as a result of lower prices plus growth that redistributes income toward the poor has a dramatic impact. The estimated number of food insecure falls by 65 percent—300 million persons fewer than FAO's 1996–98 estimate.

If the Rate of Economic Growth Falls . . .   If economic growth falters, the consequences are dire. Global hunger rises by 36 percent, to more than 1.1 billion people, compared with the FAO 1996–98 estimate, if economic growth is halved. In Sub-Saharan Africa, the number of chronically underfed climbs by 136 percent. Although insufficient in and of itself, economic growth is crucial, especially in the poorest countries.

Banishing Hunger   As a final exercise, we calculated the regional economic growth rates necessary to *end* hunger by 2025 and 2050, assuming that income distribution and real food prices remained unchanged (Table 2.5). If 2025 is the target, per capita income growth rates of 6.3–7.0 percent annually are required. These are far higher than can be achieved over a period of a quarter century. To see this, the first column in Table 2.5 gives the actual 1975–99 GDP per capita growth rates achieved (in constant 1995 U.S. dollars). But if 2050 is the target, sustained economic growth of between 3.5 and 3.9 percent could essentially end hunger. Even if economic growth does not reach such levels, hunger reduction can be significantly advanced by technological changes leading to lower real food prices, together with growth strategies that favor the poor. These are the rudiments of polices to end hunger in our lifetimes.

TABLE 2.5 • Annual average growth rates in GDP per capita
needed to end hunger, and actual 1975–99 rates

Country/region	1975–99 (GDP per capita in constant 1995 US $)	2025 (%)	2050 (%)
Sub-Saharan Africa	0.5	6.3	3.5
East Asia	1.8	7.0	3.9
China	7.5	7.0	3.9
South Asia	3.2	6.8	3.7
Latin America	1.5	7.0	3.9
Middle East/North Africa	1.1	6.6	3.7
Newly Independent States	0.1	7.0	3.9

SOURCES: 1975–99 data are calculated from World Bank 2001c; 2025 and 2050 data are authors' estimations.
NOTE: The Newly Independent States include countries of the former Soviet Union and Eastern Europe.

THAILAND: AN EXAMPLE OF PRO-POOR GROWTH

Thailand provides an example of the potential impact of sustained, robust economic growth combined with a commitment to poverty alleviation. Between 1988 and 1996, the proportion of the Thai population living in poverty fell from 32.6 percent to 11.4 percent. Among preschool children the incidence of mild malnutrition fell from 35 percent to 8 percent between 1982 and 1998, with moderate malnutrition declining from 13 percent to less than 1 percent and the severe cases from 2 percent to an insignificant level (FAO 2000f). Economic growth per capita averaged 5.9 percent per year between 1980 and 1991 and for the entire period 1980–98 household consumption grew by an average of 5.1 percent annually. By 1998–99 Thailand had recovered from the 1997 Asian financial crisis and the economy expanded by 4.1 percent per capita (World Bank 2001d).

In addition to rapid economic growth, Thailand has had a strong orientation toward investing in people, emphasizing agriculture, and directly addressing poverty. Primary school enrollment was 92 percent in 1980 and secondary school enrollment reached 47 percent in 1997. Adult literacy rates were 97 percent for men and 93 percent for women in 1998. In terms of basic investments in people's health, 94 percent of the urban population had access to improved water sources in 1990 and 88 percent in rural areas (World Bank 2001b). Moreover, the importance of growth in the agricultural sector was not overlooked. Annual growth in agricultural value added averaged 3.9 percent for 1980–90 and 2.7 percent for 1990–99 (World Bank 2001b).

Thailand also has had a well-organized poverty alleviation program. The program was initiated in 1982, starting in the 286 poorest districts in the country; it became nationwide in 1984. The efforts concentrated on ensuring a minimum subsistence level for all and took a participatory approach that stressed community involvement. The initial focus was on the most serious nutritional problems, and it combined nutrition surveillance and supplemental feeding of young children, access to primary health care, and the production of nutritious foods. In 1990 the collaboration among various levels of government was strengthened, but local community involvement remained central (FAO 2000f). Thailand has also had one of the most successful HIV/AIDS education and prevention efforts, targeted especially at those most at risk, such as prostitutes. South Africa and Thailand had roughly the same rate of infection of about 1 percent of the adult population in 1990. South Africa's infection rate rose to 20 percent by 1999, whereas Thailand's was only 2 percent (IFPRI 2000).

ECONOMIC GROWTH AND THE ENVIRONMENT

We have made the case here that broadly shared economic growth can end hunger. However, environmentalists would rightly raise concerns about the impact of such widespread economic growth on the environment. The concept of sustainable development, while seemingly laudable, has in the words of Daniel Esty of Yale University been turned into "a buzzword largely devoid of content" (cited in *The Economist* 2002b, 4). Virtually all human activity, and certainly all economic growth, affects the environment. The real issues are how to limit environmental degradation and achieve the appropriate balance between development and the environment. Development advocates and environmental champions have frequently been at loggerheads. However, Kenneth Arrow and Larry Goulder of Stanford University feel that the ideological differences are narrowing. "Many economists now accept the idea that natural capital has to be valued, and that we need to account for ecosystem services. Many ecologists now accept that prohibiting everything in the name of protecting nature is not useful, and so are being selective" (*The Economist* 2002b, 4).

In a recent study of the total impact of human activity on the environment, Wackernagel et al. (2002) analyze human demands on the environment for the production of food and other goods and for the absorption of waste. They conclude that human demands, which amounted to 70 percent of the regenerative capacity of the global biosphere in 1961, reached 120 percent in 1999, exceeding that capacity by 20 percent. However, almost the entire increased burden between 1961 and 1999 results from greater energy use in the form of fossil fuels and the resulting carbon dioxide (CO_2) emissions. One of the major impacts of the increased use of carbon-based energy is the likelihood of global climate change, which will be discussed in the next chapter. Between 1961 and 1999, Wackernagel et al. (2002) calculate that crop production directly placed very little additional burden on the earth's regenerative ability. A more detailed assessment of agriculture's environmental impact will also be presented in Chapter 3.

The fundamental message from Wackernagel et al. (2002) and many other studies is that if continued global economic growth is not to have devastating environmental impacts, we must use energy with much greater efficiency and do a better job of controlling pollution. Beyond that, sustained global growth will require a systematic "transition to a low-carbon energy system" (*The Economist* 2002a, 10). Alternative energy sources, such as solar energy and hydrogen-powered fuel cells, may be part of the solution, but so may other approaches such as biological "sequestration" (storage) of carbon. Perhaps the most immediate need is to reduce the dependence on coal (the heaviest CO_2 producer per unit of energy) and to develop technologies that drastically cut its emissions, including carbon dioxide. What is clear is that the solution will have to be global, which suggests the compelling need for a global environmental organization, which will be discussed in Chapters 5 and 6.

THE GLOBAL CHALLENGE

The World Food Summit goal of reducing the number of food-insecure persons by half by 2015 will not be achieved, even by 2025, based on current estimates of economic and population growth. Business as usual will not do the job. Much more will need to be done. First, the world's poor must share broadly in the gains from sustained, environmentally compatible, global growth. Growth that increases the poor's share over time, together with declining real food prices, would have a dramatic impact on hunger.

The actions necessary to achieve robust pro-poor growth and meet the environmental challenge will be explored in subsequent chapters. They include key investments in poor people and developing-country agricultural research and development and changes in global trade policy and institutions. Investing in human capital, principally through primary education and basic health care, together with employment creation for the poor, are key elements of such a pro-poor policy. Lower food prices will require a major commitment to agricultural research and development in the developing world. In the current round of global trade negotiations, industrial-country markets need to be opened to poor countries' exports to spur their economic growth. More funding will be crucial from international development assistance, private investment, and philanthropy. On a regional basis, making significant progress against poverty and hunger will be most difficult in Africa.

Our analysis thus points to the need for significant innovations in national policies, but it has larger implications as well. We believe that nations, acting individually, are unlikely to provide their people with the requisite tools to end hunger and protect the environment. Food security will require an additional level of effort and organization at an international level. Global changes have outpaced national institutions because many of the most pressing issues are transnational. In the next chapter, we turn to the global nature of these challenges to food security.

3 • ENDING HUNGER SUSTAINABLY

As the world's population continues to grow, shortages and degradation of both land and water will challenge the sustainability of the global food system. In a widely recognized research report appearing in *Science* in 2001, ecologist David Tilman of the University of Minnesota and his coauthors forecast the impact of increased population and food demand on a variety of environmental variables at a global level (Tilman et al. 2001). These forecasts, extrapolated to the years 2020 and 2050, focus especially on agricultural nutrients applied to crops, such as nitrogen and phosphorus, which pollute surface and groundwater and contribute to eutrophication—excessive nutrients—in lakes and rivers. In recent years this has created a "dead zone" where the Mississippi enters the Gulf of Mexico. Eutrophication results in oxygen starvation of organisms living in the water, loss of biodiversity, and changes in species composition. In groundwater, nitrogen raises nitrate and nitrite levels, increases greenhouse gases and ozone levels, and turns soils and fresh water acid.

Human activity, most of it agricultural, already contributes as much nitrogen and phosphorus to the land as all natural sources. If these levels continue at present trends in response to population and income growth, nitrogen fertilization will increase by an average of 60 percent over present amounts by 2020 and 170 percent by 2050 (Tilman et al. 2001). Phosphorus levels are projected to rise by 40 percent by 2020 and 140 percent by 2050.

In another set of projections, global pesticide use is forecast to increase by an average of 70 percent over current levels by 2020 and by 170 percent by 2050. Some of these pesticides will accumulate in food chains and affect human and animal health years after their use. However, major uncertainty surrounds the future impact of pesticides because new bio-technologies are being developed that substitute pest-resistant crops for traditional crops, perhaps reducing pesticide use significantly.

Land use for agriculture is also projected to increase as forests, grass-lands, and other natural habitats are converted to agricultural uses. As a consequence, highly managed ecosystems will be substituted for more complex habitats, resulting in losses in biodiversity on the converted lands. Land used for agriculture is projected to increase by 18 percent above pres-ent levels by 2050, although this net increase masks an actual decrease in agricultural lands in developed countries and an increase in developing countries of 10 billion hectares. Such an increase would result in a world-wide loss of natural ecosystems larger than the land mass of the entire United States. Most of this loss will occur in Latin America and Sub-Saharan Africa, including a third of remaining tropical and temperate forests, savannas, and grasslands (Tilman et al. 2001).

How can we face these pressures on land and water resources, while still responding to the food needs of both poor and rich nations? "Sustain-ability" is, of course, a widely invoked idea, with many possible interpre-tations. In the context of food security, we adopt the reasoning of the U.S. National Research Council's assessment of a "pathway to sustainability," in recognition of incomplete knowledge of both future and current eco-logical conditions. As the Council noted,

> reducing hunger while sustaining life support systems will require
> a dramatic overall advance in food production, distribution, and
> access. Sustainable increases in output per hectare of two to three
> times present levels will be required by 2050. Productivity must be
> increased on robust areas and restored to degraded lands, while
> damage to fragile areas is reduced. (NRC 1999)

How will key resources be protected in the face of global food demands, and what policies will be needed? In this chapter, we integrate land and water constraints with a global assessment of agricultural production and food demand to help answer this question. The basis of this assessment is a model developed and maintained by IFPRI, covering 36 countries or country groups and 16 commodities including all cereals, soybeans, roots and tubers, meats, and dairy products (see Appendix B). There have been

other world agriculture projections, but at this point IFPRI's work projecting global food security represents the major effort in this area (see Mc-
Calla and Revoredo 2001 for a critical appraisal of these projections). The
IFPRI model links international demand and supply through trade. Food
demand results from the key factors discussed in Chapter 2—commodity
prices, per capita incomes, and population growth—while feed demand is
derived from livestock production, feed prices, and feeding efficiency.
Changes in food production or supply result from changes in the area
and yield of various crops,[1] and advances in management and plant
breeding. Growth also results from private and public sector investments
in agricultural research, extension, and education, as well as marketing
efficiency, infrastructure, and irrigation. Added to these results are estimates of water constraints and their effects.[2]

Based on these factors, we examine global food markets and hunger up
to the year 2025. What is the influence of increasing land and water
scarcity on the sustainability of food production and prices? What might
happen to cereal prices and consumption on a global scale if China or
India suffered significant shortfalls in cereal production growth due to
land or water constraints? In the face of these constraints, what would be
the impact of trade liberalization, or a slowdown in population growth,
or increased government spending on agricultural research? Considering
these factors drives home the lesson that whether future food production
is sustainable will depend on the choices of governments acting collectively and individually, as well as on NGOs, private companies—and the
inherent limits on land and water resources themselves.

SUPPLY AND DEMAND: A PRECARIOUS BALANCE

The population and income increases described in Chapter 2 have led to
dramatic shifts in the global production and consumption of food. These
include a surge in grain production and a spectacular rise in meat consumption. Another factor is the increasingly important role of international
trade. The surge in grain production largely resulted from the high-yielding
varieties of wheat and rice that swept across much of Asia during the 1970s
and early 1980s (see Chapter 4). Recent cereal yields have risen more
modestly but have still outstripped gains in other crops such as cassava,
potatoes, and beans. Cereal grain production in some countries, such as
India, kept up with population growth (although India's nutritional status

is less clear), but many other countries turned to imports, either because domestic production fell short, or because rising incomes pushed up the demand for food and feed.

Developed-country crop exporters, led by North America and Europe, quadrupled their net cereal exports between 1970 and 1990, reaching 93 million tons by the late 1990s. The expansion in cereal production and trade, especially in Western Europe and North America, was fueled by government subsidies that supported the price of grain and underwrote exports, driving down food prices on world markets. Following the 1986–93 Uruguay Round of multilateral trade negotiations, North America and Western Europe reduced some of these subsidies modestly and made others less directly tied to production. Partly as a result, growth in the production of cereals slowed in these regions and net cereal exports declined between 1990 and 1997, with Argentina and Australia partly compensating through significant export expansion. The new U.S. farm bill with its large subsidies may help to reverse these trends.

Livestock now consume a growing share of cereals, because of a boom in meat consumption, particularly poultry. Per capita consumption of meat in the developing world more than doubled from 11 kilograms per capita in 1967 to 24 kilograms per capita in 1997; even greater relative increases occurred in poultry consumption. Even so, the developing world still consumes only a third as much meat per person, on average, as the developed countries. Large-scale, concentrated (referred to as industrial) livestock operations, still primarily in the developed countries, are the source of serious environmental problems. The huge amounts of animal waste are kept in liquid form in open ponds (called lagoons), usually with the eventual intention of applying it as organic fertilizer on fields. However, these open lagoons can cause both air pollution (odor) and contamination of groundwater (streams, rivers, and lakes) and aquifers (underground water). The failure thus far to address these issues through necessary regulation is inexcusable.

Although both India and China managed to meet most of their own cereal demands, India did so with slow income growth and policies that raised food prices and depressed demand. China was much more successful at raising both food supplies and income. In addition to the growth in production in those countries, supply expansion, especially among the net exporters, helped worldwide prices for maize (corn), rice, and wheat decline by 50 percent or more over the past 20 years, signifying that there was more food available to satisfy demand. Many, however, lacked the income to buy this food; food insecurity thus remained not because of shortfalls in production but because of the poverty and access limitations discussed in Chapter 2.

Yet it would be wrong to conclude that an adequate supply of food and feed is assured. Efforts to fight hunger require both greater income growth *and* increased agricultural productivity. The two are linked because agriculture is of critical importance to development, especially for poor people in the poorest countries, for whom it accounts for more than half of employment and half of household expenditures. Without increased productivity, food prices will escalate beyond the reach of the poor, and hunger will persist for hundreds of millions of people. At the same time, policies that artificially depress food prices undercut incentives to raise productivity. We turn now to an assessment of the policies and investments needed to sustain the precarious balance between supply and demand in the face of key resource needs and policy constraints.

THE WORLD IN 2025

Based on current trends, what will the supply/demand balance for food look like in 2025, and how will land and water constraints affect it? While developing countries continue to drive increases in the global demand for cereals, growth in demand is slowing, partly as a result of decelerating population growth, and partly because diets change as prosperity rises. Growth in cereal demand globally is projected to decline to 1.3 percent per year during 1997–2025 from 1.9 percent per year in 1969–97. Even so, the absolute demand for cereals during 1997–2025 will approach the increase experienced in the preceding period (Figure 3.1). Developing countries in Asia, with larger and more urbanized populations and rapid economic growth, will account for half the increase, with China alone accounting for a quarter (Figure 3.2).

Global demand for meat will grow much faster than that for cereals: we estimate it will increase by 69 percent between 1997 and 2025, mostly in developing countries (Figure 3.3). China alone will account for 40 percent, compared with India's 4 percent. Demand for meat is expected to double in South Asia, Southeast Asia, and Sub-Saharan Africa, but consumption will remain far below that of the developed world, indicating scope for further increases. Poultry is expected to account for 42 percent of global meat demand growth during 1997–2025, compared with 28 percent in 1997,

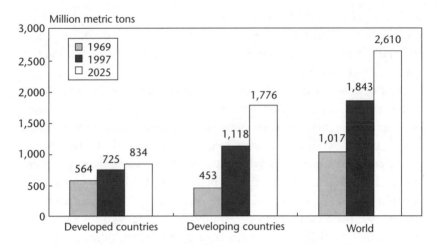

FIGURE 3.1 • Total cereal demand by region, 1969, 1997, and 2025

SOURCES: Authors using 1969 data from FAOSTAT (FAO 2001c) and IMPACT-WATER model projections, June 2001.

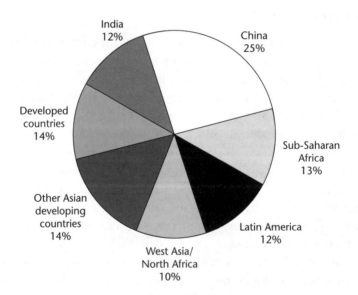

Total demand increase = 767 million metric tons

FIGURE 3.2 • Share of various regions in cereal demand increase, 1997–2025

SOURCE: Authors using IMPACT-WATER model projections, June 2001.

NOTE: The classification West Asia/North Africa, used throughout this chapter, includes Cyprus and Turkey, whereas Middle East/North Africa, used elsewhere in the book, does not.

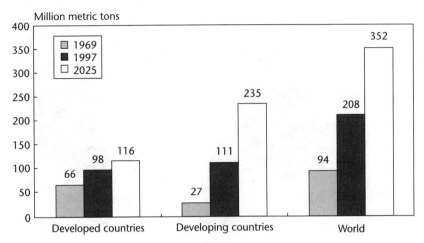

FIGURE 3.3   •   Total meat demand by region, 1969, 1997, and 2025
SOURCES: Authors using 1969 data from FAOSTAT (FAO 2001c) and IMPACT-WATER model
projections, June 2001.

reflecting a shift from red meat to poultry (Figure 3.4). Cereal crops will therefore increasingly be grown for animal feed rather than for direct consumption (Figure 3.5). Maize—mainly used for animal feed—will gain in importance. By 2025, maize will be the world's leading cereal, accounting for an estimated 30 percent of global cereal production, compared with 29 percent each for wheat and rice.

Demand growth for other staple food commodities will also be strong. In many parts of Sub-Saharan Africa, roots and tubers—especially cassava, sweet potatoes, and yams—are major food sources. In the late 1990s they accounted for 20 percent of calories consumed in the region and an even higher proportion in the diets of the poor. In much of Asia and Latin America, roots and tubers provide important carbohydrates and vitamins. Total demand for these crops is forecast to increase by 65 percent (294 million tons) between 1997 and 2025. Sub-Saharan Africa accounts for 46 percent of this increase, East Asia 21 percent, and South Asia 14 percent (Figure 3.6). Improving yields for roots and tubers thus remains a vital component in the food security of the poorest countries.

A constraint on production from land scarcity is rapidly approaching in many parts of the world. In these areas, raising production by clearing more land for farming—expanding the "extensive margin"—is almost over. Production can only be raised at the "intensive margin" through increases

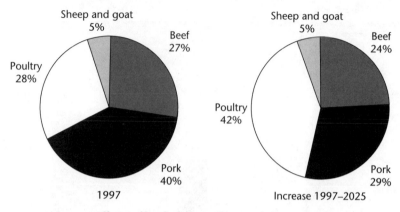

FIGURE 3.4 • Share of beef, pork, poultry, and sheep and goat meat in world demand for meat, 1997–2025

SOURCE: Authors using IMPACT-WATER model projections, June 2001.

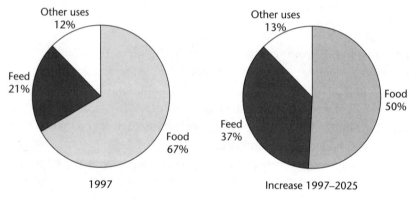

FIGURE 3.5 • Share of food, feed, and other uses in total cereal demand of developing countries, 1997–2025

SOURCE: Authors using IMPACT-WATER model projections, June 2001.

in yields. In parts of Asia, almost all available land is already under cultivation, and urban land encroachment and degradation are serious problems in some places. Sub-Saharan Africa and Latin America have more potential for area expansion: some 23 million hectares in Sub-Saharan Africa and 8 million hectares in Latin America will likely become cropland during 1997–2025. However, these two regions will be the exceptions.

As a result, cereal production must increase by raising productivity. Unfortunately, increases in crop yields have been slowing for all cereals in all regions since 1980, except for Sub-Saharan Africa, where they are recov-

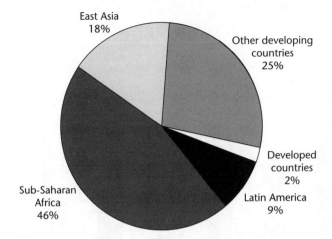

FIGURE 3.6 • Share of increase in roots and tubers
demand by region, 1997–2025
SOURCE: Authors using IMPACT-WATER model projections, June
2001.

ering slightly from past stagnation (Figure 3.7). In the rich countries the
slowdown was partly a response to lower production subsidies, which
reduced incentives to apply high levels of fertilizers and other inputs. In
the NIS encompassing the former Soviet Union and Eastern Europe, economic collapse and uneven economic reforms depressed productivity. In
Asia, the main culprit was slowing public investment in crop research and
irrigation infrastructure, combined with water shortages as growing nonagricultural demands divert water from agriculture. Globally, cereal yield
growth rates are projected to fall from 1.6 percent per year from 1982–97 to
0.9 percent per year from 1997–2025.

An underlying factor of special concern is the growing shortage of water.
Water available for irrigation is falling relative to the amount needed—the
demand for irrigation water in developing countries is forecast to rise
13.4 percent by 2025, but actual available water will rise by only 4.4 percent. Table 3.1 shows the irrigation water supply reliability index (IWSR)—
the ratio of water supply available for irrigation over the amount actually
demanded—between 1995 and 2025 for developed and developing regions
and selected countries and river basins. For developing countries, the IWSR
declines from 0.79 to 0.71 in 2025. Increasing water scarcity is thus a direct
contributor to slowdowns in cereal yields in developing countries in our

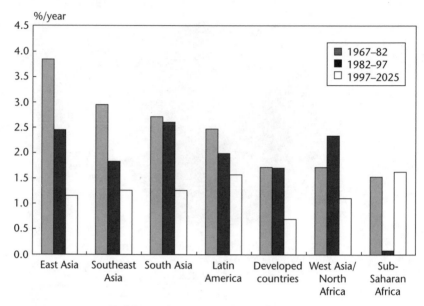

FIGURE 3.7 • Yield growth rates by region for all cereals, 1967–82, 1982–97, and projected 1997–2025

SOURCES: Authors using 1969 and 1982 data (FAO 2001c) and IMPACT-WATER model projections, June 2001.

NOTE: The classification West Asia/North Africa, used throughout this chapter, includes Cyprus and Turkey, whereas Middle East/North Africa, used elsewhere in the book, does not.

TABLE 3.1 • Irrigation water supply reliability index, 1995, 2010, and 2025

Region	1995	2010	2025
Developed basins/countries/regions	0.91	0.89	0.93
Developing basins/countries/regions	0.79	0.73	0.71
World basins/countries/regions	0.81	0.75	0.74

SOURCE: Authors using IMPACT-WATER model projections, August 2001.

baseline estimate, costing developing countries almost 140 million metric tons of reduced production annually by 2021–25, roughly equal to the total cereal production of China in the 1990s.

Table 3.2 shows the relative crop yield for cereals in irrigated areas in developing countries. This is the ratio of actual yields to maximum economically attainable yields. The ratio is projected to decline from 0.86 in 1995 to 0.74 in 2021–25. The fall in the relative crop yield index is a significant drag on future yield growth. For developing countries as a group, the

TABLE 3.2 • Relative crop yields for cereals in irrigated area, 1995, 2010, and 2025

Region	1995	2010	2025
Developed basins/countries/regions	0.89	0.86	0.86
Developing basins/countries/regions	0.86	0.80	0.74
World basins/countries/regions	0.87	0.81	0.77

SOURCE: Authors using IMPACT-WATER model projections, June 2001.

drop from 0.86 to 0.74 represents an annual "cost" in crop yields forgone due to increased water stress, compared with the base year, of 0.72 metric tons per hectare or an annual loss of cereal production of 139 million metric tons, which is slightly greater than the total rice production in China in late 1990s.

Given these constraints, developing countries will frequently be unable to meet cereal demands from their own production, increasing their reliance on international trade and thus on the trade policies of the mainly industrialized countries that make up the Organisation of Economic Cooperation and Development (OECD) and global trade rules. North and South America and Europe appear able to meet this demand and are likely to expand their roles as agricultural exporters by 2025 (Figure 3.8). Net cereal imports by developing countries are expected to more than double. The Asian nations, particularly China, will boost their imports enormously. Countries that falter economically, unable to raise sufficient foreign exchange to buy this grain, will become increasingly vulnerable.

Although sharp decreases in food prices benefited the poor in the 1980s and 1990s, it seems cereal prices under current trends will decline only slightly in the years leading up to 2025. As a result, any shocks occurring from drought or other factors will put serious pressure on food prices and poor consumers.

WHAT IF?

The Picture in Africa What if the efforts to end hunger falter, and the trends noted above turn downward? The requirements, and pitfalls, of sustaining agricultural production in various regions can be estimated using the same methods established under the baseline conditions for 1997–2025. In projections to 2025, Sub-Saharan Africa's problems stand out starkly. It is the only region where the number of malnourished children will rise over the next 20 years; even the 6 million predicted under current trends

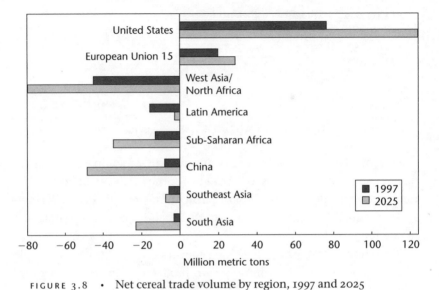

FIGURE 3.8 • Net cereal trade volume by region, 1997 and 2025

SOURCE: Authors using IMPACT-WATER model projections, June 2001.

NOTE: The classification West Asia/North Africa, used throughout this chapter, includes Cyprus and Turkey, whereas Middle East/North Africa, used elsewhere in the book, does not.

may prove optimistic. If production of most crops does not increase at rates approaching those during the past decade, hunger will expand its scope. More than half the gains in African agriculture over the past decade have come from cultivating more land (see Chapter 4), not from more intensive use of fertilizer or improved crop varieties, with resulting losses in ecosystem biodiversity. Yields are now far below other regions, such as South Asia, whereas they were nearly equal in the 1960s (Figure 3.9). Without more intensive production on existing land, accompanied by measures to maintain and replenish the soil and improvements in rural infrastructure, yields will likely stagnate. Particular threats are the environmental degradation of many vulnerable areas and the inability to move food through Africa's miserable transportation routes to larger towns and cities. Such changes will require policies promoting investment in agriculture, notably well-targeted crop fertilization and irrigation projects, as well as roads, clean water, and education. This is easy to say, and very hard for Africa to do.

But what if such efforts falter? What if political turmoil or the toll of HIV/AIDS or lack of political will cause needed investments to fall short, so that crop area and yield increases are cut by half and life expectancy and access to education and sanitation fall? The results of such a pessimistic

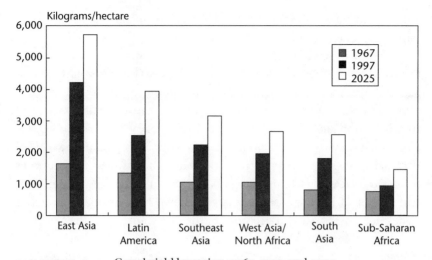

FIGURE 3.9 • Cereal yield by region, 1967, 1997, and 2025

SOURCES: Authors using 1967 FAOSTAT data (FAO 2001c) and IMPACT-WATER model projections, June 2001.

NOTE: The classification West Asia/North Africa, used throughout this chapter, includes Cyprus and Turkey, whereas Middle East/North Africa, used elsewhere in the book, does not.

picture would be tragic. Sub-Saharan Africa's net food import bill in 2025 would jump from US$8.5 billion to an estimated US$15 billion, driving incomes down as imports account for 18 percent of total domestic food production value. Calorie consumption per person would fall by 11 percent. The blow would fall heavily on Africa's children. The number of malnourished children would increase by 42 percent, to 51 million. To make matters worse, required food imports would be unsustainable because of a shortage of foreign exchange. Without a massive increase in food aid, the resulting food shortages and malnutrition would be catastrophic. This pessimistic scenario can be thought of as similar to a combination of the higher food price and slow growth cases in Chapter 2.

What kinds of growth, education, and health care would be necessary for Sub-Saharan Africa to battle childhood malnutrition as effectively as the rest of the developing world? According to our best estimates, reducing the number of malnourished children by one-third—equal to the rate now prevailing in the rest of the developing world—would require an increase in total African investments on roads, irrigation, clean water, education, and agricultural research of just over 80 percent, compared with the baseline investments from 1997 to 2025.[3] Crop yields would have to grow 3 percent annually and total GDP by 8 to 10 percent each year.

This optimistic case is in many respects akin to the pro-poor people scenario in Chapter 2, with lower food prices.

Although they seem far out of reach, such rates of growth are not unprecedented. They occurred in Asia during the Green Revolution. Sub-Saharan Africa, however, faces different constraints: climate and soil conditions are more difficult, water is much more scarce in many areas, and transportation and communications infrastructure is far more limited. As a result, the costs of staving off hunger in Africa are high, but the costs of *not* making the necessary investments are huge. Failure of African countries to act would lead to a significant global failure to end hunger and malnutrition. But Africa's fate is also a larger, shared responsibility, related to trade, aid, and investment decisions in the rich countries of the North.

The Asian Picture Because China and India are home to a third of the world's people, it is often said that they hold the fate of global food security in their hands. Shifts in food production or in consumer behavior there are often predicted to produce enormous changes in demand for food that reverberate around the world. What if income growth caused India to add more meat to its diet, as in other developing countries? While religious proscriptions reduce this tendency somewhat, such shifts would spell major changes for India, but fewer for the world as a whole. If meat consumption in India reached 21 kilograms in 2025, similar to Indonesia in 1997 and China and Pakistan during the past decade, major expansion in domestic livestock production and imports would be necessary.[4] Resulting increases in demand for livestock feed would raise needed cereal production and imports. Meat imports in 2025, we estimate, would rise to 1.5 million metric tons (compared with virtually zero in the baseline), and cereal imports to 27 million metric tons, instead of 6 million. Surprisingly, this would affect international prices only a little, since international markets could accommodate India's increasing demands. Global beef prices would increase only 3 percent by 2025, wheat prices by 7 percent, and maize prices by 8 percent. These price increases would fall most heavily on countries that are large net food importers.

But other vulnerabilities face India and China. Both may have great difficulty in further expanding agricultural production due to degraded land, water shortages, and growing competition with cities and industry for land and water, although in some parts of China, soil quality remains high even after hundreds of years of cultivation (Lindert 2000). Environmental degradation, unsustainable groundwater extraction for irrigation, and slowing agricultural investments could result in a sharp decline in agricultural growth, especially where soils are not protected and soil nutrients replenished. If these factors cause yields and cultivated area to increase only half as much as expected by 2025, what would be the result? Some effects would be offsetting. Higher prices would help induce increased food production. If economic growth rates declined, demand for meat in rapidly growing India and China would also abate. Even so, both India and China would be forced to turn to even more food imports. With no other significant changes, China's trade deficit in cereals would nearly double from 49 million metric tons to a forecast 91 million by 2025. India's imports of 6 million tons would rise to 30 million. India's small agricultural trade surplus in 1997 would give way to a deficit of US$9.5 billion in 2025, while China's agricultural trade deficit would soar to US$35.7 billion. Yet even rising imports of this magnitude could largely be met by net exporters, raising global wheat and maize prices by about 10 percent and rice prices by 28 percent.

We estimate that slowdowns in agricultural growth in India and China would also leave 2 million more children malnourished in 2025 in each country, assuming that the enormous increases in food imports could be paid for. Should these countries resist reliance on foreign suppliers and attempt to go it alone, domestic food prices could increase dramatically, with children suffering most.

Population's Role   What if the current slowdown in global population growth discussed in Chapter 2 occurred even more rapidly than the United Nation's medium-fertility forecast, resulting in a low estimate of 7 billion in 2025? In addition to putting less pressure on natural ecosystems, dramatic declines in the number of malnourished children would result. As the population declined, consumption would rise because food prices would be lower and per capita incomes higher. Consumption in calories could increase by 2.2 percent relative to the 2025 baseline (and by 10.8 percent compared with 1997 consumption levels). The projected number of malnourished children in the developing world could fall by more than 25 percent, to 76.9 million. While this number is still unacceptable, it shows that the hunger burden of high population growth in already poor regions falls heavily on children. South Asia stands out: with lower population growth, the number of malnourished children would fall by 29 percent, or

15 million children. And as emphasized in Chapter 2, even such optimistic population trends do little for Sub-Saharan Africa, where the number of malnourished children would still be 30 million, just 3 million less than in 1997.

People or Livestock?   Rapid growth in meat demand in developing countries, added to already high demands in rich countries, has raised questions about whether using cereals to feed livestock contributes to shortages for humans. The answer is a qualified yes. If humans did not eat meat, then some of the land area now devoted to feedgrains could be re-directed to foodgrains or other plant foods. Apart from the radical departure from meat in the human diet (a consumption trait dating to the Neolithic period), this conversion would not be one-for-one. Livestock, especially ruminants such as cattle, are able to graze on many areas unsuitable for arable crops and to digest grains in rough form (such as maize silage) unpalatable to humans. Moreover, livestock—especially poultry—are more efficient than humans in converting grain into edible proteins. Without this protein, major expansions in plant-based proteins would be needed, such as edible beans and peas. The environmental consequences of such a radical transformation are difficult to project but they would no doubt add to pressure on land and water resources.

While this type of wholesale conversion is unlikely, many feel that the efficiency with which grain is used to feed livestock can be substantially improved. Such improvement in feeding efficiencies, combined with some reduction in meat consumption in developed countries, could help improve nutrition in the developing countries. Feeding efficiencies have improved markedly since the 1980s. From 1967 to 1982, the ratio of feed-to-meat produced stayed almost constant, so that every step up in meat demand required more feedgrains. Beginning in the 1980s, changes in live-stock management—including hormone use and genetic improvements in cattle, swine, and poultry—allowed less feed to be used per unit of meat. A major reason was that poultry, the most efficient converter of grain to protein, accounted for an increasing share of meat production. Moreover, improved feeding efficiencies cut the total amount of waste product per animal, reducing the load of nitrogen from animal waste. In addition, meat production in some developing countries such as China (where each household traditionally owned a pig fed on household garbage) is shifting rapidly toward commercial enterprises, which rely heavily on cereal feed.

As a result, demand for feed will likely match meat production more closely than in recent years.

However, technological advances—for example, improved breeding in developing countries—could cause feed ratios to continue falling. Meat would become cheaper as animals consumed less feedgrain. The price of maize could fall by almost 30 percent by 2025, compared with current trends. This shift would set off a cascade of consequences. Falling animal feed demand and declining maize and other coarse grain prices would cause feedgrains—particularly maize—to in effect move away from large feed-importing countries in East and Southeast Asia and to flow instead toward South Asia and Sub-Saharan Africa, where cereals are mainly eaten by people. With improvements in feeding efficiencies, we estimate that net imports of cereals into Sub-Saharan Africa could increase by 90 percent and into South Asia by 82 percent by 2025, compared with current trends.

The result would also be felt in the number of malnourished children, which would fall by 3 million globally. While not a huge gain, compared with the global total of 129 million malnourished children, the effect is significant in Sub-Saharan Africa. Because maize is mainly a foodgrain in Africa, reduced animal feed usage would translate directly into more food for people, resulting in 1.8 million fewer malnourished children there in 2025.

In addition to benefits from improved feeding efficiency, could reduced meat demand in rich countries also help to reduce global malnutrition? The primary effect would be a reduced world price for meat, making it more affordable to poor consumers. A drop in meat prices would also reduce production in both developed and developing countries, further reducing the demand for feedgrains. Reduced feed demand in turn would drop feedgrain prices, allowing an increase in the use of grain for food.

Rosegrant, Leach, and Gerpacio (1999) explored the consequences of a 50 percent decline in meat demand in rich countries from 1993 to 2020. They found that prices for beef, pork, sheep and goat meat, and poultry fell by 22–31 percent. A corresponding fall in maize and coarse grain demand lowered their prices 11 and 10 percent respectively in rich countries. Globally, wheat and rice prices fell by 5 percent and wheat prices by 1 percent. The effects on wheat and rice, the primary food staple cereals in developing countries, are small because little is used for animal feed. Reduced demand for livestock feed in rich countries does not translate into significantly reduced prices for rice and wheat in poor ones. Sub-Saharan Africa would benefit more because of its greater reliance on maize as a food.

Cutting meat consumption by half in rich countries would raise consumption in poor countries by about 13 percent and cereal consumption by about 1.5 percent, mainly as a result of lowered prices and increased affordability. However, lower prices would also lead to lower production in poorer nations, which would fall by 27 million metric tons, necessitating increased cereal imports of 11 million tons.

Overall, our estimates indicate that the improvement in calorie availability in poor countries from reduced meat consumption in rich ones is only 40 calories per person per day. The main point is that the improvements in food security are smaller than many observers would imagine. Even so, the number of malnourished children in developing countries would likely decline by 3.6 million children and by 1.2 million in Sub-Saharan Africa, results comparable with gains in feeding efficiency. However, a 50 percent reduction in rich countries' meat consumption is far less likely than the improvement in feeding efficiency that we considered here.

Can Productivity Gains Stave Off Hunger?   Growth in staple crop yields has slowed, largely because one-time improvements in planting density, multiple harvesting, plants bred for fertilizer responsiveness, and better management cannot be repeated every year. Environmental constraints add extra uncertainty. Farmers generally prefer flatter lands without important soil quality constraints, but much of the world's agricultural land is less than ideal. As most gardeners know, neutral soils (those with a pH between 6.0 and 7.0) increase the availability of nutrients and promote beneficial microbial activity. But naturally acidic soils with a pH of less than 5.5 are prevalent throughout the humid tropics, and acid soils can also develop from long-term use of ammonia-based nitrogen fertilizers. Acid soils tend to be saturated with exchangeable aluminum, in some places to the extent that they are toxic to plants. They can also "fix" natural or applied phosphorus, making it effectively unavailable to plants. Such soils also have low reserves of other plant nutrients like potassium. These types of soil nutrient problems are evident on significant areas throughout Latin America, Southeast Asia, and Sub-Saharan Africa.

Poorly drained soils (including areas with high groundwater tables, stagnant surface water, or where the slope of the land promotes flooding), saline soils, and excessively alkaline soils (which, like the acid soils, affect nutrient availability) constrain crop and pasture yields. Wood, Sebastian, and Scherr (2000) estimate that only 16 percent of the world's agricultural land is free of soil and topographical constraints. Nearly 25 percent of the land in agriculture is acidic, 18 percent has low potassium reserves, 14 percent is poorly drained, and 3 percent suffers from salinity problems.

The environment thus affects farming, just as farmers affect the environment. For example, different land management practices are associated with different types and degrees of soil degradation. Salinization is linked with intensification of irrigated land and clearing of deep-rooted vegetation; soil compaction with mechanized farming; nutrient depletion with intensive, sparsely fertilized cropping systems; water erosion with clearing and poor cultivation practices on steeper-sloped land; and soil pollution with industrial waste. With the exception of the recent work by Tilman (2001) and global assessments undertaken by IFPRI in conjunction with the World Resources Institute, much of the evidence of the nature and extent of degradation induced by agriculture is scarce, controversial, and based on dubious scientific measurement (Wood, Sebastian, and Scherr 2000). In some locales, agriculture can severely degrade the land, but at a global scale these effects currently appear to be of limited consequence for food production. In addition, some (but by no means all) of this degradation is reversible. However, agriculture also leads to significant off-farm effects, such as nutrient runoff and greenhouse gas emissions that contribute to global warming. As Tilman et al. (2001) noted, "Existing knowledge, if widely used, could significantly reduce the impacts of agriculture and increase productivity. Integrated pest management, application of site- and time-appropriate amounts of agricultural chemicals and water, use of cover crops on fallow lands and buffer strips between cultivated fields and drainage areas, and appropriate deployment of more productive crops can increase yields while reducing water, fertilizer, and pesticide use and movement to nonagricultural habitats" (Tilman et al. 2001, 283–284).

Two scenarios can be envisioned. In one, environmental problems and reduced investment in agricultural research cause the growth in crop yields to slow. In the others, governments, international organizations, and private firms raise investments in agricultural research and environmental protection to new levels. To estimate the effect of these alternatives, we represent changes in these fundamental factors by assuming both low- and high-yield situations, compared with current trends to the year 2025. The low-yield scenario entails a decline in yield growth rates for meats, milk, and all crops of 50 percent from the baseline level in the developed world and of 40 percent in all developing regions. It is also associated with a zero growth in irrigation. The high-yield scenario results from an increase in the expansion of irrigated area of 1 percent per year, together with an increase in the annual growth in yields of 20 percent in the developed world and of 40 percent for the same products in the developing world.

Slower growth in yields would mean that supplies of food would not keep pace with population and income growth, resulting in sharply higher food prices. Projected rice prices would more than double by 2025, and maize prices would rise 59 percent. Global rice prices are particularly sensitive to low yield growth because developing countries where rice is grown are most seriously affected. Conversely, faster growth in yields produces more abundant food and falling prices. Maize prices fall by an estimated 28 percent and rice prices by 46 percent. The overall conclusion is that the price of food in 2025 is especially sensitive to the rates of crop yield growth—or lack thereof—from investments in agricultural research, irrigation, and environmental protection.

WATER—A DWINDLING RESOURCE

Water scarcity has already become a pressing problem in certain areas, such as the Middle East, and is generally accepted to be the most serious environmental constraint on global agricultural production in the future. Even given current trends, water scarcity will contribute to declining crop yields, but if water scarcity is even more severe—as nonagricultural water uses or an underinvestment in water supplies and water management occur—the prospects for food security and its sustainability are further threatened. A joint survey by the World Resources Institute (WRI) and IFPRI of global agroecological conditions (Wood, Sebastian, and Scherr 2000, 56–61) emphasized that 30–40 percent of the world's crop output comes from the 17 percent of the world's cropland that is irrigated, equal to 264 million hectares.[5] As irrigated area has expanded—by 1.5 to 2.0 percent a year for the past 20 years—water demands and more intensive land use have grown apace. Irrigated area varies widely, as does its efficiency (see Table 3.3). When these irrigation demands are put in the context of

TABLE 3.3 • Regional and global summary of irrigation indicators, 1990

Region	Total irrigated area (thousand hectares)	1990 irrigation indicators included in the Seckler et al. analysis			
		Area growth rate (%/year)	Irrigated area (thousand hectares)	Irrigation abstraction (cubic kilometers/ year)	Average irrigation depth[a] (meters)	Average irrigation efficiency (%)
North America	21,618	0.90	21,618	202	0.93	53
Latin America and the Caribbean	16,182	2.38	16,111	163	1.17	45
Europe	16,743	0.59	16,272	103	0.90	56
West Asia/North Africa	22,570	2.45	21,805	219	1.17	60
Sub-Saharan Africa	4,773	1.20	4,604	53	1.59	50
South Africa	1,290	0.77	1,290	15	1.16	45
Asia	154,449	1.87	136,564	1,324	1.02	39
India	45,144	2.73	45,144	484	1.07	40
China	47,965	1.31	47,965	463	0.97	39
Rest of Asia	61,340	1.70	43,455	377	0.92	32
Oceania	2,113	3.57	2,112	6	0.29	66
World	243,028	1.57	220,376	2,086	0.95	43

SOURCES: Total irrigated area and area growth rate compiled from 1999 FAOSTAT data (FAO 2001c); irrigated area and irrigation abstraction based on Seckler et al. 1998, 32–38; average irrigation depth and average irrigation efficiency calculated by IFPRI based on Seckler et al. 1998, 32–38.
NOTES: Seckler et al. (1998, 32) provide summaries for countries grouped by water scarcity. Total global irrigation abstraction in 1990 is estimated at 2,353 cubic kilometers.
[a]Gross equivalent depth abstraction divided by area.

water availability by region, they compete with other water uses (such as urban and municipal use) with direct implications for food production.

Results from our assessment for the period 2021–25 consider the effect of raising nonagricultural water use from 22 percent of all water usage at current trends to 32 percent, crowding out water available for irrigating crops. We also consider a scenario in which water management and investments remain static, so that global water withdrawal capacity in 2025 is no different than in 1995. The results of both situations exacerbate food security problems around the world, especially in the poorest countries.

As water becomes increasingly scarce and management remains unchanged, irrigation water becomes scarcer and irrigated areas decline. Cereal prices rise as cereal production falls. Irrigated area is projected to fall by a total of 30 million hectares globally under the pessimistic scenario. Even on irrigated fields, production is lower because water use is reduced, leading to net losses of 285 million metric tons of cereals and dramatic price increases. Prices for rice, an especially water-intensive crop, are the most sensitive to changes in water availability. If nonagricultural water uses rise from 22 to 32 percent, rice prices will likely be 45 percent higher in 2025. If investments in water management and the efficiency of water use remain unchanged, rice prices rise another 65 percent. Maize prices are 28–29 percent higher under each scenario, while wheat prices are 35 percent higher with low management investments and 29 percent higher if expanding nonagricultural uses crowd out the agricultural use of water. Each situation also results in an increase in international price variability, posing added risks for farmers and consumers. Moreover, the fall in irrigated area and production creates additional pressure on the relatively fragile rainfed land base. As increasing cereal prices and water scarcity push production into rainfed areas, they account for 63 million metric tons in increased production by 2025, but at added environmental costs.

CONSEQUENCES OF CLIMATE CHANGE

Related to resource constraints is the prospect of a changing climate worldwide. In the same way that demand for energy increases fossil fuel consumption and therefore greenhouse gases, so demand for agricultural products can reduce the capacity of natural ecosystems to store carbon, mitigating the greenhouse effect. Climate change includes global warming and associated changes in hydrological regimes and other climatic variables, such as higher temperatures, altered growing seasons, changing moisture, and extreme weather patterns, as well as secondary effects on social and economic systems (Wolfe 1996; Downing 1993; Kendall and Pimentel 1994). These changes would result from increasing concentrations of greenhouse gases from human activities, especially carbon dioxide (CO_2) release, which is projected to double by the year 2100 with a temperature rise that is presently predicted to be in the range of 1.5–6.0 °C (Pielke 2001).

The consensus of studies of the impact of these forces on agriculture has been relatively sanguine: world food supply will not be adversely affected, assuming farmers take adequate steps, and additional CO_2 leads to increased yields as anticipated by many researchers (Adams and Hurd 1999). However, one study found significant negative impacts, with estimated reductions in grain production of approximately 20 to 30 percent (Darwin et al. 1995). When the same study allowed farmers to adapt by modifying crops planted and techniques used, shifting cropped area, and responding to market changes, small yield increases of 0.2 to 1.2 percent resulted.

Although some studies suggest that climate change may lead to a slight increase in global food production, regional impacts are expected to vary considerably. At higher latitudes, increased temperatures can lengthen the growing season and reduce cold temperature effects on growth (Mendelsohn, Nordhaus, and Shaw 1994). In warmer or tropical environments, the effects are more negative: the impact of pests and diseases on crops and livestock is greater, soil erosion and desertification from more intense rainfall and prolonged dry periods increases, and water resources for irrigation are reduced (Downing 1993). Many of these areas are located in developing countries where land may already be less agriculturally productive, thus increased development into marginal lands may put these areas at even greater risk. In addition, smallholder farmers in these countries have less capacity to adapt their operations to changing climate than developed countries with more commercialized agriculture sectors. The rising food prices projected in these scenarios depress food demand and worsen food security globally, especially in poor countries. Cereal imports into these countries increase by an average of about 55 million metric tons per year to 2025, as higher household expenses lower the real income of poor consumers whose income goes mainly to food.

Despite the many studies on global warming in recent years, however, there is no consensus on the effects of three major variables that may mitigate the impact of climate change on agriculture: the magnitude of regional changes in temperature and precipitation, the magnitude of the beneficial effects of higher concentrations of carbon dioxide on crop yields, and the ability of farmers to adapt to climate changes (Wolfe 1996).

THE ROLE OF TRADE

Most governments have been unwilling to fully expose domestic food production to international markets, for reasons explored in detail later in this book. They intervene to promote domestic food production, to lower domestic food prices, or to limit imports. The resulting distortions produce inefficiencies that have been a major subject of recent trade negotiations. If agricultural subsidies and trade barriers were largely eliminated, even if other parts of the economy were unaffected, what shifts could be expected in global agricultural production and trade, and what environmental consequences might ensue?

Many analysts of international trade liberalization have underscored its importance for developing countries—and the environment. While the new round of multilateral trade negotiations launched at Doha, Quatar, in late 2001 is a promising start, the proof will be in achieving a balanced package of market-opening measures granting expanding access to developing-country agriculture in the rich markets of the OECD countries. Whether the United States and the European Union will be willing to trade off existing and, in the U.S. case, new levels of subsidies to rich, powerful farm interests remains an open question. At the same time, the developing countries will need to reduce protection for manufacturing and service sectors in their own economies in order to correct long-standing biases against agriculture (Hoekman and Anderson 1999). In a study of Indonesia, trade liberalization envisioned under the next round of trade negotiations could improve the environmental condition of Indonesia's air and water, even if it stimulated more rapid economic growth, and even if environmental regulation was not substantially toughened (Strutt and Anderson 2000).

Despite these gains, it is important to emphasize that in general, liberalization[6] would reduce production, especially in the rich countries. World prices in 2025 would increase for all cereals, benefiting farmers but posing serious challenges for poor countries. Our analysis suggests that rice prices would increase the most of any major crop (by 15 percent) followed closely by wheat and maize (9 and 10 percent, respectively). Meat prices would increase more sharply. Sheep and goat meat prices would rise

18 percent and beef prices 16 percent by 2025. Pork and poultry would both rise by 12 percent.

These results are broadly consistent with other estimates. In effect, the protection of agriculture from trade competition in rich developed countries has acted like a tax on net agricultural exporters in developing countries. A 2001 USDA study showed an increase in aggregate world prices of 12 percent if trade barriers, subsidies, and other trade distortions were removed, with livestock product prices rising more than any other commodity (Diao, Somwaru, and Roe 2001, 25). However, the overall benefits of trade liberalization in agriculture are less pronounced in developing countries than in many developed countries, and some poor countries will experience net losses resulting from continuing internal biases against agriculture and reductions in terms-of-trade. In other words, countries that must import food in the face of higher overall prices lose out to net exporters.

In an analysis of 67 low-income, food-deficit countries, higher food prices in the wake of agricultural trade liberalization reduced food imports but also encouraged farmers to produce more, which more than offset the negative effect of rising prices on food security, at least on average (Shapouri and Trueblood 2001, 96–97). Certain regions, however, are more negatively affected, notably North Africa, which is heavily reliant on imports. Sub-Saharan Africa, which is not, improves its food security situation, despite the price increases. The effect of expanded exports from developing countries helps food security in many that are export-oriented (such as Ethiopia and Nicaragua) but hurts those that have few exports and import much of their food, such as Algeria.

Taking into account the overall effects on producers, consumers, and taxpayers, removing agricultural subsidies for 16 commodities would generate annual global benefits of $32.4 billion in 2025 (Table 3.4). Both developed and developing regions benefit, gaining $13.2 billion and $19.3 billion respectively. These gains are significant compared with the value of agricultural production. In proportion to the size of their agricultural sectors, the biggest gainers would be Japan and South Korea (included in "Other East Asia" in Table 3.4). The biggest overall regional gains would be by Sub-Saharan Africa, at $4.6 billion, or 10.5 percent of the value of agricultural production. This is in part because African farmers would face less competition from subsidized exports from Europe and other developed

TABLE 3.4 • Net welfare effects of global trade liberalization for IMPACT commodities, 2025

Region/country	US$ billion	Percentage value of agricultural production, 2025	Percentage of GDP, 2025
Developed	13.2	2.9	0.03
United States	4.1	2.4	0.03
European Union 15	3.8	2.8	0.03
Japan	2.9	22.4	0.04
Developing	19.3	2.6	0.10
Latin America	2.7	1.8	0.05
West Asia/North Africa	2.1	5.5	0.10
Sub-Saharan Africa	4.6	10.5	0.91
China	2.1	0.8	0.05
Other East Asia	2.4	28.1	0.04
India	1.7	1.5	0.09
Other South Asia	1.1	2.8	0.25
World	32.4	2.7	0.05

SOURCE: Authors, using IMPACT-WATER model projections, June 2001.
NOTE: The classification West Asia/North Africa, used throughout this chapter, includes Cyprus and Turkey, whereas Middle East/North Africa, used elsewhere in the book, does not.

countries. It also would result from the removal of taxes that most African governments impose on food production and consumption, which tend to discourage investment by farmers and make food more expensive for consumers. It should be noted that if the removal of agricultural trade barriers were accompanied by boosts in industrial production, food consumption would increase as economic growth raised incomes.

In sum, the impacts of trade reforms on food insecurity are largely beneficial but hardly sufficient to remedy its complex causes. Internal reforms, which reduce biases against agriculture, coupled with special attention to the needs of highly import-dependent countries, will be critical to the overall success of more liberal trade policy. And environmental benefits, which are sometimes advanced by eliminating distortions and subsidies, will ultimately depend on decisions to implement and enforce resource-conserving strategies at the national and local levels.

THE CHOICE OF POLICIES

Apart from trade policy, some of the forces that determine food security, such as weather, are not something that individual nations, acting alone, can control. Many others are a matter of social and economic factors affected by policy choices at the national level. They include rates of population growth, levels of investment in technologies that allow increased food production, environmental policies to preserve and protect land and water and improvements in the capacity of farmers to take advantage of methods for growing food. But how much of a difference do such choices make? How would the world be different in 2025 as a result of choices focused on improving global food security?

Consider two futures, one characterized by positive national choices to enhance food security (akin to a pro-poor, lower food price strategy), the second by comparative neglect (basically an anti-poor, slow growth, high food price scenario).[7] In the first, economic growth accelerates by 25 percent and population growth rates decline. Access to clean water and access by women to secondary education both increase by 10 percent. Regional agricultural yields increase 10–20 percent faster. Irrigated land increases substantially, but measures are undertaken to mitigate harmful environmental effects. The second future scenario involves a reversal of these developments. Economic growth slows, populations grow more rapidly, access to clean water and to education declines, the growth in agricultural yields slows, and no additional land is irrigated.

Global cereal production is expected to increase by 6 percent in the first case and to decrease by 5 percent in the second. In the first case, the rice price falls by 42 percent by 2025. In the second case, by contrast, its price rises by 48 percent. These shifts reverberate through world food markets. In the first case, Asian countries become less dependent on imports because they grow more of their own food. Sub-Saharan Africa, on the other hand, imports *more* food as it becomes more affordable. In the second case, by contrast, South Asia's food imports rise by 93 percent. Sub-Saharan Africa is priced out of world food markets—it needs just as much food but is unable to afford it.

The most dramatic results are the enormous differences in the ability of families to feed their children. In the first or pro-poor case, malnourished children in developing nations are forecast to decline from 166 million in 1997 to 57 million in 2025, far below the 105 million in the baseline trend scenario. In China, Latin America, and Middle East/North Africa, widespread childhood malnutrition is eliminated by 2025 (Figure 3.10). In Sub-Saharan Africa, progress is less dramatic but still substantial. Instead of increasing to 36 million, as in the baseline scenario, the number of malnourished children would fall to 22 million in 2025 under the optimistic

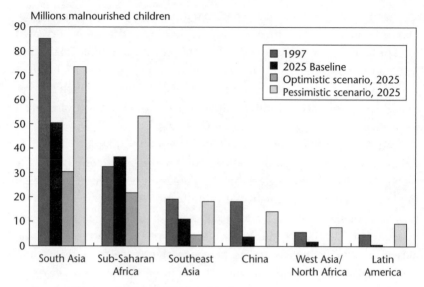

FIGURE 3.10   •   Malnourished children in 1997 and 2025, alternative scenarios

SOURCE: Authors using IMPACT-WATER model projections, June 2001.

NOTE: The classification West Asia/North Africa, used throughout this chapter, includes Cyprus and Turkey, whereas Middle East/North Africa, used elsewhere in the book, does not.

scenario (Figure 3.10). The improvement in child nutrition results from broad-based and rapid agricultural productivity and economic growth, reductions in population growth rates, and increased investment in education and health. Each accounts for about a third of the improvement. These issues will be further explored in Chapter 6.

The second (pessimistic) case depicts a slowly unfolding catastrophe. Instead of substantial declines in childhood malnutrition, the problem becomes much worse, especially in Sub-Saharan Africa. There the number of malnourished children increases from 36 to 53 million by 2025. On a global scale, the developing nations become home to 178 million malnourished children, compared with 57 million in the first case. This is one of the human costs of these choices.

LESSONS FOR FOOD SECURITY

Our major results may be summarized as follows. In the period leading to 2025, results arise from the following key trends:

• Fundamental shifts in diets will cause meat consumption in the developing world to rise, escalating demand for cereals for animal feed. As meat plays an increasing role, cereal consumption will slow. Raising cereal yields will continue to be important, but the efficiency of meat production will become equally significant.

• World cereal prices are likely to decline more slowly, compared with historical trends, as the result of a gradual slowdown in the rate of cereal production growth.

• Cereal production will face land constraints and the area planted to cereals may fall in most regions except Latin America and Sub-Saharan Africa, where additional land is still available. Yield growth must thus account for most production growth. In most countries and regions—Sub-Saharan Africa being the notable exception—a gradual slowdown in crop yields that began in much of the world during the early 1980s will pose major challenges.

• Land and water resource constraints will have major implications for sustainable food production and food security. These include issues of nutrient levels, such as nitrogen and phosphorus, pesticide use, and loss of habitat. These constraints are linked in turn to the possibility of global climate change. Although many developed countries, particularly the United States, can expect only modest changes in agricultural yields resulting from climate change and should be able to adapt, developing countries—especially those in tropical areas—may have more difficulty. An increase in developed-country production could also lead to decreased world food prices, making developing countries even worse off. To help mitigate the effects felt by developing countries, environmental and economic policies that increase the flexibility of adjustment and reduce adaptation costs should be implemented. These include policies to improve the flexibility of resource allocation in agriculture in the broadest sense: removal of subsidies and taxes that distort incentives, establishment of secure property rights in water and land; greater investment in agricultural research, especially for crop breeding to improve adaptation to moisture and temperature stress; enhanced investment in education and training and public infrastructure to improve the adaptive ability of farmers and the rural economy more generally; better integration of international commodity markets; and a greater inclusion of populations in developing countries into these markets.

- With demand for agricultural output projected to outstrip supply in many developing countries, fewer nations than ever will be self-sufficient in food production, and agricultural trade will grow to fill the gaps. China is likely to become a major net importer, as will East and South Asia and the Middle East/North Africa. This will not necessarily produce global shortages, because agricultural exporters are capable of keeping pace with the world's growing and urbanizing populations.

- Despite modest declines in real food prices and expanding world trade, food security for the poor will most likely improve only modestly in many regions and deteriorate in others, unless significant changes in national priorities occur. Sub-Saharan Africa will experience little improvement if current trends are simply carried forward, in which case the number of malnourished children in 2025 will be higher than in 1997. Slowly declining world food prices and buoyant international trade will coexist with continuing—and even rising—malnutrition in some regions, suggesting that trade liberalization is an insufficient basis for food security.

- Sub-Saharan Africa stands out. Many experts see the pessimistic case we examined in this chapter as the most likely outcome for the region. Deteriorating natural resources, stagnant technologies, and rising population densities can only be alleviated by a major transformation from subsistence to commercialized agriculture capable of supporting a growing urban population. And without associated investments beyond agriculture in education, health services, and environmental services, few changes are possible or sustainable. Despite the magnitude of the challenge, a sense of urgency and commitment by African leaders has been lacking to date.

- Significant improvements in sustainable food security worldwide requires renewed efforts by national governments, international and research institutions, and civil society to forge a combination of increases in productivity and enhanced environmental protection.

4 • SCIENCE AND FOOD SECURITY

Scientific research in agriculture has saved hundreds of millions of people from starvation. Without it, Malthus and the neo-Malthusians would have been proven right. The technical and environmental wonder of the past four decades is that today's farmers are feeding better diets to a world population 80 percent larger than in 1960 with a comparatively modest increase in the cropland base. In 1961 1.06 billion hectares of land were harvested for crops; in 2000 1.37 billion hectares produced twice the cereal grain and four times the oilseeds, providing the average developing world citizen 29 percent more calories. Except in countries devastated by AIDS, or disrupted by the collapse of the Soviet Union, people today will live much longer than 50 years ago. The steady accumulation of new knowledge and the productivity consequences of new technologies are arguably the most crucial factors overlooked by doomsayers. Land and labor productivity growth throughout much of the world has allowed global food supplies to outpace increases in demand.

Selection of plant varieties and management of crops, improvement of animal breeds, mechanization of farm tasks, uses of new inorganic fertilizers, sophisticated genetics-based breeding techniques, and new methods of controlling pests and diseases have resulted in increased supplies of food per person and the lowest food price levels in history. They have also reduced the land required for agriculture. Increasing feeding efficiencies for livestock has also reduced animal waste per unit of food.

Partly as a result, the remaining problems of food security are largely hidden from view in rich counties. While the homeless and those dependent on food banks are still features of some rich countries, they are seen as exceptions. The overall affluence and diets of the rich countries obscure the fact that the agricultural successes of the past were not inevitable, nor necessarily a triumph of Adam Smith's "invisible hand." Rather, they resulted from massive public and private investments that allowed successful interactions between farmers, input suppliers, and a publicly supported research and extension system. Despite this success, there is no room for complacency. As noted elsewhere in this book, world population is projected to increase by some 50 percent by 2050, and increased income will expand food demand even further. If hunger among the world's poorest families is to be reduced and ultimately ended, the future contributions of scientific research to agriculture will be critical.

This research can pull the Hassans, and millions like them, from the edge of subsistence by sharply raising what they can produce on their small plots of land. It can also contribute to protecting what they produce from the vagaries of weather, for example with rice varieties resistant to salination. If global warming generates even greater extremes in weather, this kind of adaptability will become a key to sustainable agriculture. Unfortunately, public attitudes toward agricultural science appear increasingly hostile, and public spending on agriculture is slowing in many countries. Partly as a consequence of its success, some question the need for further productivity gains in agriculture. Others seek to stop, or at least restrict, the use of modern technologies in agriculture, especially biotechnology and the larger field of genomics, as well as technologies that enhance the conversion of feed to food.

This chapter examines the past and potential effects of agricultural science on food security. We first consider how productivity increases—getting more from the same resources—resulted from the historical research and development process. We then look forward to potential advances, especially in the field of biotechnology. Without strong research performance, we cannot continue to meet world food requirements and sustain resources and the environment at the same time. Because the lags between investment in research and output gains are often decades long, decisions made today may not pay dividends until years later. Although much new research investment will be private, the private sector usually demands more immediate results and returns. Hence, a continued public and nonprofit role in agricultural science will be crucial. However, government and nonprofit agencies must increasingly form partnerships with private firms, who now account for significant shares of agricultural research—at least in the developed countries—and are typically more adept at getting technologies into the hands of farmers, food processors, and marketing chains.

WHAT IS AGRICULTURAL PRODUCTIVITY?

Worldwide, about 95 percent of major cereal production gains during the past four decades came from increased yields, which have more than doubled since 1961 (Figure 4.1). In Sub-Saharan Africa, by contrast, less than 40 percent of the gains came from increased yields; the rest came from expanding the area of land in agriculture. As noted elsewhere in this book, Africa must depend increasingly on yield gains. In Western Europe, the former Soviet Union, and Eastern Europe, the area sown to cereals

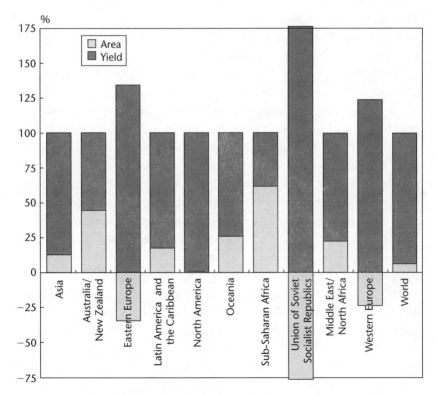

FIGURE 4.1 • Sources of agricultural production growth, 1961–2000

SOURCE: Compiled by authors based on data from FAO 2001c.

NOTES: Union of Soviet Socialist Republics includes the former Soviet Union from 1991 to 2000. Area represents area in agriculture and counts multiple cropped areas as a single unit within a cropping season.

actually declined, but yield increases were able to maintain growth in production. In South Asia, the rice and wheat growing area per person shrank from 0.11 hectares in 1961 to about 0.07 hectares in 2000. Although increased rates of planting are an option, many areas already support two and even three crops a year. Yield increases, which have proceeded steadily since the 1930s, appear the only way out.

Looking Backward   Wheat and rice, the principal foods of more than half the world, have a very long history. Archaeological evidence places the domestication of rice 9,000 years ago, most likely along the Yangtze River in eastern China. Sedentary hunter-gatherers began cultivating the weedy ancestors of modern wheat varieties about 10,000 years ago in the Fertile Crescent around Jericho in the southern Jordan Valley.[1] Over thousands of years, yield gains were eked out by the collection, selection, and replanting of the best and most productive seeds, augmented by improved techniques of cultivation soil fertility management and migration to more favorable agricultural lands. Yield increases using these methods rose slowly, though substantially over long periods.

Starting in the late nineteenth century and growing more rapidly during the last half of the twentieth, major crop yields in the United States and other developed countries increased at rates well above historic trends. From an average wheat yield of 11 bushels per acre in 1866 (the earliest year for which reasonably reliable time-series data are available), 91 years were to pass before U.S. yields doubled (Figure 4.2). Just 43 years later yields had almost doubled again, averaging 42 bushels per acre in 2000. Wheat yields are substantially higher in Europe than in the United States, partly because of heavier fertilizer use per unit of land. American farmers also grow primarily maize and soybeans on the best agricultural land, while wheat, a lower-value crop, is relegated to lower rainfall areas like Kansas and North Dakota. Yield accelerations occurred in many other crops in the United States over the past century as improved varieties spread rapidly and increasing amounts of yield-enhancing inputs were used.

These accelerations were all based on developments in the early twentieth century as mainly public (but some private) breeding programs began applying the lessons of Mendelian genetics. In the developing world, scientific crop breeding lagged behind. Beginning in the 1950s and 1960s, improved varieties became available to farmers and yields rose; wheat went from 1 ton per hectare or less in China and India in the mid-1960s to

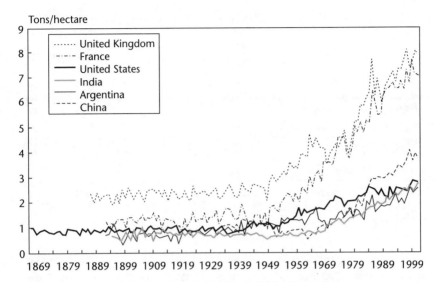

Tons/hectare

FIGURE 4.2 • Long-run trends in wheat yields, 1800–2000
SOURCES: FAO 2001b and various sources compiled by Pardey, Chan-Kang, and Alston for a forthcoming paper.

more than 2.5 tons in India and almost 4 tons in China by the late 1990s (Figure 4.2). Table 4.1 shows the rapid spread of modern rice and wheat varieties throughout the developing world. Asia embraced these new varieties most rapidly, while adoption lagged in Sub-Saharan Africa (Lipton with Longhurst 1989).

Similar patterns of productivity growth have occurred in staple food crops the world over. Globally, yields have climbed steadily for all major cereals since the 1960s. Although concerns have been raised that the rate of yield growth for some crops (like rice and wheat) seems to have slowed in some regions,[2] the pattern is not uniform. Indeed, an absolute yield ceiling seems far off. Researchers estimate that under ideal conditions maize yields of 450 bushels and soybeans of 250 bushels per acre are a technical possibility, compared with current average U.S. yields of 128 bushels per acre for maize and 40 bushels per acre for soybeans. But land and climate are often far from ideal, and these natural inputs into agriculture are prone to degradation without careful stewardship.

Apart from yield growth, another source of gain has been the productivity of seed. In Medieval England, farmers saved one-quarter of their wheat harvest for seeding the next crop; only three-quarters remained for

TABLE 4.1 • Share of area planted in modern varieties of rice and wheat

Region	Rice			Wheat			
	1970	1983	1991	1970	1977	1990	1997
	(% of area planted)						
Sub-Saharan Africa	4	15	n.a.	5	22	52	66
Middle East/North Africa	0	11	n.a.	5	18	42	66
Asia (excluding China)	12	48	67	42	69	88	93
China	77	95	100	n.a.	n.a.	70	79
Latin America	4	28	58	11	24	82	90
All developing countries	30	59	74	20	41	70	81

SOURCES: Byerlee and Moya 1993; Byerlee 1996; Heisey, Lantican, and Dubin 1999.
NOTES: Modern varieties refer to semi-dwarf varieties; n.a. indicates that data were not available.

food and feed consumption. In times of privation, breaking into seed maize stored for spring was punishable by death. Death was also nature's verdict if seed rotted due to fungus, as in the wet, cold summers that occurred periodically during the Middle Ages in Europe. Over time, the ratio of seed-to-grain produced has fallen sharply. In 1961, the global average planting rate of wheat was about 11 percent of output, by 1999 it was only 6 percent. The average planting rate of rice in 1961 was only about 5 percent, and by 1999 it had fallen as low as 3 percent, as germination rates and other crop protections improved. In addition, mechanization released land formerly needed to feed draft animals (oxen, mules, horses) for production of food and fiber. Therefore, yield growth actually underestimates the real gain in net harvest from changes in technology. Improvements in harvesting, storage, and transportation technologies have added to the food available to consumers from a given harvest by reducing losses and spoilage.

The result of these additions in production capacity has been to "save" land. Producing today's global food supply with 1960 crop yields would require an additional 300 million hectares of land. In other words, modern farming has dramatically reduced the cropland necessary to meet demand—by an area equal to the entire land mass of Western Europe. One important result has been to relieve areas only marginally suitable for agriculture from potentially serious environmental degradation.

Labor versus Land Farming, to paraphrase John Locke, involves "mixing one's labor with the land." Yet the particular mix varies dramatically over time and place. In Australia, Canada, and the United States for example, the history of agriculture has been of little available labor and vast stores of land. In Asia, especially Japan, the picture is reversed: ample labor working relatively little arable land (Hayami and Ruttan 1985). These differences show up in calculations of the value of crop production per unit of land and per farm worker. Figure 4.3 shows international comparisons of the average total value of agricultural output in 1998–2000 per unit of agricultural land and per agricultural worker. (These country averages obscure significant variation within countries for both measures.) Globally $279 worth of agricultural output at 1989–91 prices was produced for every hectare in agriculture (a hectare is equal to 2.47 acres). Areas with more irrigated land where multiple crops can be grown over a one-year cycle (as in East Asia), produced, on average $1,354 of crop output per hectare. Value of output is also related to the use of other inputs such as water, labor, and fertilizer, and to the mix of outputs—the livestock grazing systems of Sub-Saharan Africa and Oceania are where the value of output per hectare is lowest.

The two panels of Figure 4.4 show that the geographical pattern of labor productivity is quite distinct from the pattern of land productivity. In 2000, the United States ranked 89th of 198 countries in land productivity, but second (to Belgium-Luxembourg) in labor productivity—output per agricultural worker—an estimated $57,532 for every person working in agriculture. Sub-Saharan Africa did poorly on both counts, with low land and labor productivity.

As global land productivity doubled from 1961 to 2000, the fastest rate of land productivity growth was in land-scarce Asia, where agricultural output per unit of land was 200 percent more in 2000 than it was in 1961. The former Soviet Union had the slowest gains. Output per unit of land changed little; it was 1.5 percent lower in 2000 than in 1961, with a marked decline throughout the 1990s. Labor productivity grew more slowly, increasing by 50 percent. Labor productivity grew fastest in Western Europe due to strong growth in agricultural output and an exodus of labor from European agriculture. Labor productivity also increased reasonably rapidly in the United States (2.65 percent per year since 1961, compared with 4.40 percent for Western Europe) but barely budged in Africa, growing by only 0.25 percent per year since 1961, with a higher rate of growth during the 1990s (0.57 percent per year) than the 1980s (0.42 percent).

Value of production per hectare of agricultural land, 1988–2000 average

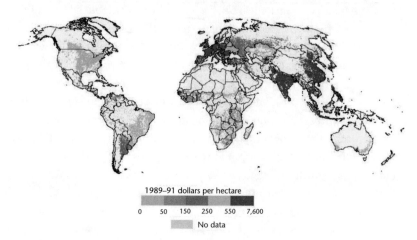

1989–91 dollars per hectare

| | | | | | |
0   50   150   250   550   7,600
No data

Value of production per agricultural worker, 1988–2000 average

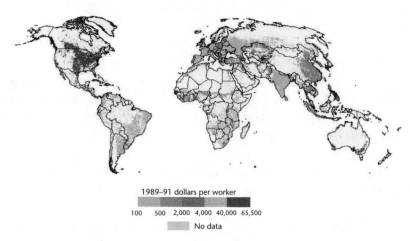

1989–91 dollars per worker

100   500   2,000   4,000   40,000   65,500
No data

FIGURE 4.3 • International comparisons of agricultural land and labor productivity

SOURCES: FAO 2001c; Wood, Sebastian, and Scherr 2000.

NOTES: The maps are average national values for 1998–2000 shown within the global extent of agroecosystems as defined in Wood, Sebastian, and Scherr (2000). The value of agricultural production was calculated by weighting 134 primary crop and 23 primary livestock commodity production quantities by their respective international prices in U.S. dollars, for the 1989–91 period.

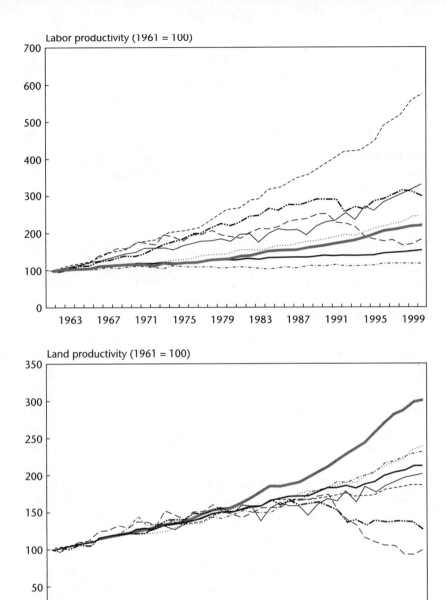

Labor productivity (1961 = 100)

Land productivity (1961 = 100)

▬▬ Asia	─··─ Eastern Europe	········ Latin America and
── North America	─·─· Sub-Saharan	the Caribbean
─ ─ ─ Western Europe	Africa	·─ ─ Union of Soviet
	▬▬ World	Socialist Republics

FIGURE 4.4 • Trends in land and labor productivity in global agriculture, 1961–2000

SOURCES: FAO 2001c; Wood, Sebastian, and Scherr 2000.

The implication of these different measures is that each shows only part of the picture defining increases in agricultural productivity. A full picture would capture not only all of the contributors to yield growth (land, labor, human capital skills such as education, fertilizer, chemicals, water, soil, and others), but also would reflect the multiplicity of outputs, including such unmarketed goods as rural landscapes, greenhouse gases, and off-farm pollution of water.

ENTER SCIENCE

In the broad sweep of agricultural history, organized scientific research is a recent phenomenon, although farmers have tinkered with different techniques for about 10,000 years, and kings and emperors have collected plants on an ad hoc basis for millennia. (Thomas Jefferson, risking penalty of death, smuggled rice seeds out of Italy in the lining of his coat to encourage cultivation of the crop in South Carolina [Fowler 1994].) Science-based solutions to agricultural problems did not take root until the formation of agricultural societies throughout the United Kingdom and Europe beginning in the early to mid-1700s. By the mid-1800s the evolution of these societies gave rise to agricultural "experiment stations," beginning in Germany and England and spreading to the rest of Europe and eventually to the New World. Colonization spread them to the developing world. Japan, a much less economically developed country than America or Europe in the nineteenth century and most of the twentieth century, when measured by per capita income, paralleled developments in the West by publicly funding and conducting agricultural research beginning in the mid-1800s (Maddison 2001).

Scientific agriculture developed hand-in-hand with these research institutions. Darwin's theory of evolution, the pure-line theory of Johannson, the mutation theory of de Vries, and the rediscovery of Mendel's Laws of Heredity all contributed to the rise of plant breeding in the beginning of the twentieth century. Pasteur's germ theory of disease and the development of vaccines opened up lines of research in the veterinary sciences. The effectiveness of this body of science in raising yields and solving farmers' production problems became evident in the first half of the twentieth century. This success encouraged similar developments in the newly independent colonies, where agricultural research had been largely confined to export crops, and had ignored the needs of farmers growing food for local consumption. Crops like cassava, yams, and other root crops, significant in many African diets, and sorghum, pearl millets, pigeon peas, and chickpeas common in diets of the poor throughout South Asia and parts of Africa, still suffer in comparison to the major export crops.

Progress in the science of genetics gathered pace around the middle of the twentieth century after Hersey and Chase, Watson and Crick, and others uncovered the role and structure of DNA.[3] These findings engendered a huge, largely publicly funded, research effort directed mainly at the application of the modern recombinant DNA methods to human health. This also led to the development of genetic markers and plant transformation techniques useful to agriculture. The result was a wave of biological innovations which, combined with changes in intellectual property rights regimes, attracted both public funding and private investment. In 1995 about half a trillion dollars (nearly US$500 billion) was invested in public and privately financed science worldwide—around 85 percent of it in rich countries (Pardey and Beintema 2001). Agricultural research accounted for $32 billion of this total (1993 prices) or nearly 7 percent of all private and public spending on science.[4]

The public share of agricultural investment was substantial but is now flagging. Worldwide, public investments in agricultural research have nearly doubled in inflation-adjusted terms over the past two decades, from an estimated $11.8 billion in 1976 to nearly $21.7 billion in 1995 (Figure 4.5). Yet for many parts of the world, growth in spending during the 1990s slowed dramatically. In the rich countries, public investment grew just 0.3 percent annually between 1991 and 1996, compared with 2.3 percent per year during the 1980s. In Africa, there was no growth at all. In Asia, annual growth in investment was 4.4 percent, compared with 7.5 percent in the previous decade.[5]

The distribution of spending on agricultural research has shifted as well. In the 1990s, for the first time, developing countries as a group spent more on public agricultural research than the developed countries. Among the rich countries, $10.2 billion in public spending was concentrated in just a handful of countries. In 1995, the United States, Japan, France, and Germany accounted for two-thirds of this public research, about the same as two decades before. Just three developing countries—Brazil, China, and India—spent 44 percent of the developing world's public agricultural research money in 1995, up from 35 percent in the mid-1970s.

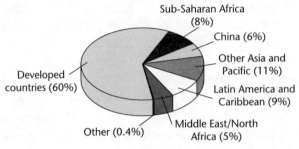

1976: $11.8 billion (1993 international dollars)

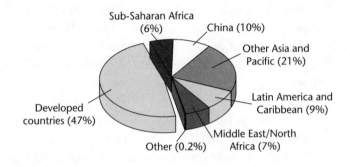

1995: $21.7 billion (1993 international dollars)

FIGURE 4.5   •   Global agricultural research expenditures, 1976 and 1995

SOURCE: Adapted from Pardey and Beintema 2001.

NOTE: Agricultural research intensities represent research spending as a percentage of corresponding agricultural gross domestic product.

Science without Borders   These figures refer to national investments, but agricultural innovation need not be homegrown. A striking feature of the history of agricultural development is that technology can be bought, borrowed, or (as Jefferson showed) stolen. The result is that it moves across borders both by design and by accident. Nonetheless, most agricultural technologies are sensitive to local climate, soil, and other attributes, so effective transfer often requires adaptation. Soybeans, for example, are sensitive to the length of days, so different varieties must be developed for different latitudes (Pardey et al. 2002). Crops that thrive in temperate soils can fail or falter under tropical conditions. Unlike many medical, mechanical, or veterinary innovations that are applicable from Tijuana to Tokyo, local adaptation is generally required for crop technologies. This has implications for the diffusion of agricultural research results, and for the biases that are introduced when it is concentrated in a relatively few places. About 63 percent of the nontropical world's agricultural research occurs in developed countries. Countries such as Argentina, China, and South Korea, with broadly similar growing conditions, will find this research relatively easy to adapt. However, transferring technologies from nontropical regions to tropical areas like northern Brazil and southern India often requires research fitted to local realities.

For these reasons, grouping countries according to their agroecology is useful. One option is to divide them into tropical and nontropical. Tropical countries have year-round average adjusted temperatures greater than 18°C (64°F). In 1997, about 1.44 billion hectares (or 62 percent) of the world's agricultural land and 2.6 billion people (45 percent of the world's population) were in tropical countries. This greatly exceeds the tropical-country share of public research spending (about 28 percent) but almost exactly matches the share of agricultural output by value that comes from the tropics, almost all of it from the developing countries.[6]

International Research Initiatives   In order to overcome the biases against the diffusion of agricultural technologies to developing countries, internationally conceived and funded agricultural research began in the mid-1940s and accelerated through the 1950s. The Ford and Rockefeller foundations placed agricultural staff in developing countries to work alongside scientists in national research organizations on joint-venture projects. These efforts evolved into the International Rice Research Institute at Los Baños, the Philippines, in 1960 and the International Maize and Wheat Improvement Center (CIMMYT) at El Batan, Mexico, in 1967 (Baum 1986; Gryseels and Anderson 1991). Hoping to show that the model of international agricultural research could achieve success in broad agroecological regions as well as specific commodities, the foundations also established the International Institute for Tropical Agriculture at Ibadan, Nigeria, in 1967 and Centro Internacional de Agricultura Tropical (International Center for Tropical Agriculture) at Cali, Colombia, in 1968.

In 1971, these institutions joined together to form the Consultative Group on International Agricultural Research (CGIAR, or CG for short), a funding and governance mechanism for international agriculture involving both bilateral (between two countries) and multilateral (an international effort involving multiple countries) donors. Funding for the CGIAR system grew rapidly until the 1990s, after which spending began to fall in inflation-adjusted terms. Even as funding fell, the number of centers continued to grow, largely through the addition of new centers concerned with forestry, agroforestry, irrigation management, and fisheries. In 2000, the CG included 16 institutions with a budget of $338 million.[7] Although the CG markedly accelerated the spread of new varieties of wheat, rice, and other technologies (commonly called the Green Revolution), it spent only a small, and of late declining, fraction of the global agricultural research investment. In 1995 it spent just 1.5 percent of the nearly $22 billion (1993 international dollars) in public-sector agricultural research by national agencies worldwide.

The Growing Private Sector   Innovation in agriculture has always had a strong private dimension, beginning first with farmers and in the past 200 years involving individual innovators working on and off farms and in private companies. In the United States, entrepreneurs such as John Deere or Cyrus McCormick and the Wallace family (founders of Wallace Seed Corn, later Pioneer) were part of agriculture's long affair with capitalism. Most herbicides, insecticides, and veterinary medicines were developed in the private sector (although drawing on discoveries made by public research), as were many food storage, transport, and processing technologies, including the refrigerated railroad car and the grain elevator, to name but two. Private investment in chemical, mechanical, and food-processing research is now substantial; it rose rapidly in the latter part of the twentieth century. Attention is presently riveted on biotechnology research. In 1994 the commercially unsuccessful Flavr-Savr™ tomato (genetically engineered to retain its "fresh picked" flavor)[8] set in train a series of innovations derived from genetic engineering. In the mid- to late 1990s, commercially successful herbicide- and insect-tolerant crop varieties such as Roundup Ready® and Liberty Link™ maize, cotton, and canola, or *Bt* maize and cotton followed.[9]

By the mid-1990s about one-third of the $32 billion total public and private agricultural research investment worldwide was private (Table 4.2). But little of this private research takes place in the developing world. The overwhelming majority ($9.8 billion, or 94 percent of the global total in 1995) is conducted in developed counties, where private research accounts for more than half of all expenditures. In LDCs, the private share of research is just 5 percent, and public funds are still the major source of support.

TABLE 4.2 • Estimated global public and private agricultural R&D investments, 1995

Group	Public	Private	Total	Public	Private	Total
	Expenditures			*Shares*		
	(million 1993 international dollars/year)			(% per year)		
Developing countries	11,770	609	12,379	95.1	4.9	100
Developed countries	9,797	10,353	20,150	48.6	51.4	100
Total	21,567	10,962	32,530	66.3	33.7	100

SOURCE: Pardey and Beintema 2001.

Private research is displacing public research in areas like commercial crop breeding for the seeds of crops with high commercial value. Such investments, fueled by agricultural biotechnology research, gravitate to techniques that promise large markets, are protected by intellectual property rights, and are easily transferable across agroecologies. These include food processing and other postharvest technologies and chemical inputs such as pesticides, herbicides, and fertilizers. Hence, while private research is much more geographically concentrated than public research, many of its fruits may be more easily transferred across borders and agroecological zones. Even so, private research is far less likely to be involved in research on products or methods with small markets, weak intellectual property protection, and limited transferability, precisely the situations in which most poor farmers are found.

One way in which to gauge the commitment of agricultural research funds, public or private, is to compare them to national agricultural output, rather than measuring them in absolute terms, much as development aid is often measured as a percentage of GDP.[10] This relative measure captures the *intensity* of investment in agricultural research, not just the *amount* of total research spending.[11] Figure 4.6 presents a public agricultural research intensity measure as a percentage of agricultural GDP.[12] In 1995, as a group, developed countries spent $2.68 on public agricultural research and development (R&D) for every $100 of agricultural output; a sizable increase over the $1.50 they spent per $100 of output two decades earlier. Since the mid-1970s, research intensities have risen for the developing countries as a group, but unevenly. Despite gaining a much greater absolute share of the developing world's public spending on agricultural

Public agricultural R&D intensities by region

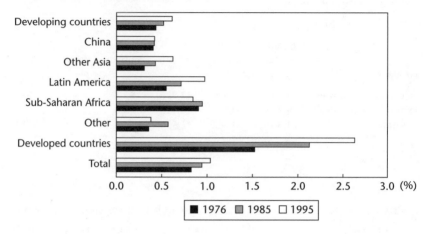

Public and private agricultural research intensities, 1995

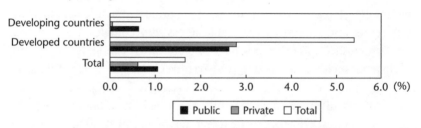

FIGURE 4.6 • Agricultural research spending intensities, 1976, 1985, and 1995

SOURCE: Adapted from Pardey and Beintema 2001.

research (see Figure 4.6, top panel), China's agricultural research intensity in the mid-1990s was no greater than in the mid-1980s. In other words, China's research spending grew, but its agricultural sector grew just as fast. Although public research throughout the rest of Asia and Latin America appears to have grown in intensity, Africa has lost considerable ground, with research intensities lower than in the 1970s. The large and growing gap between rich and poor countries has widened further in terms of total (that is, private and public) research spending (Figure 4.6, bottom panel). In 1995, total spending intensities were more than eight times higher in rich countries than they were in poor ones—they were four times higher when only public spending was used as the basis of the intensity calculation.[13]

THE GLOBAL GAP IN APPLIED SCIENTIFIC KNOWLEDGE

The eightfold difference in total research intensities illustrates the present gap in agriculture between rich and poor countries. Moreover, the situation is growing worse. The difference in public research intensity ratios was 3.5-fold in the 1970s, compared with 4.3-fold now (an even wider gap would have opened up if private spending was also factored in).

These trends may actually understate the scientific knowledge gap. Science is a cumulative endeavor, with a snowball effect. Innovations beget new ideas and further rounds of innovation or additions to the cumulative stock of knowledge. The mutually beneficial effects of accumulating and exchanging ideas is why lone innovators have largely given way to institutional approaches to research, why scientific disciplines formed and spawned journals to capture and carry forward findings, and why scientists seek out other scientists at conferences, via the Internet, or other venues. And so the size of the accumulated stock of knowledge, not merely the amount of investment in current research and innovative activity, gives a more meaningful measure of a country's technological capacity.

The sequential and cumulative nature of scientific progress and knowledge is starkly illustrated by crop improvement. It generally takes 7–10 years of breeding to develop a variety of wheat, rice, or maize that is uniform, stable, and superior (due to improved yield, grain quality, or some other attribute). But breeders of today build on a base of knowledge built up by breeders of yesteryear. Breeding lines from earlier research are used to develop new varieties, so that research of the distant past is still feeding people today. New crops not only carry forward the genes of earlier varieties, they also carry the crop breeding and selection strategies of earlier breeders, whether they be the farmers who made the crop selections for the first 10,000 years of agriculture or the researchers making the scientific crosses and selections for the past 100 years.

Figure 4.7 is a partial pedigree of the wheat variety Pioneer 2375, released in February 1989 by Pioneer-Hybrid International, the private company mentioned in connection with the Wallace family, based in Ames, Iowa (and now part of DuPont). Pioneer 2375 was one of several commercially significant wheat varieties in Minnesota during the early 1990s.[14] This pedigree reveals the persistent effects of distant past research spending on current innovative activity. Pioneer 2375 was developed by crossing the varieties Olaf/Era/Suquamuxi 68 and the varieties Chris/ND487/Lark.

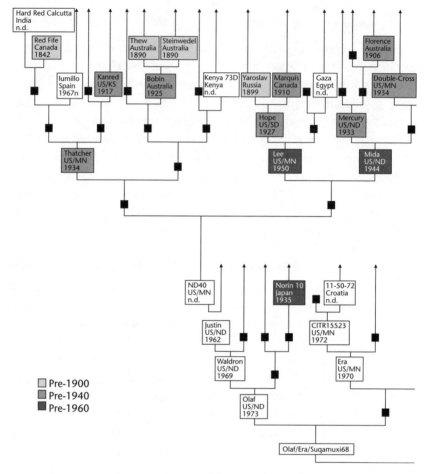

FIGURE 4.7 • Partial pedigree for Pioneer 2375 wheat

SOURCE: Pardey and Beintema 2001.

NOTE: "n" following some dates signifies the date that the variety was introduced in the United States but not necessarily the date of development.

Moving back through successive generations reveals its grandparents, great grandparents, great-great grandparents, and so on. Varieties developed as long ago as 1873 (Turkey Red), 1901 (Federation), and 1935 (Norin 10) are part of this pedigree. Over 14 percent of the varieties or breeding lines incorporated into Pioneer 2375's pedigree were discovered or developed prior to 1900, and at least 36 percent before 1940. The cumulative nature of this process means that past discoveries and related research are an integral part of contemporary agricultural innovations. Conversely,

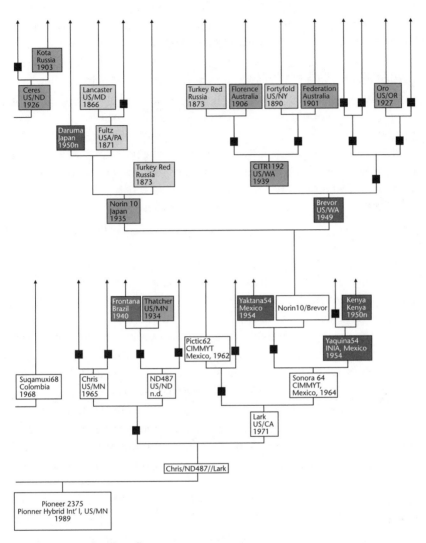

FIGURE 4.7 *(continued)*

the loss of a variety (or the details of the breeding histories that brought it about) means the loss of accumulated past research to the present stock of knowledge.

Providing adequate funding for research is thus only part of the science story. Putting in place the policies and practices to *accumulate* innovations and increase and preserve the stock of knowledge is an equally important and almost universally unappreciated foundation. Discoveries and data that are improperly documented or inaccessible (and so effectively exist only in the minds of the relevant researchers) are lost from the historical record when researchers retire from science. These "hidden" losses seem particularly prevalent in cash-strapped research agencies in the developing world, where inadequate and often irregular amounts of funding limit the functioning of libraries, data banks, and gene banks, and hasten staff turnover.

There can also be catastrophic losses, tied to the political instability that is a root cause of hunger. Civil strife and wars cause an exodus of scientific staff, or at least a flight from practicing science. Much of Uganda's scientific facilities, for example, were totally destroyed by the time its civil war ended in the early 1980s. It is hard to imagine today that the Congo once had one of the most sophisticated scientific infrastructures in colonial Africa, with facilities and staff comparable to those found in most developed countries in the middle of the twentieth century albeit with an all-European scientific staff (Eicher 2001).[15]

Pardey and Beintema (2001) have estimated the stocks of scientific knowledge arising from public and private research conducted in the United States and Sub-Saharan Africa. Historical research spending (running from 1850 for the United States and 1900 for Africa and allowing for a gradual diminution of the effect of distant past R&D spending on money measures of the current stock of knowledge) is compared with the agricultural GDP for 1995 (Figure 4.8). The accumulated stock of knowledge in the United States was 10 times more than the amount of agricultural output produced in that year. In other words, for every $100 of agricultural output there existed a $1,000 stock of knowledge to draw upon. In Africa the stock of knowledge in 1995 was actually less than the value of African agricultural output. The ratio of the U.S. knowledge stock relative to U.S. agricultural output in 1995 was nearly 12 times higher than the corresponding amount for Africa. This measure suggests the immensity, if not the outright impossibility, of playing "catch-up," in addition to the need to transmit knowledge across borders and continents.

THE SLOW MAGIC OF RESEARCH

Although Pioneer 2375's release in 1989 was part of the payoff to investments in breeding Turkey Red in 1873, the Turkey Red investors could have cared less. This case illustrates not only the lags between investing in

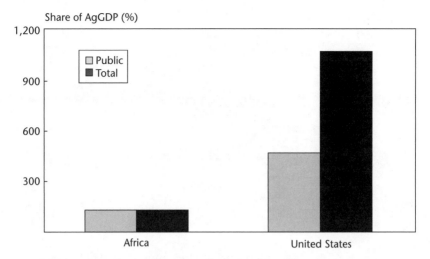

FIGURE 4.8 • Knowledge stocks and research intensities, 1995

SOURCE: Adapted from Pardey and Beintema 2001.

NOTES: Past additions to the knowledge stock were presumed to depreciate by 3 percent per year when constructing these 1995 stocks of knowledge. Given the instability and lack of infrastructure in Africa, knowledge depreciation rates are likely to be higher there than in the United States, leading to an even lower intensity ratio for Africa than indicated here.

research and reaping some return but the problem of "selling" them either to private investors or public figures in the short run. These lags are an important reason why there is underinvestment in research. Even the most public-spirited politicians see less benefit in supporting research that develops a new crop variety in seven years than in subsidizing farmers directly today.[16]

Figure 4.9 illustrates the timing and flows of benefits and costs from investing in a successful agricultural research project. The vertical axis represents the flow of benefits and costs in a particular year, and the horizontal axis represents years after the commencement of the project. The project involves expenditure without benefits during the "gestation" or research period.

Even if the research is successful, there may be further delays including a "development lag" of several years and an "adoption lag" that may extend further. Shortening the adoption lag may help to achieve benefits earlier, but the flow of benefits will eventually decline as old technologies lose their effectiveness—when, for example, pests and diseases evolve to

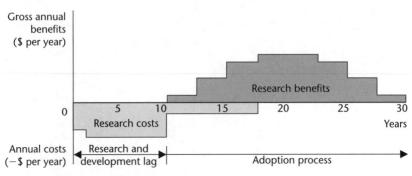

FIGURE 4.9 • Flows of research benefits and costs

SOURCE: Alston et al. 2000.

overcome resistance bred into crop varieties. Indeed, research directed at maintaining yields and profitability in the face of pressures that would otherwise lead them to fall is a major component of successful agricultural research and development. Estimates indicate that 35–70 percent of U.S. agricultural research is needed simply to maintain previous research gains (Adusei and Norton 1990; Heim and Blackslee 1986).

Even when the long horizon of agricultural research is fully accounted for, the rates of return are still impressive. Comparing nearly 2,000 such estimates taken from 292 studies published since 1958, the average annual rate of return for all studies combined was found to be an extraordinary 81 percent (70 percent for nominal rates of return and 77 percent for real returns after adjusting for inflation), although there is a large variation around this average (Table 4.3). U.S. government bonds, by comparison, yielded less than 6 percent in 2001. Part of the reason for the large variation in returns to research is that eventual outcomes are highly uncertain. For many projects costs of research exceed the benefits. But other research is highly successful, leading to very large benefits compared to costs. This variation is an additional strike against investments in any individual line of research. Government bonds, which pay paltry returns in comparison, seldom result in losses and are thus far less risky. Despite these risks, on average the rates of return to research have not declined over time. Recent analysis suggests that returns are likely to be higher when the research is conducted in developed versus developing countries, further biasing the flow of investments away from the location of the hungry.

TABLE 4.3 • Rates of return by commodity orientation

Commodity orientation	Number of observations	Rate of return		
		Mean (%)	Minimum (%)	Maximum (%)
Multicommodity	436	80.3	−1.0	1,219.0
All agriculture	342	75.7	−1.0	1,219.0
Crops and livestock	80	106.3	17.0	562.0
Unspecified	14	42.1	16.4	69.2
Field crops	916	74.3	−100.0	1,720.0
Maize	170	134.5	−100.0	1,720.0
Wheat	155	50.4	−47.5	290.0
Rice	81	75.0	11.4	466.0
Livestock	233	120.7	2.5	5,645.0
Tree crops	108	87.6	1.4	1,736.0
Resources[a]	78	37.6	0.0	457.0
Forestry	60	42.1	0.0	457.0
All studies	1,772	81.2	−100.0	5,645.0

SOURCE: Alston et al. 2000.
[a] Includes fishery and forestry.

THE BRAVE NEW BIOSCIENCES

The latest, most exhilarating, and most controversial chapter in agricultural science is the biotechnology revolution. We have now moved beyond understanding the structure of DNA to the analysis of the complete sequence of genes in humans, plants, animals, and other organisms. The mapping of this genetic landscape is known as *genomics,* and includes the recently completed gene sequences for *Arabidopsis thaliana,* a mustard-like weed, and for rice. Both plants provide genomic blueprints for a host of basic plant functions, dramatically accelerating crop improvement efforts. By coupling the biosciences with new computing and informatics technologies, researchers are developing databanks of DNA sequences for individual plants and animals and linking them to various functions and traits, such as resistance to certain pests and diseases, tolerance to drought, frosts, saline soils, and improved grain quality or yield.

Some argue that the genetic modification that scientists can now make involves a distinct break from more "natural" processes of plant breeding used in the past. But manipulation of crops through some form of breeding has occurred since domestication began. For all but the last hundred years, humans succeeded largely through trial and error, until the application of Mendel's Laws of Heredity at the turn of the twentieth century. Conventional plant breeding led to new varieties of crops by crossing and back-crossing different varieties (as illustrated by the pedigree for Pioneer 2375 wheat in Figure 4.7). These techniques shuffled tens of thousands of genes among individual plants in a structured but somewhat haphazard fashion.

Using modern biotechnologies, scientists can now snip a single gene from one plant and insert it into another to create a new variety with a desirable trait. It is also possible—but harder—to use the same technologies to incorporate traits that are controlled by multiple genes. And, somewhat more disquieting to some, scientists can move genes from other organisms to plants. DNA that codes for a desirable trait in one species (such as a soil bacterium) is inserted into a maize plant to provide pest resistance, using so-called transgenic techniques. To the new science of functional genomics, genes are recipes for proteins, and proteins are the workhorses of living cells. The even newer science of proteomics catalogues proteins within living things and probes deeper to understand the molecular structure of these proteins and the complex biology linking them to specific genes.

All these discoveries have spurred a rapid restructuring of the scientific institutions and industries engaged in science that affects agriculture, at least in the United States and other rich countries. The incentives for research and the public and private roles in that research are changing, shifting the balance between locally provided and internationally traded goods, part and parcel of the globalization of agricultural research.

The disquiet over biotechnology both reflects and affects these many changes. Some critics are concerned over environmental and human health consequences. In Europe, consumer resistance to transgenic plants and animals has engendered trade bans and restrictive labeling. The majority of consumers in other markets, including Argentina, China, and the United States, seem less concerned and more accepting. Other critics of biotechnology focus on its relationship to consolidation and concentration in the agriculture industry, especially the many mergers and acquisitions in the seed and agricultural chemical companies during the 1990s. The concern is that oligopoly will stifle competition, shift profits away from farmers, and drive research toward private profitability but not necessarily toward society's food security, environmental, or ecological inter-ests. An additional criticism is that the proliferation of patents and other forms of intellectual property protection demanded by large biotechnology companies will slow progress in the agricultural sciences and make new innovations inaccessible to farmers and scientists in developing countries. Joined to this is the worry that many of these countries lack the capacity to regulate and monitor the use of modern biotechnologies in ways that will satisfy consumers in potential export markets. Each of these criticisms merits attention in the context of science and food security.

TECHNOLOGICAL PROMISE AND PESSIMISM

Genetically modified (GM) crops have proved exceptionally popular with farmers given the chance to grow them. The most widely adopted biotechnologies to date are insect-resistant maize and cotton and herbicide-resistant varieties of soybean, cotton, maize, and canola.[17] Resistance to insects like the European corn borer in the case of maize or the bollworm-budworm complex in the case of cotton is achieved through the incor-poration of toxin-producing genes from the soil bacterium *Bacillus thuringiensis* (*Bt*). For decades, farmers have sprayed *Bt* spores on crops as an effective bio-insecticide, a practice that is especially popular among organic fruit and vegetable growers. The other popular class of biotech crops incorporates various genes for herbicide tolerance, enabling farmers to optimize the timing of their herbicide sprays to control weeds without damaging the crop. Indeed it is the potential to shift away from chemical toward biological control of pests and diseases that drew many bio-scientists to work with these technologies and farmers to grow them.

Absent *Bt* technologies, farmers typically spray vulnerable crops much more frequently to control for insects. With *Bt* technologies the reduction in spraying is often substantial, especially in cotton. Herbicide-tolerant technologies have reduced the amount of herbicides used and eliminated the need for repeated plowings (tilling) after the emergence of the crop to control for weeds. Most of the benefits to date from these first generation biotechnologies accrue to farmers and technology suppliers, with more modest and indirect pluses for consumers in the form of lower prices, reduced toxicity of chemical residues on crops, and other environmental benefits. For some farmers the technologies have raised yields, and for most the costs of chemicals are lower. In addition, less tractor time lowers the cost of fuel and labor and reduces soil compaction and erosion. In fact, many U.S. soybean farmers are using herbicide-tolerant crop technologies to switch entirely to low-tillage cropping systems.

In the United States, regulatory approvals for commercial plantings of genetically engineered cotton, maize, and soybeans were first given in 1995. By 2001, one-quarter of the U.S. maize crop was planted with GM pest-resistant or herbicide-tolerant varieties, almost 70 percent of the cotton acreage was genetically modified, as was 68 percent of the area in soybeans.[18] GM versions of some of these same crops (and others, like canola) have also proven profitable for farmers in Argentina, Australia, Canada, and China, but more widespread adoption of these and other GM crops is limited by a lack of local regulatory approval and crop release.

The lack of consensus and the sense of disquiet among critics of these technologies stems not only from different perceptions of the consequences of using them, but from divergent views about the farming practices that would prevail if we avoided them. Similar controversy accompanied hybrid crop technologies in the 1930s and the semi-dwarf (short-stemmed) rice and wheat technologies of the Green Revolution. Indeed, many critics of the environmental and distributional consequences of the Green Revolution have re-entered the fray as leading critics of GM technology.

Technological pessimists point out that using GM seeds is more expensive, offsetting reductions in other production costs.[19] Many assert that adverse human health effects, such as allergic reactions,[20] may result from eating GM food, and mistrust the approvals granted by the U.S. Food and Drug Administration, the USDA's Animal and Plant Health Inspection Service, and the Environmental Protection Agency. Although the National Research Council (NRC 2000) and a panel of seven scientific academies from around the world (NAS 2000) concurred that the risks to human health or to the natural environment posed by genetic engineering are no different in principle from those posed by conventional plant breeding, pessimists are undeterred, alleging that corporate influence tainted the objectivity of these experts. As an April 2000 report from the U.S. House of Representatives Subcommittee on Basic Research noted "No product of conventional plant breeding . . . could meet the data requirements imposed on biotechnology products by U.S. regulatory agencies. . . . Yet, these foods are widely and properly regarded as safe and beneficial by plant developers, regulators, and consumers" (2000, 37).

Although most public concerns focus on the health effects of GM food,[21] far less is known or understood about the environmental consequences of GM technology because of the complexity of ecological systems and the short history of the techniques. The most common environmental concerns focus on the possibility of "super weeds" if herbicide-tolerant genes from transgenic crops spread through pollen to weedy relatives. An alternative nightmare is the emergence of "superbugs"—pesticide-proof insects that evolve in response to crops with enhanced chemical defenses, such as *Bt* maize or cotton. These risks are not unique to transgenic types of biotechnology and apply equally to use of existing plant protection technology.

Herbicide resistance is unlikely to persist in a weed not subject to selection pressure, and if it did, it could be controlled by another herbicide (just as farmers now rotate herbicides in continuous cropping systems). Pesticide resistance affects all spray technologies used by farmers, and it must be managed in any crop, including GM varieties. In the United States, for example, farmers growing *Bt* cotton must plant either 20 percent of their cotton land to a conventional variety with conventional pest control, or 4 percent to a conventional variety with no pest control to preserve pest susceptibility to *Bt*.[22] Restrictions also exist affecting how much *Bt* maize can be planted in a county with significant cotton acreage. Similar requirements for "refugia" apply to *Bt* maize.

So far, most of the benefits of GM crops have gone to farmers in the rich countries of the North. From the perspective of poor developing countries, biotechnologies have yet to deliver on their promise. But it would be unreasonable to expect applied GM research to reach them after less than a decade of commercialization. As shown in previous chapters, food production worldwide must increase to meet growing demands. If the poor and hungry are to be aided in raising yields, conserving land, and avoiding postharvest losses, then plant-breeding technologies, including but not restricted to GM crops, will play a vital role. There are real prospects of broadening the base of beneficiaries. Some, but still comparatively little, of current biotech research is targeted to technologies that tackle production problems facing LDC farmers (Jefferson 2001). But there is every reason to think developing-country producers could gain. New generations of biotechnologies with traits that improve the quality of the crops in ways that directly benefit consumers are in the works. A continuing stream of cost-reducing technologies will further reduce the costs of production and help keep food prices from rising as demand continues to grow. As these technologies spread, the beneficiaries will be precisely those who spend most of their incomes on food.

For consumers, mainly in the North, who opt for foods produced from GM-free crops and animals, markets are already beginning to segregate products in ways that satisfy these demands (Anderson et al. 2001). These choices need not preclude others from enjoying the lower prices and new quality traits that biotechnology products can offer to the developing world. Per Pinstrup-Andersen, the former director general of IFPRI, placed the North/South issue in the context of access and ethics:

> We need to talk about the low-income farmer in West Africa who, on half an acre, maybe an acre of land, is trying to feed her five children in the face of recurrent droughts, recurrent insect attacks, recurrent plant diseases. For her, losing a crop may mean losing a child. Now, how can we sit here debating whether she should have access to a drought-tolerant crop variety? None of us . . . has the ethical right to force a particular technology upon anybody, but neither do we have the ethical right to block access to it. The poor farmer in West Africa doesn't have any time for philosophical arguments as to whether it should be organic farming or fertilizers or GM food. She is trying to feed her children. (Pinstrup-Andersen quoted in Bailey 2001, 29)

SCIENCE AS PROPERTY

One of the most challenging areas of agricultural research for developing countries results from the expansion of property rights doctrine to include the intellectual property of agricultural and biological innovations. The elaborate web of legal patent protection in Western countries, and its extension to international trade law under the World Trade Organization (WTO), has provoked anxiety that the "genetic commons" may be enclosed by biotechnology companies seeking to protect their profits by locking developing countries out and blocking their access to new developments by public and nonprofit researchers (Herdt 1999). In response, well-publicized "donations" of intellectual property have been undertaken by major multinational corporations to developing countries for certain noncommercial crops. While dramatizing the potential usefulness of biotechnology, these exercises in largesse reinforced the impression that developing countries are locked out of access to modern technologies.

In principle, intellectual property rights protect incentives to innovate and promote innovation by mandating disclosure of patented technology. With legal protection enabling investors to recoup their research investments, a stronger incentive exists to pursue innovation. Absent such protection, underinvestment in research or hiding and hoarding information can result. Intellectual property rights also clarify ownership, helping innovators reap more of the rewards of their research. In practice, there is tension between incentives for innovation and allowing innovators to build on one another's work. Owners of a technology may be willing to share or license it only after costly negotiations, making it difficult for others to obtain the tools to advance their own research. They may also litigate against alleged infringers, forcing those who hope to use a protected technology to weigh the risk of litigation against the costs of obtaining licenses.

Modern methods of crop development are based on a wide range of components with the rights to each component possibly held by competing parties—be they patent rights or assigned use rights via commercial contracts or licenses (Nottenburg, Pardey, and Wright 2002). As biotechnology advances, the number of separate rights needed to produce a new innovation will escalate. If ownership of these rights is diffuse and uncertain, it can be difficult or impossible for potential users to negotiate successfully with all of the relevant parties.[23]

One misconception, at the heart of the "lockout" apprehension, is that a patent awarded in one country, such as the United States, confers property rights in the rest of the world. This is not so; there is no such thing as an "international patent." To protect an innovation in more than one country, a patent must be awarded in each. The cost of obtaining a patent varies from country to country; the cost of obtaining protection in all important markets can be hundreds of thousands, if not millions, of dollars. Thus, most inventions are patented in just one or a few developed countries with large markets; the chance that any given patent has been awarded in developing countries is small.

The freedom to operate in developing countries is also not well understood. For example, recent biotechnology-based innovations creating a vitamin A–enhanced rice (so-called *Golden*Rice™), reportedly requires permission to use more than 70 patent rights (Kryder, Kowalski, and Krattiger 2000). The well-publicized donations by major corporations of their intellectual property relevant to vitamin A rice left a strong impression that crucial patent rights were being relinquished in favor of poor developing countries. In fact, in many major rice-consuming countries, there are no valid patents, and in most there are very few (Kryder, Kowalski, and Krattiger 2000). Similarly, well-publicized donations of virus resistant technology for some noncommercial potato varieties in Mexico and for sweet potatoes in Kenya apparently do not involve any local patents at all. Crop breeders in the developing world are free to produce crops as long as the inputs and processes used and the crop varieties grown are not protected under local intellectual property laws. But those crops cannot be legally exported to countries where they fall under intellectual property protection. In such cases, the importer, not the breeder, may be infringing on intellectual property rights.

The result of these misunderstandings is widespread apprehension, particularly among LDC researchers and international agencies, that ignoring the claims of intellectual property rights holders, even in jurisdictions where they are not valid, could injure collaborations with them and threaten support from donors. Yet private firms routinely ignore patents not valid in a given jurisdiction, and donors and developing-country researchers can currently do likewise in most cases regarding research on staple food crops (see Binenbaum et al. 2003).[24] Freedom to operate may still be a problem for developing-country research on export-oriented cash crops such as horticultural products. As intellectual property protection becomes more pervasive, it may also constrain Southern science geared to food staples. The policy and practical implications of these possibilities are discussed in Part Two of this book.

THE FUTURE OF AGRICULTURAL SCIENCE

The knowledge available to tackle food and hunger is much greater than in the past. But this knowledge is biased toward the rich countries—both in absolute magnitude and relative to the size of the agricultural sectors. From the 1960s until the early 1980s, developing countries were bridging the divide, as technologies spread, spurred by science conducted in or financed by rich countries. Public agricultural research spending grew faster than in rich countries, funds flowed from international donors to universities and public research agencies in the LDCs, and a consortium of aid agencies and private foundations created institutions like the CGIAR, designed expressly to stimulate technology sharing. Moreover, most of the relevant technologies were unencumbered by intellectual property rules.

As a new century begins, these initiatives are waning and the South-North knowledge gap is widening. Agricultural science spending, public and private, has slowed in many regions of the world and for many countries. In the 1990s, public spending actually shrank in Africa and stalled in the rich countries, and many aid agencies massively reduced their support for agricultural research. The pool of science and technologies that can spill over from rich to poor countries is growing more slowly. The slowdown in science spending in the developing world (especially Africa) also limits the capacity of poor countries to develop locally relevant technologies and tap into stocks of knowledge developed elsewhere.

The notion that private science is a substitute for public research in tackling hunger and poverty is mostly wrong. As profitable markets develop, private research can play a larger role. But for the majority of the poorer countries of the world, these prospects are in the future. The right approach is to strike a balance between public and private initiatives, not to remove government from agricultural research. Even in rich countries, agricultural research still relies very significantly on public support, as we will discuss in more detail in the next chapter.

Private science in rich countries concerns itself mainly with crop and animal technologies orientated to capital-intensive forms of commercial agriculture with high added value. Private research will steer clear of areas where benefits are difficult to capture commercially. Public as well as private research will find the technological tools of the trade increasingly proprietary, requiring increasing attention to intellectual property issues. Gaining access to proprietary science for public research—especially for research oriented to Southern agriculture—is a new and yet unresolved challenge.

Nor is funding alone sufficient to close the knowledge gap between rich and poor countries. Public-private partnerships—easier said than done—are another requirement. Making efficient and effective use of the dollars invested in Southern science is yet another. Science, especially for agriculture, is not a stop-start affair. It requires persistence, not least because of the long lags from investing in research to realizing benefits. Despite the political and market challenges, the past shows that sustained scientific effort over the decades can have profound growth and development consequences. Relegating hunger to history cannot be achieved without the necessary scientific research and development.

5 • HUNGER AND INSTITUTIONAL CHANGE

With the new millennium has come an outpouring of anxiety over globalization and criticism of the institutions that service the global economy. The International Monetary Fund (IMF), the World Bank, and the World Trade Organization (WTO) are derided for supporting rich multinational corporations, while giving short shrift to the poorest countries and the poor within them. This criticism is paired with an emphasis on local self-reliance and recognition of the many noneconomic factors that define a civil society.[1] While largely hostile to international institutions, this critical perspective is nonetheless implicitly international and begs the obvious question: if not *these* institutions, then what others?

In this chapter we consider the role of both national and international institutions in responding to hunger and food insecurity and the need to rethink globalization progressively and constructively in order to achieve growth that affects poor people positively. While many criticisms of the global economy and global institutions are well founded, it is hard to think of a future in which international trade, global institutions, and economic growth will play little or no part. Accordingly, the task is to *redefine* national objectives in a global economy and to *restructure* institutions to meet these objectives. We focus mainly on redefining objectives; detailed proposals for restructuring institutions are the subject of later chapters.

There is little doubt that much in the world has changed since the creation, in the wake of World War II, of the IMF, World Bank, and the General Agreement on Tariffs and Trade (GATT) (since 1994 the WTO). Yet the essential rationale underlying these institutions—the need for some form of international economic and trade policy coordination to facilitate growth in income—remains more important today then ever before. One of the most obvious international changes since the mid-twentieth century is the rise of LDCs as a force that will increasingly have to be reckoned with, with a new set of needs, especially in the area of food security. Yet, as critics have often charged, many of the policies promoted by the IMF, World Bank, or WTO mainly seem to support already rich industrialized OECD countries,[2] with relatively minor benefits to LDCs. Notwithstanding striking gains in global agricultural productivity and growth, many LDCs remain chronically food insecure.

Nowhere are the potential benefits of growth through expanded trade more obvious than in agriculture. Since World War II, as tariffs on manufactures fell from an average of 40 percent to as little as 4 percent, agricultural tariffs stayed in the 40–50 percent range and in some cases actually rose. Moreover, agriculture experienced increases in the use of nontariff barriers (such as health and safety restrictions) primarily aimed at keeping competitive foreign imports out. The result of this set of protective devices is clear in terms of trade volume: while manufacturing trade grew more than 17 times larger after World War II, agricultural trade expanded less than sixfold, despite the fact that it remained the largest sector in nearly all developing countries (*The Economist* 2001b).

In recognition of the need for a renewed emphasis on agricultural trade reform, the WTO began negotiations in 2001 at Doha, Quatar, to set a new trade agenda giving greater weight to developing-country concerns, most importantly expanded market access to the rich markets of the North. One of the key points of contention was food aid, which is most popular in donor countries when they have surplus supplies and international prices are low. As a result, food aid often clears rich countries' shelves, while further undercutting prices for farmers in recipient nations (Ruttan 1993). Despite efforts to better incorporate agricultural issues of greatest concern to LDCs in a new round of trade negotiations, many poor countries remain highly skeptical that they will see opportunities to access rich countries' markets. This skepticism was reinforced in 2002 as the United States raised protectionist tariffs on steel imports and passed a grossly distorted set of agricultural subsidies as part of a new farm bill (Becker 2002).

In the face of these challenges, how can national economic policies, development assistance, and especially trade policies be redefined to respond to the food insecure? First, food security is not only a national concern but a global issue that inevitably involves economic and political interdependence. Efforts to deny this interdependence and to nationalize food and agricultural policies have resulted in inefficient and distorted "go it alone" responses to the food problem. Like ozone depletion or climate change, food security operates on a global scale and must be considered in large part as a shared international responsibility.

Recognizing the global nature of food security does not, of course, absolve national governments of responsibility for their own agricultural policy decisions. What it suggests is that policies to support or tax farmers or consumers should be developed with global trade and markets in mind, and that international forces should become increasingly important factors in national planning. To date, the primary reaction by national governments, especially in food-deficit nations, has been a defensive emphasis on self-reliance at all costs and the erection of protective barriers to food imports. These policies are driven by a fear of global market forces and a somewhat justified sense that LDCs are their victims. As noted, the 2002 U.S. farm legislation has undercut efforts of economic reform advocates who oppose such protectionism.

We emphasize that international institutions should seek not only to increase the efficiency of the global food distribution system but also to increase its fairness and justice. A fair or just distribution of food is central to dealing directly with the poor and providing an underpinning for a world system based not only on economic logic but also on the logic of civil society. Only if participants in the international market economy believe that they have a fair opportunity for success will they become stakeholders in market institutions, including global trade liberalization.

How, then, should institutions be restructured to meet these objectives? Such a redefinition has three dimensions: one horizontal, one vertical, and one psychological. The horizontal dimension involves the breadth or reach of global institutions: their coverage of issues such as food production and trade and related issues of environment, health, and the conservation of scarce resources such as soil and water. The vertical dimension turns on the authority and control that international institutions and organizations exercise in relation to national governments and local authorities. These, too, are issues not only of efficiency but also of justice, and they go to the heart of debates over national sovereignty, local self-reliance, and the definition of "development as a form of freedom."[3] Institutional reform, especially directed at food security, must also come squarely to terms with the meaning of "security" itself, a psychological condition in which confidence about future prospects offers the assurance of economic and social opportunity (Runge 1981).

A set of broad policy innovations can take these principles and implement them in specific and tangible ways. While detailed recommendations will appear in later chapters, here we present architectural sketches for a set of global reforms, with particular proposals for steps designed to fill gaps in the current international food system that can be undertaken by national and international actors in both the public and private sectors. We will give particular emphasis to building and complementing human assets through scientific and policy research and education, and to targeting and directing the huge concentrations of wealth held in private foundations to the objectives of food security, as well as to more general reforms in trade and development policies.

FOOD SECURITY: A GLOBAL PUBLIC GOOD

The global food system is the result of hundreds of millions of production decisions and billions of consumption decisions by farmers and consumers in every country on earth. The supply chains connecting food producers, processors, handlers, and ultimately consumers are longer than ever before and cross many national borders, as food moves through the system to its ultimate destinations. While some farmers and consumers, especially in LDCs, remain locked inside local food systems, many more are looking outside for both production and consumption, from fertilizer and seed to grain and meat. From an ecological perspective, these longer supply chains consume more resources in transit and further processing than local production, and they result in a variety of unwanted environmental side effects such as agricultural pollution from fertilizers or large, concentrated animal feeding facilities (Runge 1997; Runge and Fox 1999). At the same time, they offer consumers, especially in high-income countries, a cornucopia of choice. Even low-income consumers in Chicago or Paris can afford to shop in supermarkets loaded with fresh, frozen, and processed foods that would have astounded shoppers even half a century ago. Most of these products are not locally produced, but many, such as fruits and specialty cheeses, represent the best local traditions of other parts of the world.[4]

Because this system of food production and consumption has many effects (both positive and negative) that transcend borders, its operation is not just a national or local issue but a global one. Food security is really part of an overall strategy to improve human health and nutrition through preventive measures designed to promote the welfare and productivity of people whose immunity to disease is strengthened by balanced and nutritious diets. Food security, health, and the environment are a complex of global "public goods," which define how people depend on the earth and its resources and how these resources are used and conserved in return. Economists consider public goods to have two distinguishing attributes. Once provided, it is difficult or prohibitively costly to exclude anyone from enjoying the benefits of public goods (a "nonexcludability" criterion), nor does one person's consumption diminish the amount available to others (a "nonrivalry" criterion). Thus the benefits (or costs) of many public goods cross groups and national boundaries—and thereby are dubbed international public goods. Many goods may be quasi-public or mixed public and private goods in that they are either partially excludable or partially nonrival, or excludable or nonrival but not both.

While not a "pure" public good, food security, like human health, has strong public good characteristics. First, food security for one group, except in cases of extreme privation and scarcity, does not generally imply a reduction in this security for other groups (nonrivalry). Second, if food security is attained by a group or country in the form of an adequate and nutritious diet, it is difficult to exclude others from benefiting, except through the use of naked political denial of entitlement (Sen 1981). Food security also results from commodity flows (and relates to transborder environmental issues), which make it a global public good.[5] Notwithstanding this intricate web of agricultural, human health, and ecological connections, many people (especially politicians) persist in the notion that food is primarily a national or a local product, or that it should be. Hence, "foreign" sources of food are distrusted and discriminated against both culturally and more formally through tariffs and nontariff trade barriers. While it is true that all food is produced locally (somewhere), it is also increasingly true that much of it is consumed far from where it was produced.

An essential challenge posed by global food security is that perceived national interest too often leads governments to hoard food stocks, artificially encourage production, and limit imports—ostensibly to buffer consumers from food shortages or swings in market prices and to preserve rural traditions. Even where the international market offers an alternative source of food, the notion of dependence on external sources is anathema to many politicians and their constituents in both North and South. Food self-reliance and independence from foreign interference, even at demonstrably higher costs to the nations involved (many of which are poor), are extremely popular forms of nationalism. Food exporters too, such as the United States, erect protectionist regimes for commodities where foreign competition is perceived as a threat, as in the U.S. sugar program. This program, among others (such as the U.S. subsidy to wool and mohair) has been defended on "national security" grounds, in the same spirit as government stores of strategic metals, where the argument is usually more plausible.

The appeal to self-sufficiency is even greater where historical memories of privation and food shortage exist, as in the European Union and Japan. In the postwar period, the Europeans consciously erected a protectionist regime encouraging domestic food production to reduce their net imports from the rest of the world. Unfortunately, the regime survived to see Europe become a net exporter of wheat in the 1970s; wheat was then subsidized for export in order to clear European markets, creating a domestic constituency dedicated to perpetuating both domestic and export subsidies and setting the stage for the continuing battles over these subsidies with Australia, Canada, the United States, and others. Japan, which remains the largest net importer of U.S. agricultural products, clings to a policy for rice that grossly subsidizes its domestic production, shutting out competitive rice from much lower cost producers in Asia. Now the United States has joined the ranks of grossly subsidized agriculture.

Among developing countries, India represents an especially striking case of the drive for self-sufficiency. Efforts to raise food production and reduce reliance on imports have been a hallmark of every Five-Year Plan since independence in 1947. With substantial government subsidies to wheat and rice, largely to the exclusion of other crops, India has raised wheat production 10 times over since 1947; it is now the world's second-largest producer of rice and tied with the United States as the second-largest producer of wheat (Hopper 1999). It reduced food imports from a high of 10.5 percent of production in 1965 to become, for a period in 1995, a net exporter of both wheat and rice. Yet behind these achievements lurk more disturbing trends. As wheat and rice production and consumption have grown, production and consumption of pulses (chickpeas, pigeon peas, mungbeans, lentils), the main protein source for most of India's population and nearly all of its poor, have fallen. This is also partly due to the lagging yields of pulses relative to wheat and rice. The result is that from 1960 to 1995, per capita supplies of protein from all plant products increased only modestly from 47.3 to 48.7 grams per day, and supplies of critical proteins actually fell from 9,384 to 8,790 milligrams per day (Hopper 1999, 456).

Moreover, as mentioned in Chapter 2, India has a larger number of undernourished people (in terms of calories) and malnourished (under-weight) children than any other country. To overcome these deficits, greater food imports are a cheaper alternative than subsidization of domestic production. This is especially true of wheat, the world's most widely traded and available crop. As one expert said, "If the government chooses to pursue its present path of self-sufficiency, its single-mindedness may serve not only to delay the country's social and economic development, but also to prolong the misery of millions of malnourished people" (Hopper 1999, 475).

The consequence of national policies such as these has been to reduce the reliance of many nations on international trade as a source of lower-cost food supplies, allegedly on the grounds that the international market is "insecure." While total reliance on food imports is unlikely in most nations (with some exceptions such as Singapore or Hong Kong), excessive protection against imports in one nation has negative consequences for many others. The collective consequence of hoarding and protection is actually to destabilize the international market, withholding supplies when prices are high and exporting them when they are low, further reinforcing a global sense of food insecurity. Hoarding and protectionism help to guarantee that fears of instability will be realized, driving countries deeper into calls for national self-reliance.

Of course, world trade in foodgrains does not guarantee food security, especially when low levels of purchasing power limit access to these supplies. Yet, a careful review of the relationship between global grain markets and food importing needs, especially of poor countries, reveals many potential opportunities forgone in order to avoid, as India's Congress Party put it, exposure to the "whirlpool of economic imperialism" (T. N. Srinivasen, quoted in Paarlberg 1999, 139). India's sense of vulnerability during the food crises of the 1960s and 1970s was real and deeply felt. If countries are averse to food imports, it is not only because of their purported unreliability or instability, as Paarlberg notes, but also "because of a larger policy aversion the governments in these countries have to all markets, both grain and nongrain, both domestic and foreign" (Paarlberg 1999, 140).

The case of India nonetheless demonstrates both the appeal, and the fallacies, of the argument for national as well as for local self-sufficiency. At its base, this argument rests not only on a distrust of markets, but on a deeper psychological aversion to dependence on foreign sources of goods. The same aversion underpins the resistance to foreign sources of agricultural technologies such as the biotechnology and to corporations such as Monsanto. Even if it is less efficient (and even unfair, especially to the very poor) to rely largely on one's own sources of production, it is better, in this line of reasoning, not to lose the assurance that comes with local or national self-reliance. The psychological dimensions of this "assurance problem"[6] are important to resolving it: if international markets and trade do not offer the same or greater assurance, then national leaders may reject them in favor of less efficient self-sufficiency schemes.

The very phrase "food security" speaks to this psychological dimension. At its base is a sense of predictability and stability of supply: if global markets offer a predictable and stable source of food, then they can be relied upon and are "secure." Many arguments for food security begin with claims that foreign sources are unpredictable and therefore unreliable, given the intrinsic vagaries of agricultural markets, or that other countries may use food as a "weapon," cutting off supplies for political or ideological reasons, as in fact the United States did as a response to rising soybean prices in the early 1970s and in reaction to the Soviet invasion of Afghanistan in 1979.

This view has been shown to be largely false in research conducted since the 1970s and 1980s. More open trade in agriculture smoothes out the bumps and gyrations in markets, rather than aggravating them as is popularly believed (Newberry and Stiglitz 1981; Anderson et al. 2000). This is an important finding, because it turns the conventional wisdom on its head: if countries want the assurance of stable and predictable food supplies, they should seek *more* open trade, not more self-sufficiency. More open trade allows food to move from areas where it is in surplus to areas of deficit, and it enhances the capacity of deficit regions to feed themselves. This requires, of course, that they can afford to pay for the food, a central issue to which we will return. However, generating the income to be able to pay in poorer countries can be dramatically improved by expanding market access to developed-country markets, again by opening trade.

In a global assessment of the potential gains to developing countries of agricultural trade liberalization in the wake of the 1986–93 Uruguay Round of trade negotiations, Anderson found that the potential gains from further agricultural trade liberalization are "huge, both absolutely and relative to gains from liberalizing textiles or other manufacturing." Moreover, the next round of trade negotiations "offers the best opportunity yet for developing countries to be pro-active in seeking faster reform of farm (and textile) trade by OECD countries. In return, the developing countries will need to offer to open their own economies more. Fortuitously, that too is in the economic interests of rural people in poor countries" (Anderson quoted in Schuh 2000a, 1).

Consider the case of sugar. The Caribbean Basin produces a substantial amount of the world's sugar, yet still depends largely upon food imports. If the Caribbean countries rely on imports for food security, then they must be able to earn sufficient foreign exchange from sugar and other exports to purchase this food on the open market. It has been estimated that if the United States opened its sugar market by an additional 25 percent, by reducing tariffs and quotas on foreign imports, it would have a greater impact on incomes in the Caribbean Basin than 25 years of foreign aid (Messina and Seale 1990). This example shows that trade liberalization and food security are a two-way street: if poorer countries are to benefit from more open markets in food and primary products, then developed countries like the United States must be prepared to reduce their protection of imported products like sugar. Such changes would also benefit U.S. consumers, who pay several times the world price for sugar. Unfortunately, powerful vested interests in the U.S. sugar industry vociferously defend its protection at the border.

The sugar example thus underscores the political and ideological dimensions of the problem. In the United States, an unwillingness to liberalize the sugar program is at least in part related to the possible benefits to Cuba, which has been subject to a U.S. trade embargo for 40 years. When agricultural policy is tied to ideology, farmers and consumers tend to suffer, as when President Carter employed food as a weapon in the largely unsuccessful food embargo against the former Soviet Union in the wake of the Afghanistan invasion in 1979–80. Such actions undermine confidence in the trading system as a basis for food security and further encourage the rhetoric of self-reliance.

The economic importance of trade in providing for food security is readily shown. About 75 million people will be added to the world's population every year between 1997 and 2025. As noted in Chapter 2, most population growth will occur in developing countries, much of it in urban areas. Depending on how rapidly incomes also increase, households will purchase more meat and animal products. To meet these demands, the world must produce 40 percent more grain by 2020. Expanding the amount of land in production will likely account for only about one-fifth of this increase. Yet yield increases are slowing from the heady days of the Green Revolution in the 1970s.

As a result, trade will play an increasingly vital role. Net cereal imports by developing countries will need to almost double by 2025 to fill the gap between production and demand, and net imports of meat will need to increase by a factor of eight. While many of the critics of global trade advocate a return to locally produced goods, including food, the truth is that about 60 percent of world net cereal imports in 2025 will come from the United States. And not only America must respond. This estimate assumes that Eastern Europe, the former Soviet Union, the European Union, and Australia will also substantially increase their net exports. If any of these groups, notably the former Soviet Union, fail to do so, the burden of supplying the rest will fall to the remaining exporters.

As described in detail elsewhere in this book, the challenge of food security is thus essentially a race between productivity and populations with rising incomes. Whether the world can feed itself in the next century will depend in part on whether the international community turns to or away from growth through trade as a way of moving food from surplus to deficit regions. It will also depend on whether countries adopt resource-conserving methods to sustain water, land, and forests, or deplete them in order to meet other needs.

In summary, a strong case can be made on efficiency grounds for a reduced emphasis on self-sufficiency as a basis for food security and an increasing emphasis on trade (coupled, as we shall argue, with global programs of environmental protection). These issues cross national boundaries and cannot be confronted by nations, or localities, operating in isolation. This does not mean countries should abandon local or national food production, nor that national policy reforms should take a back seat to global ones. But national resources that could be better employed in areas other than food production should be allocated accordingly, and national agricultural programs should be reformed with an eye to international markets. In addition, national policies that promote food production in areas with highly vulnerable soils or with scarce water resources should be redirected.

However, the efficiency gains of such a redeployment will not occur unless developing countries consider international markets predictable and reliable sources of supply. This will require additional safeguards (discussed in the chapters to follow), including enhanced access to international funding and development assistance and, most importantly, a more balanced structure of rights and obligations under international trade agreements and access for all nations to trade benefits. Only if both the efficiency and fairness of the system are guaranteed will nations be prepared to commit themselves to trade-based avenues of food security, confident that the system assures them of access to food when and where it is needed.

GLOBALIZATION AND JUSTICE

Economic analysis sometimes fails to deal adequately with questions of distributive justice—meaning who gets what and whether such a distribution is just. These questions (around which society is, after all, largely organized) are ethical issues for which economists often feel unequipped.[7] But they are central to understanding arguments for food security, especially in the context of civil society. The most powerful argument in favor of distributive justice, defined as a type of fairness, was put forward over 30 years ago by John Rawls (1971) emphasizing the "priority of liberty," interpretable as freedom from want. Rawls proposed a hypothetical (but, at least to low-income societies, not altogether unrealistic) "original position" in which one is uncertain as to how society's goods and resources will eventually be distributed.[8]

As a simple example let us say that you know you are going to be born, but you do not know into what type of family. Your chances of becoming a member of any given household anywhere in the world are equal, from the Rockefellers to the Hassans. You have a chance of being born into a well-off family in a high-income country, but you face an equal chance of being born into a family like the Hassans. Given this, what degree of inequality would you consider appropriate and just? In this position, most would probably opt for a world of greater equality and an absence of extreme poverty and hunger, with particular attention to those worst off. If Rawls' argument has merit, individuals who face uncertain prospects are naturally concerned over being left in the bottom position and will develop institutions to protect themselves and others from such outcomes. These institutions will be defined by rules of equal division (or equal access) of basic needs, including food, as well as attention to those at the bottom.

Here it is important to distinguish between rules that provide for equal division at the "starting line" and at the "finishing line." There is tension, in other words, between equality of outcome and equality of opportunity. If equality of outcome is too rigidly guaranteed, it can destroy the incentive to compete and win. Yet individuals, regions, and nations do not come to the starting line equally endowed with skills and resources, and some provision must be made for a "safety net" to protect those who cannot overcome these disadvantages. The challenge is to develop an institutional framework that guides global capitalism toward such justice.

Rawls' arguments suggest that gaining the assurance of ample food supplies, locally or internationally, will be unlikely without *rules* that guide its distribution. These rules need not stipulate total equality, nor always mandate compensation to those worst off, but giving weight to such principles will lend support to any system of food distribution.[9] Ironically, in light of the hostility in the social justice community to the international economic system, the entire structure of international trade rules is based on a form of fairness, enshrined as "reciprocity" and "nondiscrimination," both of which are forms of equal treatment.[10] In cases in which discrimination results in trade injury, provisions also exist for compensation to those made worse off.[11] However, there is a widespread perception in LDCs that the wealthy nations who created the GATT/WTO system in the postwar era did so in their own image, and that the developed countries are first among equals. At least until the Uruguay Round, the United States and the European countries were largely responsible for keeping agriculture off the trade reform agenda. Most LDCs continue to believe that large, food-exporting countries dominate agricultural trade negotiations, granting only secondary status to LDCs and especially net food importers. Until they begin to see and experience real evidence to the contrary, the LDCs are less likely to support the system of trade rules that defines the WTO or programs of agricultural trade liberalization. Increased LDC support for a system of international trade rules based on the GATT/WTO system can only be achieved by a system seen as less weighted in favor of the rich.

In addition to the need for rules guaranteeing more equal treatment, the idea of justice suggests the need for expanded access to opportunity (Rawls 1971). In the context of trade, this implies a need for greater market access, as discussed above, but has a deeper meaning as well. In his 1999 book, *Development as Freedom,* Amartya Sen argues that a full understanding of development cannot come only from economic indicators but must capture some larger sense of human potential.[12] A precondition to realizing this potential, Sen argues, is *access* to the ways and means of improved welfare, including food. In the same broad sense that Rawls defines justice as fairness, Sen relates development to freedom of access, which is itself a form of fairness. Sen links the idea of *economic* freedom, on which a liberal trading regime is based, back to the idea of *individual* freedom, on which liberal societies and civil liberties must be based.[13]

The relevance of distributive justice to food security thus operates at several levels. First, it relates directly to the perception that LDCs have been left out of many benefits of a global trading system, not least in agriculture, and have not been given equal standing at many of the world's important economic and political fora. It cannot be emphasized enough that the new round of world trade negotiations finally launched in late 2001, the Doha Development Round, must truly reflect the needs and interests of LDCs to succeed. First, a new set of initiatives will be required to open access to developed-country markets, especially in commodities reflecting LDCs' comparative advantages, such as sugar, tropical fruits, horticultural products, and textiles. As detailed below, this suggests the need to redefine the objectives of the agricultural negotiations around the broader theme of food security itself.

Second, a concern with distributive justice suggests that the low incomes that aggravate LDC food insecurity must be raised not only through expanded access to developed-country markets, but by an increased ability to tap private investment credit and development aid. Relieving the income constraints of these countries will require careful review of the role of the IMF and World Bank in providing such funds and a rethinking of their objectives to achieve pro-poor growth.[14] These issues will be taken up in greater detail in Chapter 6.

Inside national borders, the relevance of distributive justice for food security is that people cannot be chronically malnourished and reasonably productive at the same time. Food, at least in terms of its provision of the basic nutrition necessary for an active, healthy life, is one of the clearest examples. To be deprived of food is a denial of a fundamental right to a full and active life. For most consumption goods, society cannot say what or how much is best or whose consumption pattern is better because no minimum standards exist; food is an exception because standards are in place to evaluate dietary adequacy based on physiological requirements. As noted in Chapter 2, food security is defined by the FAO in terms of calorie adequacy, providing a relatively clear and objective measure.

A right to food has been widely recognized as fundamental. It was first formalized in the 1948 Universal Declaration of Human Rights of the United Nations. The International Covenant on Economic, Social, and Cultural Rights, adopted by the United Nations General Assembly in 1966, also recognized "the fundamental right of everyone to be free of hunger" (Pinstrup-Andersen, Nygaard, and Ratta 1995). The inability to realize one's productive potential is thus not just an economic issue but also a civil and moral one, amounting to a form of bondage. Breaking these chains will require explicit attention to maldistribution of resources within nations and efforts to assure economic and social security, especially for those worst off. By providing for this security, the narrow appeal of self-sufficiency will be lessened, as the opportunity of all segments of society to participate in the income-generating marketplace expands.

A final, highly personal dimension of distributive justice, with special relevance to food security at the household level, concerns the role of women and children. Despite their central role in many traditional (as well as modern) agricultural households, women have been undervalued economically, and many also lack civil liberties. Without equal access and opportunity in areas such as secondary and higher education, their productive potential has been stunted (Harriss 1991). Perhaps more important than their economic potential, denial of access and opportunity inhibits their individual freedom and the broad realization of their social participation. Expanding food security at the household level will expand opportunities for women, while promoting efficiency and fairness.[15] The link from food to individual freedom is also clear when we think of children's nutrition, which allows them to develop physically and mentally and achieve their full potential.

THREE DIMENSIONS OF INSTITUTIONAL REFORM

We argue that if global food security is to be achieved in this century, policymakers must cooperate nationally and internationally. Food security cannot be accomplished by nations operating in isolation. However, the criticism directed at existing international institutions by many opponents of globalization raises questions about the commitments that nations and groups within them are prepared to make to new rules and methods of organizing international food security. More specific objectives for these reforms must be identified. All three dimensions of the problem—horizontal, vertical, and psychological—require attention; together they define the scope of needed institutional reforms. The role of NGOs is an important part of the vertical dimension.

Horizontal Dimension First, the current breadth of international institutions is inadequate to the task of meeting the food security challenge. Although critics decry the expanding influence of "international bureaucrats," the current reach of international institutions actually falls short of covering many of the most prominent issues of global concern. Indeed, it is arguable that the architecture of international governance is less far-reaching than proposed after World War II (UNDP 1999b, 98). John Maynard Keynes then proposed not only the establishment of the World Bank, IMF, and an international trade organization, but expansion of many United Nations agencies, including FAO, to work alongside the Bretton Woods institutions to achieve global full employment. During the post–World War II economics conferences, Keynes proposed a working fund equal to half the value of the world's imports (compared with 1999 IMF liquidity of 3 percent of total imports), and the establishment of an international reserve currency based on Special Drawing Rights (which today amount to only about 3 percent of global liquidity). Keynes' conception of an international trade organization included the creation of global commodity stockpiles to help stabilize prices and fixed price ratios for primary commodities indexed to nutritional and standard-of-living targets. In light of these ambitious objectives, some widening of global institutions today seems less radical than many might imagine (see Skidelsky 2001).

Two areas of needed "horizontal" expansion linked to food security stand out. The first concerns human health and nutrition. The World Health Organization (WHO) in Geneva, its resources stretched to confront the burgeoning crisis of AIDS and other infectious diseases, requires additional support, especially in preventive health. Vaccinations are a well-known example. The Gates Foundation of Seattle, Washington, formed from the huge financial resources of Bill and Melinda Gates, has recently committed hundreds of millions of dollars to a global vaccination effort. In June 2001, UN Secretary General Kofi Annan and U.S. Secretary of State Colin Powell joined forces to focus international attention on AIDS, especially in Africa. Annan and Powell sought to leverage government contributions to a global AIDS fund with private aid from corporate and foundation sources. (This objective was reinforced by additional U.S. funding commitments to AIDS in Africa in President Bush's 2003 State of the Union Address.) The goal was to raise $7–$10 billion compared with the $1 billion available in 2001. The fund is to be administered outside the UN system. As an example of the private sector's potential contributions, Annan pointed to the distribution of AIDS medicine by the Anglo-American Mining Company in Botswana and the anti-AIDS effort by the Volkswagen Corporation in Brazil. Coca-Cola, the largest private employer in Africa, is planning an AIDS effort modeled on its polio vaccination efforts in India (Perlez 2001, A3).

These examples of coordinated public and private aid to combat AIDS and other diseases can serve to inform the design of food security initiatives as well. While life-threatening and crippling diseases such as AIDS and tuberculosis draw needed international attention, the linkages from food insecurity and poverty to infectious diseases are often missed. Nutrition—hence food security—is a critical form of preventative health care equal to any other. Like vaccination, it arms the body against many viral and bacterial ailments and contributes significantly to overall health.

A second area currently not covered by the global institutional architecture concerns environmental protection. In the past decade, in the face of criticisms of the WTO and trading systems' inability to deal effectively with a variety of environmental challenges, calls have been issued for the creation of a global environment organization (GEO) to function alongside the WTO and WHO in response to global ecological challenges (Esty 1994; Runge 2001). *The Economist* magazine and a former director of the WTO have called for such a body (*The Economist* 1999b, 18; Ruggiero 1999). While the United Nations Environment Programme (UNEP) has attempted to respond to some of the many global environmental challenges, and the WTO has made painful but important adjustments (creating a Committee on Trade and the Environment in 1995), the growing number of multilateral environmental agreements and their potential conflicts with the WTO suggest the need for a broader framework (Sampson 2000; Shaffer 2001).

The linkages from global environmental protection to food security are both important and controversial. Unfortunately, many developing countries remain suspicious that the environmental agenda is just a way to block their exports to the rich markets of the North. This is a further reason for taking environmental issues, especially those with no substantial trade implications, outside the WTO and into a separate body. We have already explored some of the linkages from environment to food security, especially the growing scarcity of freshwater for agriculture and the important potential role of genetically modified (GM) organisms.

GM organisms may turn out to be the most important—and divisive— issue linking the environment, trade, and food security in the next decade and beyond. Their rapid adoption suggests that biotechnologies presently available have major appeal to farmers, at least in developed countries. In developing world countries the appeal of GM technology remains uncertain, although major funders, such as the Rockefeller Foundation, have for more than two decades sought to harness the technology to the needs and purposes of poor farmers and other private agencies like the McKnight Foundation have joined in supporting these efforts. Unfortunately, as noted in the previous chapter, most developing countries possess few of the technical resources to develop their own scientific and management capacity for biotechnology. This will require a "massive effort," according to Robert Herdt of Rockefeller, involving substantial flows of capital, human resources, and scientific information and expertise across national borders (Herdt 1999; Smith 1998).

GM organisms connect agriculture, trade, environment, and food security in a chain of causation that demands a global structure of rules and disciplines—precisely what the WTO/GATT system, joined by a potential GEO, can provide. Ironically, these technologies have become central to the new protectionist coalition's case against the world trading system and the agreements over intellectual property that emerged from the Uruguay Round of multilateral negotiations. If agricultural competition and market access remain at the heart of global trade negotiations, if environmental and trade linkages are now an acknowledged feature of these negotiations, and if trade, environment, and GM technologies all represent pieces of the food security puzzle, then it is inescapable that food security will be linked with rules formulated to guide world trade and to deal with trade and the environment (Victor and Runge 2002a, 2002b).

The horizontal expansion of global institutional architecture is partly a question of "coverage," but it is also necessary to assure developing countries that such expanded coverage will respond directly to their needs— an aspect of a "rebalancing" of the interests of North and South. Former Canadian trade negotiator Sylvia Ostry argues that the Uruguay Round trade agreements shifted the terms of trade negotiations in ways that are only now beginning to be understood. First, agriculture was for the first time at the center of the negotiations. Second, the opening of OECD markets to agricultural (and textile) imports from the LDCs was promised (although the promise has remained largely that) in return for the expansion in WTO coverage to include "new issue" negotiations over services, intellectual property, and investment, as well as the creation of the WTO itself. As Ostry notes:

> The essence of the South side of the deal—the inclusion of the new issues and the creation of the new institution—was to transform the multilateral trading system. Indeed the full transformation is still underway and difficult to forecast (especially after Seattle). In the present context the most significant feature of the transformation was the shift in policy focus from the border barriers of the GATT to domestic regulatory and legal systems—the institutional infrastructure of the economy. (Ostry 2000, 5-6)

As a result, LDCs need technical assistance in transforming their domestic regulatory systems. As observers of the challenge posed to LDC governments note, these governments agreed to be bound to commitments to implement new regulatory and legal regimes. The OECD countries, meanwhile, were not bound by a parallel commitment to provide the necessary technical assistance, and only limited commitments to liberalize OECD agricultural and textile markets (Finger and Schuler 2000). How these current technical needs will be provided is at the center of the LDCs' capacity to take part in new trade initiatives.

In addition to the creation of new institutional breadth, existing UN institutions are in need of reinvigoration. One is the United Nations Commission on Trade and Development (UNCTAD). Created in 1964, UNCTAD has defended the special claims of developing countries, notably protection of LDC industries behind trade barriers to promote "import substitution." In the GATT (now WTO) system this was reflected in exceptions to the GATT principles of reciprocity and nondiscrimination in "special and differential treatment" for developing countries, as well as GATT provisions allowing for protection of "infant industries" and balance-of-payment exceptions (Hudec 1987). Yet in the 1990s, in part because of its declining aversion to more open trade, UNCTAD has begun to redefine its objectives. Its secretary general, a former trade minister and WTO director, has sought to establish a "positive agenda" in which, rather than seeking to be excused from the trading system through continuing exceptions, LDCs offer their own proactive proposals.

In the run-up to the ministerial meeting of the WTO in Seattle and later in Doha in 2001, more than half of the specific proposals for the meeting came from LDCs, many of them prepared in cooperation with UNCTAD (Michalopoulos 1999; Luke 2000).[16] A consensus formed around some of these proposals, including increases in technical assistance, tariff removals for exports of the poorest countries, and expanded market access for LDC agricultural products and textiles. Until the final hours of the Doha meeting, the United States and European Union were unprepared to accept these proposals and disagreed among themselves over what could and could not be part of the round. Nonetheless, the LDC agenda was largely intact at the conclusion of the trade meeting in Doha, laying the foundations for further negotiations.

The positive role for UNCTAD that has emerged is encouraging, and it may serve as a backdrop for further capacity building by LDCs, especially in the development of negotiating expertise in Geneva. This is the objective of a cooperative project by the World Bank, UNCTAD, and others, launched by former WTO Director General Renato Ruggiero as the Integrated Framework for Trade-Related Technical Assistance to Least Developed Countries. As we detail in chapters to follow, this initiative (or something modeled closely on it) deserves considerable increases in its scope and amount of support, especially from private foundations.

A second existing institution in need of reinvigoration is FAO, which remains the primary source of international data and provides technical support for policies and regulatory regimes concerned with food, forestry, and fisheries. FAO's capacity to respond to major issues of food security has been severely hampered in recent decades by chronic underfunding, part of a general lack of support for the UN system, especially at the hands of the U.S. government. Since 1994, FAO has engaged in a wide-reaching but still incomplete set of internal reforms, with a central emphasis on food security in low-income, food-deficit countries (see FAO 2000e).

Despite lack of support, the United Nations has managed to maintain three critical affiliated agencies, whose role in future food security policies will be fundamental. The first of these is the World Food Programme, responsible for delivering and supervising the distribution of emergency food aid in areas beset by natural or man-made disasters, such as

Bangladesh, Sub-Saharan Africa, or the former Yugoslavia. The World Food Programme, like FAO, has been underfunded and understaffed for most of its history.

The second agency (operated under the auspices of both FAO and the WHO and previously of interest primarily to scientific and commercial food interests) is the Codex Alimentarius Commission, known as Codex. Codex is comprised of a small group of professional food scientists responsible for developing harmonized approaches to food standards across national borders. It is of particular importance in dealing with GM foods, notably labeling issues (Josling 1999; Runge and Jackson 2000). Labeling requirements can be used to stigmatize and reduce sales of unwanted products less on grounds of health or safety than as disguised barriers to trade. An example was a European Union requirement that British sausage exported to Germany be labeled "pork-filled offal tubes" (Rosen 1995). However, the role of Codex goes well beyond labeling to include assessments of safety and risk. These are of particular significance in implementing provisions of the Sanitary and Phytosanitary Standards Agreement of the Uruguay Round in the WTO. Again, it has been both underfunded and understaffed, especially given these important new responsibilities. Apart from its linkages to food safety via the Codex, WHO will need to be more centrally engaged in food and nutrition issues, requiring some expansion of its mandate. WHO has already begun an internal transformation but more remains to be done. In addition to its central involvement in the global fundraising for AIDS and other health needs, WHO needs to emphasize food/nutrition/health linkages more explicitly.

The third agency is the International Fund for Agricultural Development (IFAD). Established in 1977 as an outcome of the 1974 World Food Conference, IFAD was created to provide funds on concessional terms for poverty alleviation and improvements in nutrition. Under its 2002–06 strategic framework, it is focused on pro-poor strategies targeted to small farmers, the rural landless, pastoralists, traditional fishing groups, indigenous people, and poor rural woman. Most of its funds are made available as long-term loans repayable over 40 years with low interest charges. Its funding comes from member countries, investment income, and loan repayments in about equal proportions, totaling about $450 million in 2001 (IFAD 2002). This level of funding could be substantially expanded, even doubled, without unduly taxing member governments.

With the emergence of GM technologies and the growing role of intellectual property regarding agricultural biotechnologies and genetic resources, several international institutions take on special significance. One is the Convention on Biodiversity, and under it the 2000 Cartagena Protocol, negotiated to deal with trade in living modified organisms (especially seed). The implementation of this protocol can help build assurance that countries trading in plant genetic resources are being carefully monitored, but it also holds the potential for interfering in the orderly flow of new technologies to developing countries (Jackson 2000). How the Convention on Biodiversity interacts with FAO, WTO, and UNCTAD will thus be of considerable importance to LDCs in defining an institutional agenda for food security.

The Trade-Related Aspects of Intellectual Property, administered by the WTO, and the Patent Cooperation Treaty, administered by the World Intellectual Property Organization (WIPO) profoundly affect intellectual property markets worldwide. Yet many poor countries are struggling to develop intellectual property policies and practices in ways that meet their obligations under these international agreements. Moreover, the agreements themselves are in need of urgent reform, especially regarding the intellectual property aspects of folkloric and traditional knowledge and international access to and use of agricultural genetic resources. These are both critical issues for many LDCs, who rely heavily on these forms of intellectual property. WIPO is doing much to strengthen intellectual property policies and markets in LDCs, but much more could be done, in concert with WTO, to bridge the intellectual property divide between rich and poor countries. The outcome of negotiations over the Substantive Patent Law Treaty launched in May 2001 regarding the harmonization of administrations and the centralization of function of the patient process will have important implications for the intellectual property regimes facing LDCs.

The Vertical Dimension   This dimension is among the most sensitive and easily misunderstood of the issues of international governance. It concerns the way in which international institutions exercise authority in relation to national governments and local groups. It is this dimension that has raised much of the suspicion and resentment against international organizations. Ultranationalists are joined by grassroots NGOs and many LDCs in decrying the power and alleged abuses of institutions such as the WTO, World Bank, and IMF. For example, an advertisement in the *New York Times,* running before the 1999 WTO ministerial meetings in Seattle and signed by a coalition of NGOs, argued

> It no longer matters what democratic societies want, what matters is what global corporations want, as expressed and enforced by global trade bureaucrats in Geneva. . . . the WTO . . . has been granted unprecedented powers that include the right to rule on whether laws of nations—concerning public health, food safety, small business, labor standards, culture, human rights, or anything—are barriers to trade by WTO standards. (*New York Times,* November 22, 1999)

Not only does this view substantially overstate the authority of the WTO, it also reveals an anxiety (or seeks to provoke it) over the growing role of international institutions. Nowhere is this more true than for the food system, which joins the issue of economic interdependence to consumer health and safety concerns. Critics of the new Sanitary and Phytosanitary Agreement, part of the Uruguay Round trade agreements, for example, have suggested that U.S. food additive standards could be undermined if levels deemed acceptable by Codex are less strict than domestic requirements (Millimet 1995).

Behind the question of unelected power exercised by multinational corporations (or NGOs) through international bureaucrats is the more fundamental issue of national and local sovereignty (Jackson 1997a). If Sen is correct in arguing that development is an issue of access to opportunity, then freedom by countries to pursue national and subnational goals, largely independent of dictates from supranational agencies, must be weighed against the arguments for an expanded role for these agencies. Freedom—self-determination—in this respect, has two faces—a positive and negative one.[17] Positive freedom—the freedom of countries, groups, or individuals to exercise their access to opportunity—is largely about the rights and capacities that they have to do so. Negative freedom, by contrast, is the freedom from interference by those outside or above one's nation or person. Thus LDCs have argued strenuously in favor of their right to maintain their own set of labor or environmental standards in food production and manufacturing, not just as a way of gaining a competitive edge (freedom *to*), but as a reflection of a desire for a lack of interference in their pursuit of national policies, given their stage of development and lack of influence over the application of these standards at an international level (freedom *from*) (Salazar-Xirinachs 2000).

The two faces of freedom can be interlocking: freedom from the dictates of supranational authority may be a precondition for the exercise of the freedom to gain international opportunities. If development requires these freedoms as a fundamental matter, it implies the need for substantial deference by international institutions to the sovereign rights of countries and subnational groups to pursue domestic goals. This argument has been made in detail for the rights of countries to maintain food standards.[18] There is, however, less evidence than the critics claim that existing international bodies have consistently failed to exercise this deference, or that horizontal expansion of their coverage to include issues of environment, health, and food security has compromised national and subnational self-determination.

It remains clear that the locus of responsibility for many, if not most, key decisions affecting food security will remain at the national level. As Paarlberg (2002, 2) argues

> Global markets and interstate institutions may be spreading and proliferating overall, but in the poorest countries where large numbers of people are still hungry, and particularly in the rural regions of those countries, international food markets and global institutions still tend to have weak influence relative to local or national food markets and local or national food governance institutions.

Yet it is equally clear that national policies should not proceed as if a larger international market does not exist. Ironically, one of the most glaring turnabouts in this respect came in 2002 with the passage of a U.S. farm bill driven almost totally by domestic politics. The $180 billion bill led delegates to the 2002 World Food Conference in Rome to roundly condemn U.S. unilateralism and self-absorption. The Cairns Group of agricultural exporters, including Australia, Brazil, Canada, and Thailand, among others, wrote in a private letter to Congress in June 2002 that "the sheer size of the subsidy package will inevitably hurt farmers around the world, particularly in developing countries" (Becker 2002, A-3). As C. Fred Bergston of the Institute for International Economics noted, the U.S. farm bill cannot even be defended on grounds of self-interest. As he noted, "The long-term

growth of U.S. agriculture is clearly in foreign markets. That requires liberalization and access to those markets. The farm bill undercuts our ability
to reach those markets" (Becker 2002, A-3).

The Role of NGOs   Part of the reason for optimism over the vibrant state
of self-determination in developing economies is the growing influence of
NGOs, reflecting increasing local and national attention to civil society
issues. These NGOs,[19] knit together through extensive Internet contacts,
have forged alliances in favor of environmental and trade policy concerns,
and they provide both knowledge and capacity-building for LDCs. As former Canadian trade negotiator Sylvia Ostry (2000) notes, "together they
constituted a 'virtual secretariat' through the increased use of the Internet
in the second half of the 1990s." Many are also directly involved in food
security and agriculture.

Paarlberg (2002) distinguishes between NGOs with an international
focus and orientation (INGOs), those operating largely within national
boundaries, and strictly local grassroots organizations. He further distinguishes between not-for-profit but still private INGOs and NGOs and the
public and for-profit private sector. His classification is shown in Table 5.1.

NGO and INGO support and assistance to food-insecure developing
countries has grown dramatically in the past decade. Today, more than a
thousand such organizations provide programs and projects including
relief, reconstruction, and environmental improvements throughout the
developing world. Their comparative flexibility and ability to work at the

TABLE 5.1   •   Taxonomy of nongovernmental organizations

Level	For-profit private sector	Public sector	Not-for-profit private sector
International	Multinational corporations (MNCs)	Intergovernmental organizations (IGOs)	International nongovernmental organizations (INGOs)
National	National corporations	National government	National nongovernmental organizations (NGOs)
Local	Local private tradespersons	Local authorities	Grassroots organizations

SOURCE: Paarlberg 2002, Table 1.

grass roots, and to lobby effectively at high levels with governments and industry, have made them important players in the network of global development organizations (Simmons 1998). One careful observer of this process has called the rise of NGOs a global "associational revolution," which may be as important as the development of the nation-state in earlier centuries (Salamon 1994). Notwithstanding their popular support and growing influence, NGOs face their own set of challenges and do not offer a "magic bullet" for food security (Edwards and Hulme 1996).

Growing disaffection with both multilateral and bilateral aid, combined with a new emphasis on private-sector initiatives and cuts in the public sector, have created a need for assistance in the developing world that numerous NGOs have filled. If development assistance was not to be abandoned altogether, but was to have a private sector and local orientation, a delivery mechanism was needed. NGOs stepped into this gap, and have been recipients of considerable government aid money. For example, under Title II of the U.S. government's Food for Peace (PL 480) program, surplus commodities from the United States can be sold for local currency in developing countries, some of which is then paid to NGOs to support their in-country projects.

At the same time, NGOs came to recognize the global reach of information technologies such as the Internet and the potential use of this technology to advance an agenda of local empowerment and civil society concerns, especially democratization.[20] Globalization thus helped to position NGOs, as governments' monopoly on information slowly dissipated and the end of the Cold War created opportunities to broker political and economic power in new ways. Notwithstanding their important role in the process of globalization, and the benefits they have derived from the process, many NGOs are ideologically inclined to criticize global economic integration, especially its effect of reducing the power of local groups vis-à-vis multinational corporations and international institutions. While operating globally, many NGOs thus emphasize that their "primary stakeholders" are indigenous organizations and groups.[21]

The range of services related to food security performed by NGOs depends on their size, ideological bent, and expertise. Catholic Relief Services, for example, is heavily involved in the administration of food aid and emergencies under the auspices of the Catholic Church in recipient countries. It is linked to broader networks and advocacy groups, such as Washington, D.C.–based Bread for the World, and in turn to efforts organized at the grass roots by NGOs such as Panos or technically oriented service groups who operate their own projects, such as Techno-Serve (Clark 1991, 34–35). This range of activity suggests a much broader agenda than simple humanitarian relief. Moreover, NGOs answer to a wide range of constituencies: donor agencies, contributors, local power brokers, and in-country governments. The result is a diverse set of aims and sources of influence, which make generalizations difficult. In fact, the increasingly militant stance of some NGOs in protests at international economic meetings such as the Group of Seven or WTO has created cleavages among them over issues such as the proper role of agricultural biotechnology, how best to protect environmental sustainability, and international trade liberalization. Because of their general focus on participation, NGOs tend to see the proper scale of economic and social organization as local and decentralized, casting them as antagonists to both private and public institutions with global scope.

Yet they are also critically involved with a variety of these institutions. NGOs that provide assistance to poor countries, according to David Beckmann, president of Bread for the World, manage more than $2.5 billion in grant funding each year. Collectively, they speak to millions of their supporters. They could do much more to be a voice for the people they serve, helping their supporters to understand what they can do in addition to sending checks. At the 1996 World Food Summit in Rome, for example, not only 185 countries were represented, but more than 1,200 NGOs. They agreed to a goal of reducing undernourishment by 50 percent by 2015. When an Action Plan was released, however, the NGOs simultaneously released a forum statement that differed from the official action plan in numerous ways, from the impact of structural adjustment programs to the right to food and the role of civil society. While the event achieved global consensus on the importance of food security, it showed that NGOs were prepared to question the official version of what was to be done. In contrast to the NGOs' positions, the official Action Plan focused on increasing productivity, markets, and trade, and put less emphasis on access by small farmers to inputs and participatory decisions.[22] Such differences in emphasis continue at the parallel meetings organized by NGOs at meetings of the WTO, World Bank, and IMF (Kuchinsky 2000).

There is evidence that these parallel efforts have made inroads in the official proceedings. In the United States, for example, an official emphasis on trade liberalization has been blended with calls for more participatory procedures. Two 1999 initiatives of the U.S. government, the 1999 Africa Food Security Initiative to improve food security in selected African states, together with Africa: Seeds of Hope (Public Law 105–385), reflect the substantial influence of NGOs over official policies relating to Sub-Saharan Africa. The Seeds of Hope legislation emphasized smallholder production, women's roles in agriculture, and participatory programs (Kuchinsky 2000).

Deference to national and local sovereignty, or to NGOs and participatory democracy, requires that national and local institutions are viable and legitimate. Yet throughout Africa and in other parts of the developing world, national governments are unable to launch the initiatives necessary to combat hunger. Beleaguered by a lack of private or public capital, plagued by corruption and cronyism, it is not an exaggeration to say that the state as an agent of change is often hollow: "The state collapses from within, leaving citizens bereft of even the most basic conditions of a stable existence: law and security, trust in contracts, and a sound medium of exchange" (World Bank 1997, 19). NGOs have, unsurprisingly, been drawn into this space, functioning as extensions of developed-country aid agencies, both national and multilateral. In one sense they fill a role left empty by the hollow state, providing needed support, infrastructure, and technical skills. But in another sense, they often project the values and preferences of the North, lowered onto the stage of the South.

There are thus risks attending their growing influence over food security. The first, and most obvious, is that they supplant and substitute for the functions of representative and responsible government in poor countries, preventing it from assuming its proper role. Second, they encourage a view that developing world states cannot function without external support. Third, they risk imposing the priorities and views of developed world interests, even if those are not the interests of multinationals or the usual targets of external interference. Fourth, they may function in ways for which non-NGO interests are often criticized, with a lack of transparency and accountability. In short, if NGOs are asked to bear too much of the burden of food security, their contribution may not be in *addition* to that of the state, but *instead* of it, in ways that may not be consistent with the long-term interests and priorities of indigenous people. These aspects of NGO activity are often unaccounted for in the praise usually granted them as a group (Roberts 2001). Those promoting local self-reliance often have sided willingly with narrow protectionist interests, and a strong strain of technological pessimism makes many of them hostile to the scientific possibilities of plant and animal research for the global food system. Despite these risks, NGOs will continue to fill important niches in developing-country food security.

And given the growing role of NGOs as a countervailing influence to governments and corporate interests, it would be wrong to see them only as antagonists to corporate or government power. Their role in civil society is in fact highly complementary to the private sector, governments, and international organizations. Korten (1987, 1990) argues that instead of substituting for the state, NGOs would be better off supporting government efforts to promote long-term development efforts, such as food security. As a recent analyst of NGOs' role and function noted, "NGOs and governments can disagree over service provision, policy, and even politics, without necessarily undermining the institutional capacity of each to contribute to the development process" (Atack 1999, 864).

The Psychological Dimension: Building Human Capacity   Anyone who has experienced institutional change appreciates the importance of aspirations, expectations, and confidence to the possibilities for reform.[23] In a very real sense, ending hunger in the twenty-first century is a question of mind over matter: because we know that sufficient food can be produced, whether we feed the hungry turns on the willingness to commit ourselves to a global project of reform and economic growth. The resources and technology exist to accomplish the task. Lacking are the organization and willingness to act. Giving a lift to this process will, in our opinion, require a number of specific actions that all point to the same objective: raising not only the human capacity to confront hunger but the confidence that it can be done.

Three main initiatives stand out. First, as emphasized in Chapter 6, human capacity requires educational innovations and improvements at all levels—from the primary education of women in LDCs to increases in advanced scientific training of agronomists, soil scientists, plant breeders, and social scientists (Herdt 1999; Pehu 2002). Education, applied research, and scientific training are of crucial importance if the many potential benefits of new agricultural technologies are to be realized in poor countries.

Second, at a slightly different level, developing countries will require new capacity to participate meaningfully in global trade expansion (Runge et al. 1997). Obligations stemming from WTO's Uruguay Round to raise the level of regulatory, environmental, and scientific oversight in and out of agriculture will be nearly impossible for many LDCs to fulfill without substantial technical assistance to erect, maintain, and enforce new regulatory regimes. In the context of continuing trade negotiations, delegations from developing countries in Geneva need to be meaningfully and truly integrated into the negotiating process. In later chapters, we propose that this process be consolidated in a "trade policy center," located in Geneva.

Over and above their involvement in trade negotiations, LDCs require stable and uncorrupt national governments, capable of delivering agricultural research, education, and targeted policy interventions to their poorest people. As *The Economist* (2002c) observed in a critical assessment of the 2002 World Food Summit: not only have the rich countries turned back the clock of hunger alleviation with bloated subsidies to already rich farmers, many poor countries have compounded their hunger problems with backward and corrupt regimes. "Beating hunger," *The Economist* noted, has "as much or even more to do with good governance in poor places, with sensible policies needed for education and health care as well as agriculture, as it has to do with access to money and technology from afar" (*The Economist* 2002a, 74).

A final aspect of capacity building relates directly to confidence in trade and international markets and an end to food as a "weapon" of foreign policy, especially by major exporters (and importers) such as the United States. The United States should offer a binding commitment in the WTO to refrain from export or import embargoes in the future. In addition, it should seek major increases in funding for the World Food Programme (WFP), IFAD, and FAO, and the creation of both a food emergency relief plan and standby credit terms in the event of production shortfalls, especially in the poorest countries. Together, these actions would help to bolster confidence in the international system of food delivery, and in the trading system as a whole. The details of these and other policy initiatives will be spelled out in the second part of this book.

CONCLUSION

In this chapter we have tried to chart objectives for international institutions that will facilitate a full response to the global challenges of food security. At the highest level of generality, greater efficiency and fairness in the conduct and performance of these institutions and the international trading system will encourage even the poorest countries, and the poor within them, to become stakeholders. Three sets of changes in the structure of governance are needed. First, the breadth of international institutions must be expanded horizontally, allowing better coverage of some key global issues, including human health, nutrition, and environmental protection. Greater food security is preventive medicine, which suggests a need to integrate food security with a general strategy for health by the WHO. Maintaining a productive and sustainable food system will also require greater care and protection of soil, water, and plant resources, overcoming many LDCs' skeptical view of environmental issues (in and outside of agriculture), especially in the context of trade. A GEO would separate trade and environmental issues where possible, and be especially useful in tracking global environmental questions surrounding the spread of new biotechnologies. Existing institutions also merit revitalization. UNCTAD should redefine itself less as a perennial objector to OECD trade and development policies and more as a positive force in pushing for trade openness and development. FAO, WFP, IFAD, and Codex all merit expanded attention and support. Because of the key possibilities of biotechnology for LDC food security, the newly negotiated Cartagena Protocol of the Biodiversity Convention should give priority attention to the unanswered questions surrounding trade in GM technologies, in concert with efforts led by the World Intellectual Property Organization to strengthen the policies and practices pertaining to intellectual property, especially as it relates to innovations in food and agriculture, including crop and animal genetic resources.

A second change involves the ways in which WTO, IMF, and the World Bank exercise their authority with due deference to national and subnational governments. Nations and subnational groups must not feel that compliance with international rules undermines their self-determination. Despite such deference, international aid and technical assistance will remain vital elements in food security, together with expanded trade and market access. Only as LDCs build national regulatory and food systems, based on the rule of law and uncorrupted civil services, will they be full partners in the global agricultural trading system. The encouraging growth of NGOs reflects new international emphasis on local and community self-determination. While many NGOs style themselves as opponents of globalization, in fact they are part of it, and help give weight to the need for appropriate deference to national and local voices that have often only been weakly heard in the past. Their emphasis on civil society is a humanizing element in the expansion of global systems and important in assuring that issues of distributive justice are taken seriously.

Finally, confidence by nations that the global food system can assure their food security enables them to feel capable of the task of feeding their people. This capacity is based on four foundations. Expanded educational opportunity and an increase in support for regulatory, environmental, and scientific interventions in food systems are key. Additional technical support for LDC delegations in multilateral trade negotiations and a trading system uninterrupted by political use of food as a weapon are added confidence-building measures. In the chapters to follow, we will further develop all of these dimensions of food security.

PART TWO
SOLUTIONS

6 · POLICIES AND INSTITUTIONS

Part 1 of this book has laid a foundation of understanding. Who are the hungry? Why are they hungry? What future will they have in the twenty-first century? Without substantial changes in priorities, their number will not diminish rapidly, especially in parts of Africa and Asia, and in some places may actually grow. In Part 2, we consider in detail the new priorities and innovations needed to end hunger in our lifetimes. In this chapter, we carefully assess the policies and institutions that must change. In Chapter 7, we consider the financial resources available to accomplish these tasks. Each of the areas in which new policies and institutions are needed can be thought of as an investment in a shared global future. Taken together these investments—in human capital, agricultural science and technology, environmental sustainability, and new institutional forms—constitute an agenda for reform.

A strong case has already been widely made by others that certain fundamental standards of national governance must be met before any headway can be made against hunger and poverty (World Bank 1997). Paarlberg (2002) makes a compelling argument that food insecurity largely reflects a failure of governance at the national level. Weak or despotic nation-states fail to provide such basic national public goods as civil peace and the rule of law. Although the citizens of most developed countries can take these government functions for granted, in many of the world's poorest countries, especially in Sub-Saharan Africa, they are largely lacking, and little progress can be made regardless of the international effort. Where lawlessness, corruption, and civil unrest prevail, poverty and hunger are likely to proliferate. Only limited attention is given to the prerequisites for good national governance in this book because the issue has recently been discussed in detail elsewhere, especially in Paarlberg (2002) and World Bank (1997). Moreover, the real question is what does the global community do when confronted by weak or despotic governments? Should the plight of their people simply be ignored? For this reason, this book focuses more on the necessary global agenda to end hunger and poverty.

HUMAN CAPITAL

Human capital is an investment in people. This includes education, childhood nutrition, and health care. Added to these are special attention to the needs of children and greater gender equity for young girls and women. All of these investments promote pro-poor growth, with gains accruing increasingly to the poor over time. Agricultural development plays a crucial role in such a strategy, especially in the early stages of rapid economic growth. Carefully designed food and nutrition programs can accelerate the reduction of chronic poverty and hunger and also offer a safety net in times of transitory hardship.

Education It is important to remember that poor families have few physical or financial assets and little human capital. The Hassans, who own less than an acre of land, have few household possessions, no bank account, and a few small loans. Neither the husband nor wife has any formal education. Their nutrition and health are poor. Like the Hassans, 47.9 percent of those in extreme poverty in Bangladesh own no land, and 60.1 percent have no formal education (Sen 1997). Lack of assets and low income are self-reinforcing and passed from generation to generation. Perhaps the only hope of escape for the Hassans is their sons' education.

Education and training are the most critical components of human capital. Nobel Prize winner Theodore W. Schultz was one of the first economists to stress the role of education in raising the productivity of human effort (Schultz 1961). Schultz argued that the key factor in improving the welfare of the poor is "the improvement in population quality" (Schultz 1982, 4). Much research has now clearly established that education raises the returns to effort on the farm or in the home, and a lack of it is the main way poverty is passed from one generation to the next. More than half of the 15–19-year-olds in the poorest 40 percent of households in 12 countries (including India, Morocco, and Pakistan) have no schooling at all. In Sub-

Saharan Africa, the enrollment rate in primary school was only 60 percent in 1998 (World Bank 2001d, 27; Filmer and Pritchett 1999; UN 2000). At current trends, more than 100 million primary school-age children will not be attending school in 2015 (UN 2000).

With an educated workforce increasingly the pivotal factor in production, the rewards to it have grown as well as the costs of being excluded. The United Nations has now established as a specific development goal to "enroll all children in primary school by 2015" (World Bank 2001d, 5). Getting and keeping children in school will require investments in books and uniforms, which can be real obstacles for the poor. Poor families also frequently count on the work of children on the farm or around the household, so that incentives will be needed to encourage school attendance. School meal programs are one incentive that can increase attendance and improve nutrition.

Mexico's Progresa, an integrated rural poverty program started in 1997, provides an example of successful education strategies. Reaching about 80 percent of Mexico's poor rural population, Progresa has increased school enrollment at all levels, especially in secondary school. Grants are given to families for each child attending school. These grants increase at higher grades and are somewhat higher for girls than boys. The grants amount to 46 percent of the average earnings of an agricultural laborer for a child in the third year of secondary school (Soufias and McClafferty 2001).

Although the number of girls going to school is catching up in all parts of the world, the enrollment gap is still wide. In 1998 the ratio of girls to boys in primary and secondary school was only 77 percent in South Asia and 83 percent in Sub-Saharan Africa, but it reached 97 percent in East Asia and 94 percent in Latin America (UN 2000, 10). The reasons that investment in the education of girls yields such high payoffs are several. First, women become more economically productive. A World Bank study found that per capita GNP would have grown substantially faster between 1960 and 1992 in the Middle East/North Africa, South Asia, and Sub-Saharan Africa if these regions had closed the gender gap in education as rapidly as in East Asia (World Bank 2001d, 119). Second, there is strong evidence across countries that fertility falls with increased female education (Schultz 1994). Amartya Sen (1999, 195) concludes that "women's education and employment are the two most important influences in reducing fertility rates." Because population growth is still very high in many of the poorest countries and is a serious impediment to raising standards of living and reducing hunger, investing in women's education is a vital underpinning to bringing population growth rates within bounds.

More education and greater employment options also have the effect of raising the value of women's time. Since raising children is very time-intensive, especially for mothers, the focus shifts from child quantity (the number of children) to child quality (the investment in each child). Better-educated mothers have higher aspirations for their children. Moreover, infant mortality is lower in families with more educated mothers, so that to obtain a desired number of surviving children fewer births are needed (World Bank 2001d, 49). A study of 13 African countries between 1975 and 1985 found that with a 10 percent rise in female literacy rates child mortality fell by 10 percent (World Bank 1993, 42). Better-educated women also use contraception more effectively.

Women also have central responsibility in most families for a wide range of activities that affect health and nutrition (Quisumbing et al. 1995). Education greatly strengthens the wife and mother's ability to perform this pivotal role. A study using household-level data for Brazil found that 25 percent of preschool children with mothers with 4 or fewer years of schooling were severely or moderately stunted, based on their height for their age, and that this rate declined to 15 percent if these mothers had a primary education (between 4 and 8 years of schooling) and only 3 percent if they had a secondary education (at least 11 years of schooling) (Kassouf and Senauer 1996). Child nutrition and health strongly reflect the time of the mother as caregiver (Behrman and Deolaikar 1988; Senauer and Garcia 1991). When care is informed by higher levels of education, it is of superior quality.

The mother's care is even more important for infants and preschool children. Mothers who can process information, acquire skills, and make informed decisions develop caring patterns that support infant health and hygiene. They make greater use of health care facilities, communicate better with health providers, and are better able to follow directions for medical treatment. More educated mothers are also better at coping with adversity and protecting their children from dangers such as poor community sanitation (Smith and Haddad 2000, 7; World Bank 2001d, 119).

Although education is perhaps the single most important factor, efforts are also needed to improve employment opportunities, legal rights to property, and the overall status of women in many societies (World Bank

2001a). Because those most at risk of hunger and malnutrition are young children and women themselves, enhancing women's status reduces those risks. Those families where women earn or control more income invest more in nutrition, health, and education (Thomas 1997; UN, ACC/SCN 1991).

A final aspect of the role of education concerns the allocation of food and other resources within the household. Households distribute food, health care, and education among family members. In some cultures, women and children, especially girls, are discriminated against in this allocation (Quisumbing and Maluccio 2000). Economists have begun to view household decision making as a complex bargain, with husbands and wives having both "congruent and conflicting interests that affect family living" (Sen 1999, 192; Haddad, Hoddinot, and Alderman 1997). Solutions to conflicts may not be very egalitarian, and bargaining power is affected by the perception of contributions to the household. The bargaining power of women is often particularly weak in poor, traditional cultures because of their inferior legal rights, employment opportunities, and education compared with men. Yet, research has found that an increase in women's education and their productive value leads to a more equitable intrafamily distribution (Haddad, Hoddinott, and Alderman 1997; Senauer, Garcia, and Jacinto 1988).

Overcoming Child Malnutrition   An analysis of malnutrition among preschool children by Smith and Haddad (2000) found that women's education and increased food availability are the most important factors in reducing it. Data for 63 countries over the period 1970–95 supports these conclusions. Figure 6.1 shows the percentage reduction in child malnutrition attributable to women's education, national food availability, the health environment, and women's status, listed in order of their importance. More education for women accounted for the largest share of the decline, and, together with increased food availability, was responsible for 69 percent of the improvement. Women's education was measured by female secondary enrollment rates and status by the ratio of female to male life expectancy. One-fifth of the change was attributable to a healthier environment, as reflected in the share of the population with access to safe water, and over a quarter to increased food availability, as measured by the average daily calories available in the national food supply. However, if food availability was very low, it was the most important factor.

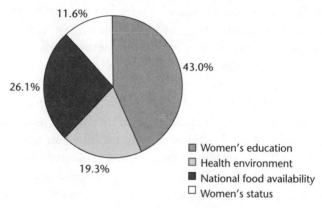

FIGURE 6.1 • Share of reduction in child malnutrition attributed to underlying variables, 1970–95
SOURCE: Smith and Haddad 2000.

Based on this analysis, Smith and Haddad (2000) estimated that the proportion of children who are malnourished could be reduced by half by 2020 if food availability per capita increased by 16 percent and the other underlying factors all improved by 25 percent. Food availability and women's education will be the most important factors in reducing child malnutrition in Sub-Saharan Africa and South Asia. Improving the status of women will also be crucial in South Asia. In East Asia, the Middle East/North Africa, and in Latin America, women's education is the key factor, followed by food availability and improvements in the health environment.

Investing in Health   Although reducing poverty and hunger and improving nutrition are crucial avenues to better health, other improvements in health are also essential to attack poverty and hunger. Health, like education, contributes to human capital. Workdays are lost and productivity falls if a person is sick and still working. School is missed and learning ability declines. There are medical costs and the burdens of providing care within the family. These burdens are greatest for the poor, who are not only ill more often but can least afford any loss in earnings because they lack savings or insurance schemes to fall back on. Again, particular emphasis needs to be given to children.

Public health experts use the concept of disability-adjusted life years to account for the overall burden of disease resulting in premature death and impairment in different countries. As of 1990 (before the HIV/AIDS epidemic had grown) the disease burden calculated in disability-adjusted life years was about five times greater in Sub-Saharan Africa than in developed countries, primarily because of premature death (World Bank 1993, 3). The infant mortality rate per 1,000 live births declined from 97 to 68 between 1980 and 1998 in low-income countries and from 115 to 92 in Sub-Saharan Africa. But it was still very high compared with only 6 per 1,000 live births in high-income countries (World Bank 2000d, 287). Most developing world countries substantially underinvest in health. Public health expenditures averaged only 1.3 percent of GDP for the period 1990–98 in low-income countries versus 6.2 percent in high-income countries (World Bank 2001d, 287).

The most cost-effective measure to improve health is preventive care, especially for children. Preventable and curable diseases were responsible for 43 percent of the disease burden in Sub-Saharan Africa in 1990 (World Bank 1993, 10). Some of the most cost-effective measures include child immunizations and school-based health services. In 1995–98, only 71 percent of children under 12 months old were immunized for measles and 68 percent for diphtheria, pertussis, and tetanus in low-income countries, excluding China and India (World Bank 2000d, 96). Many of the poor also lack access to safe drinking water and sanitation, leading to even greater disease problems as the developing world crowds into urban slums.

Only 8 percent of the $50–60 billion spent annually on health research worldwide is accounted for by developing countries and only 1 percent of medicines patented between 1975 and 1997 were for tropical diseases (World Bank 2001d, 183; WHO 1999). If climate changes lead to atmospheric temperature increases, mosquito-borne disorders such as malaria and dengue fever will become more prevalent in tropical regions and will spread to currently unaffected areas (Epstein 2000). Priority attention, similar to the international effort to find a vaccine for AIDS, is needed for these and other tropical diseases.

Oral rehydration therapy, which has been promoted by the United Nations Children's Fund (UNICEF), also costs very little and has saved millions of children from dying from the dehydration caused by severe diarrhea. Moreover, there are many other preventive health or simple medical treatment programs that are highly cost-effective. As opposed to the kinds of untargeted, general food subsidies that many countries had in the past, carefully targeted nutrition programs can be far less costly and more effective. Some of the most effective programs for malnourished children are administered through health clinics and involve careful monitoring of the child's health, preventive health care and nutrition education for the mother, as well as food supplementation (Binswanger and Landell-Mills 1995).

The HIV/AIDS epidemic in Sub-Saharan Africa remains not only a health crisis but a catastrophe for economic development. Progress against poverty and hunger is now dependent on controlling the epidemic in these countries. UNAIDS, the United Nations agency for combating AIDS, predicts that there may be more than 40 million children who have lost both parents by 2010 in Sub-Saharan Africa (IFPRI 2000). Unless a vaccine is developed, only prevention can reduce the impact. The cost of the drugs used to control HIV in rich countries, even if lowered in Sub-Saharan Africa, will still be hundreds of dollars per year—beyond the reach of most poor families (Rosenberg 2001).

ENDING POVERTY THROUGH SCIENTIFIC CHANGE

Increased agricultural productivity is driven by technologies, which transform traditional agriculture and the rural economy. Peter Timmer (1997, 3) with data for 35 countries, found that a 1 percent increase in agricultural GDP per capita led to a 1.61 percent gain in the per capita incomes of people in the lowest income quintile of the population, which was 38 percent greater than for industry. A primary reason for the slowing rate of poverty reduction in Asia and the worsening poverty in Sub-Saharan Africa is the exploitation of agriculture by governments and state marketing boards, which has been largely tolerated by international aid agencies (Mellor 1999). In returning to a Bangladeshi village he and his wife had lived in and written about 20 years earlier, John Briscoe (2001, 2) found that "today the people of Fatepur lead lives which are incomparably better." He identifies the crucial factor in this improvement as "a sharp increase in the demand for labor, as a result of more intensive and productive agriculture" (Briscoe 2001, p. 3).

Rural people account for more than three-quarters of the poor and hungry in South Asia and Sub-Saharan Africa. Even with Latin America's high level of urbanization, the majority of the poor are rural (Pinstrup-Andersen and Pandya-Lorch 1995). Productivity gains in agriculture thus translate directly into higher rural incomes for peasant farmers and landless farm laborers. The average real income of small farmers in southern

India rose by 90 percent and that of landless laborers by 125 percent between 1973 and 1994, a period of rapid adoption of the new high-yielding seeds and complementary practices referred to as the Green Revolution (World Bank 2001d, 184; Rosenzweig 1998b). Because agriculture forms the economic base of the rural economy, the increased purchasing power of farmers and agricultural laborers also spreads the economic expansion to rural nonfarm people (Hazell and Ramasamy 1991). The growth of the rural nonfarm economy provides employment opportunities for the excess labor in agriculture resulting from greater productivity, so that these people do not simply migrate to the major cities and become jobless.

Urban poverty is growing rapidly. The urban poor must devote half or more of their budgets to food. Therefore, declines in food prices resulting from rising production are equivalent to substantial increases in real income for the urban poor. Although the benefits may be quite small for each consumer, when spread across all the consumers of a staple food, such as rice or wheat, the gains are sizable (Schuh 2000b). It is estimated that wheat prices would have been 34 percent higher and rice prices 41 percent higher in 1970–95 in the absence of the international agricultural research efforts (World Bank 2001d, 184; Evenson 2000).

The essential components of investments in an agricultural growth strategy are technological change that increases output and cuts production costs, investments in rural infrastructure such as roads to reduce transport costs, and widespread participation by small peasant producers and woman farmers (Mellor 1999). It bears repeating that the majority of farmers producing food crops in Sub-Saharan Africa are women.

In his return visit to Fatepur, the village in Bangladesh, Briscoe (2001) found the people in virtual agreement that improvements in flood protection, irrigation, and transportation infrastructure have primarily transformed their lives for the better. A new embankment protected their island village and fields from devastating floods. Improved roads, bridges, and motorization of the riverboats "has meant easier access for those providing social (i.e., health care) and commercial (i.e., fertilizer) services, and lower costs in getting goods to market" (Briscoe 2001, 3). The market town can now be reached in 15 minutes. With an understanding of their importance to enhancing market access, FAO (2002a) gives a high priority to investments in the construction, upgrading, and maintenance of rural roads in its plan to reduce hunger.[1] Anyone who has bounced along at 5 miles per hour on a potholed dirt road in the developing world or become hopelessly stuck in the mud after a rain can appreciate the significance of this investment.

The unprecedented growth in agricultural productivity in the past century is primarily a result of investments in agricultural research and the innovations that followed (Borlaug 2001). Although technical change is only part of ending hunger, it may be the most crucial additional investment that can be made besides basic education. Agricultural technology development targeted at the poor and hungry cannot be entirely left to the private sector; it will involve conscious policy decisions by governments. Although the role of the private sector is critical in many respects, left to its own devices, it will provide research and innovations ill-suited to the poor. In agriculture, as in other areas such as medical research, there are few interest groups able to direct public funding to the poor and hungry. The poor simply do not have the political clout. The long lags (usually decades) between investing in agricultural research and reaping its rewards further discourage people who have more immediate needs (whether profits or poverty) from promoting their own research agenda. For many of the same reasons, donor agencies and governments must often deal mainly with short-term concerns and emergency relief, putting off investments in human knowledge and know-how that could confront the underlying causes of hunger.

If we want to end hunger in our lifetime, agricultural research investments worldwide are headed in the wrong direction. During the 1990s, public spending on agricultural R&D actually shrank in Africa, while it stalled in the rich countries. By the mid-1990s, although half of this spending was done in developing countries, much of it (44 percent) occurred in just three countries: Brazil, China, and India. As developed in Part 1 of this book, not only the amount of spending but its intensity per unit of output is the best measure of progress. By these measures, the research gap between the rich and poor is large and growing. In the mid-1990s, each developing-country farmer was supported by $8.50 per year of public research investment, compared with $594 for every farmer in the industrialized countries (Pardey and Beintema 2001, 13).

This gap has grown as aid agencies have reduced their support for agricultural research. In Africa, over 40 percent of research funding (excluding South Africa) came from foreign sources in the early 1990s (Pardey, Roseboom, and Beintema 1997). U.S. Agency for International Development (USAID) support for international agriculture declined in real terms

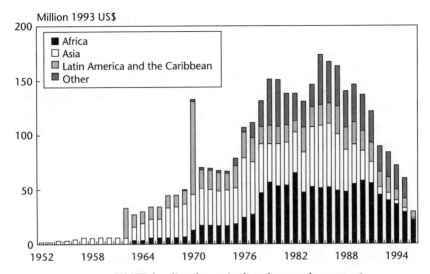

FIGURE 6.2 • USAID funding for agricultural research, 1952–96

SOURCES: Data are from Alex 1997 and Dalrymple 2000.

NOTES: USAID is the U.S. Agency for International Development. Nominal U.S. dollars were deflated to 1993 base-year prices using implicit GDP deflator from World Bank 2000d and BEA 2001. "Other" includes Europe and the Middle East.

throughout the 1990s (Figure 6.2), and it amounted to only $92.1 million in 2000 (CGIAR 2001). The most dramatic declines were in assistance to developing-country universities (Alex 1997). In 1996, just $2 million was earmarked for all these institutions, less than the budgets of most U.S. academic departments. Aid grants to government agricultural research agencies in LDCs were cut by 80 percent from the mid-1980s to the mid-1990s.

Turning these trends around is imperative, but increasing funding is only one requirement. Equally important is how funds are disbursed, how they are used, and the time frame of funding commitments. Much funding for agricultural R&D has been wasted by failing to attend to these requirements. During the 1960s and 1970s, aid dollars built up the stock of physical and human capital in agricultural research, only to be followed by cutbacks in the 1980s and 1990s. These cutbacks undermined the ability of national research agencies to replace buildings and equipment or keep trained staff. Because research is a long-term undertaking, stop-start modes of funding are ineffective.

Generating new plant varieties through crop-improvement research, for example, takes at least seven years. Erratic funding makes it impossible to accumulate new knowledge and to pass know-how from one generation of scientists to the next, building the basis for future rounds of innovation. A separate issue is whether aid dollars simply substitute for domestic dollars that would otherwise be committed to research.[2] Matching arrangements, where aid funding earmarked for research is offered contingent on funding from other sources, is one possible solution. Similar arrangements can be made for extended periods, supplementing rather than crowding out funding from national governments.

Regulations on public spending can also stifle government research by limiting the ability to offer competitive salaries and creative employment conditions for highly trained scientists. Some countries (such as Uruguay and Colombia) have spun off public agencies into public, nonprofit corporations, freeing research managers to make staff more accountable for their work and providing them with more decisionmaking authority. Others have moved toward more competitive processes, encouraging collaborative or joint-venture arrangements among public agencies, universities, and private firms. Among developing countries, these approaches have been pioneered by the national Brazilian agricultural research agency Embrapa.[3] Similar schemes have sprung up in Chile (Beintema, Avila, and Pardey 2001). Even so, competitive research allocation processes are still rare, averaging only 1 percent of Brazil's total agricultural research budget (Beintema, Avila, and Pardey 2001).

This competition can increase the flexibility of research, help attract the best talent, and provide a basis for reviewing research performance against the promises made to secure the funds. This allows resources to be reallocated to higher payoffs (Alston and Pardey 1996). Yet competing for funds also consumes scarce resources and adds an element of uncertainty. Competitive grants can also be steered for political reasons, just like public funding. Moreover, it makes no sense to introduce competitive schemes in developing countries struggling to maintain just one breeder or a handful of agronomists for each crop; there is simply no basis for meaningful competition.

Transcending Transgenic Technologies   Among the most controversial scientific frontiers in agriculture is biotechnology. Most of the news headlines and the health and environmental concerns over genetically modified crops deal with transgenic technologies that shift genes from one species to another (say from a soil bacterium to a maize plant). But modern biotechnologies encompass and promise much more. Scientific optimists believe that transgenics can produce yield gains, environmental benefits, and nutritional improvements targeted to poor people. Pessimists point to the risks involved and diminish or deny these benefits relative to the risks (Pardey 2001; Victor and Runge 2002a, 2002b).

A more balanced view would look beyond transgenics to broader genomic possibilities, including genetic mapping and techniques to splice genes among plants within a species to produce apomixis, or "seeds without sex." Perfecting this technology will open up hosts of valuable options. Saved hybrid seed would retain its hybrid vigor, and saved seed in general would maintain its traits from generation to generation, eliminating "genetic drift" and deterioration in crop performance. This would be of great value to poor farmers who cannot afford to buy new seed on a regular basis. It would also lower the cost of breeding new hybrids by eliminating costly controls over pollination. Pollen from apomictic plants is also sterile, eliminating the possibility of genetic drift from farmers' fields to nearby plants.

A second area of promise is the development of "sentinel" plants. In some parts of the world, for example, winegrowers plant fungi-susceptible rosebushes at the ends of their rows of grapes to serve as indicators of the fungi that can cause serious losses to grape production. Checking crops to see if they are under attack from certain pests and diseases or suffering from stresses such as dryness or nutrient deficiencies is a time-consuming and imprecise job; crops are prone to losses before problems can be detected. Perhaps certain plants—the sentinels—could be bioengineered to change color in response to specific stresses, signaling farmers when other crops are stressed. Farmers could then take remedial action—irrigating their crops, using biological controls, applying nutrients where needed in the field, or spraying selectively at certain times or places to control pests and diseases—before the stresses turn to economic losses.

A third area is the use of molecular markers—short snippets of DNA—as the basis for the breeders' selection strategy, instead of observed physical traits. These molecular markers offer a highly precise way to orient and guide crop breeding. Physical traits are often costly and time-consuming to evaluate (for example, growing plants and exposing them to pests to find those most tolerant requires expensive quarantine procedures). Checking for the molecular markers can be much more cost-effective.

Transgenic technologies are especially important in confronting hunger because the time frames involved in crop breeding are likely to be shorter. Yield-increasing or nutrient-enhancing traits can be introduced that are slow, expensive, or simply not possible using more conventional breeding techniques. In much of the world, environmental constraints to agriculture are constant threats to production: drought, pest infestation, waterlogging, and soils that are too acidic, too basic, or have insufficient nutrients or elevated amounts of salts or metals all take their toll. Crop management can deal with some of these problems, but crop varieties increasingly can be designed to tolerate drought, cold, and other stresses. And if predictions of climate change and increasing variability in weather conditions come to pass—causing productivity to fall in certain regions and to rise in others—the stresses that agriculturists must confront will be even more difficult without transgenic tools.

Although the first generation of herbicide and disease-resistant transgenic crops has benefited mainly Northern farmers, transgenic technologies are not inherently biased in their favor. Most farmers in poorer countries have not used them because of restrictions on their commercial use or because they have not yet been adapted to LDC conditions. Even so, the early examples of transgenics have proven popular among some Southern farmers. First released in 1996, Bt cotton is now widely grown in China (Pray et al. 2001). Smallholder producers in the Makhatini Flats of South Africa began planting transgenic cotton varieties in the 1998/99 season (Beyers et al. 2001)—the year they were given regulatory approval to do so—as have an increasing number of cotton growers throughout Mexico since 1996 (Traxler et al. 2001). In 2000, about 90 percent of Argentina's 10.2 million hectares of soybeans was herbicide resistant, compared with 54 percent of the 30.2 million hectares sown to soybeans in the United States in the same year (James 2001, 8). Southern farmers seem prepared to pay for the genetically enhanced varieties when the yield gains (or reductions in chemical, labor, or other input costs) more than offset the costs of the seed. Of course, many poor farmers cannot even buy or gain access to improved seed—transgenic or otherwise. They require subsidized seed technologies or financial credit to purchase seeds. But these constraints relate to delivery and access, not to the technologies themselves.[4]

However, much adaptation must be undertaken to respond to the needs of poor farmers. Resistance to corn borers in varieties suited to farmers in the Corn Belt of Iowa is of no use to farmers suffering losses from the same pest in tropical areas where the maize varieties are entirely different. Major investments are needed to get the right technologies to the right crops for use by poor people. Some of this is beginning to happen, but much less than is needed to really make a difference for food security. Examples that are well along the research pipeline include the development of virus-resistant sweet potatoes in Mexico and Kenya.

Managing the Scientific Commons   A critical determinant of investment flows in agricultural science and technology, especially with the advent of genomics and transgenics, is the complex structure of legal protections granted to innovators in both the private and public sectors. How these property rights are defined, assigned, and transferred will be crucial to whether poor farmers can gain access to new technologies. Until a few decades ago, most crop breeders worked with seeds and breeding know-how that was entirely in the public domain. The main exception was private research on hybrid varieties of maize: these hybrids were trade secrets and protected as such under national laws.

Now, most of the modern technologies used to develop new varieties involve a bundle of component product and process innovations, many of which are protected by patents and technology contracts and licenses.[5] As a result, nonprofit access to agricultural research may be closed off as the scientific commons is enclosed. Countries of the WTO must now comply with international rules protecting intellectual property. Ensuring public access and use of agricultural science in the face of these new rules will be critical if improved seed varieties and other agricultural technologies are to spill into poor country markets. This is not necessarily because private claims on technology will prevent its diffusion, but because the technologies of most use to poor farmers may not be privately profitable, at least in the short run.

Indeed, intellectual property rights do not currently appear to be the binding constraint on Southern science. Lack of local investment in science and limited experience and expertise in accessing, using, and regulating modern agricultural technologies are the real problems. Nevertheless, new intellectual property rules may affect the freedom to operate in the next generation of agricultural technologies, especially genomics. Guiding these changes in intellectual property regimes and responding creatively to the new environment are pressing challenges for those interested in the future of scientific research, inside and outside of agriculture. The World Intellectual Property Organization (WIPO) based in Geneva has an important role to play in helping formulate intellectual property policies and practices that stimulate technology flows into and use by private and public agencies operating in LDCs, especially regarding the Substantive Patent Law Treaty now under negotiation by WIPO member states.

Among the strategies for maintaining the freedom to operate is segmentation of LDC markets because of the largely domestic orientation of food stuffs.[6] Until recently, few developing world countries allowed patents on life forms. Patenting internationally is expensive, and corporations in many if not most cases have not obtained patent protection beyond certain OECD countries. To the extent that research agencies use technologies and cultivars that are not patented or otherwise protected where they are made, they can and should legally proceed without obtaining permission from the holder of the intellectual property rights. New international trade laws may loosen requirements for plant protection, allowing plants derived from patented or protected varieties to be free from such encumbrances. As a result, research programs in LDCs are likely to have considerable freedom to operate so long as they operate judiciously. To implement a judicious strategy, those who design research programs must have access to adequate information on patent rights and to expert legal counsel. Such access is not widely available on an international basis and does not exist for most LDC researchers and research institutions. As we will discuss in greater detail below, new forms of institutional support, working through new and existing channels, can provide access to this expertise.

One promising initiative to provide such services is the nonprofit corporation CAMBIA (Center for the Application of Molecular Biology to International Agriculture) in Australia. It has developed extensive online patent databases that are freely available to help researchers identify prior patent claims and move more safely through the international patent minefield. However, continuing access to expertise in international patenting is quite expensive. Markets for intellectual property can also be segmented using technology licenses specific to fields of use, including particular crops, lengths of time, research use versus commercialization, or restrictions on third-party services. Another option is to charge license fees based on ability to pay or the expectation of profit streams, thus distinguishing between small startup entities, be they in LDCs or developed countries, and large national or multinational corporations.

Insight into such segmentation strategies is offered by Lanjouw (2001), who developed a scheme for pharmaceuticals such as drugs for cancer or heart disease. These drugs have their largest markets in developed countries, but many potential users live in LDCs. When applying for a patent in the United States or other OECD countries, applicants would promise not to enforce them in designated developing countries. A foreign filing license, a routine requirement for filing in other countries, would effectively ask producers to choose between enforcing their patents in developed or developing countries.

Another way of lowering the cost of agricultural technology is the creation of an Internet-based clearinghouse to establish prices or pricing indicators, facilitate negotiations, and offer mechanisms for arbitration of disputes and monitoring of compliance. Such a clearinghouse could bundle together patents for biotechnologies "syndicating" inventors' technologies to make multipatent technology systems affordable to researchers (Graff et al. 2001). For many crops other than wheat, maize, some kinds of rice, soybeans, and barley, proprietary biotechnology may not require direct compensation, especially if there is little risk to commercial markets. Most staple crops for poor consumers, such as cassava, will have limited commercial markets (although cassava is imported on preferential terms to the European Union for animal feed).

Cases of technology offered without charge already exist, including several by the International Service for the Acquisition of Agri-Biotech Applications. Monsanto Corporation has made virus resistance available for several noncommercial potatoes in Mexico (Qaim 1998). It has also supported the incorporation of virus resistance in yams in Africa. Astra-Zeneca (now Syngenta) and Monsanto have announced they will make technology for vitamin A GoldenRice™ available free to subsistence farmers in developing countries. Such collaborations help solve nutritional deficiencies while generating goodwill. Care should be taken to protect such offers from misuse of their technology, especially serious in countries lacking effective regulatory oversight.

However, the publicity surrounding technology donations should not lead to an exaggerated sense of the generosity of technology producers. Multinationals' largesse is unlikely to extend in most cases to giveaways of commercially valuable patents or other intellectual property. For example, of the 70 odd patents identified as relevant to vitamin A rice technology, none are valid in Bangladesh, Iran, Iraq, Malaysia, Myanmar, Nigeria, Saudi Arabia, or Thailand, but 44 are valid in the United States, 21 in Japan, 11 in China, 6 in Indonesia, 5 in India, 9 in Vietnam, and 1 in the Philippines. Many apply only to the conduct of research and do not restrict production, sale, or importation of the transformed seed (Kryder, Kowalski, and Krattinger 2000). It is fair to conclude that the value of any intellectual property claims included in these donations is not large, notwithstanding the value of the technological know-how and assistance that the multinationals have provided in these instances.

Rather than cooperate in piecemeal technology transfer, corporations might give more general support to public research. For example, a consortium of corporations has supported a public database of genome markers called single-nucleotide polymorphisms, in preference to partaking in a competing private-sector initiative (Marshall 1998). Their actions suggest that private firms might choose to support similar public agricultural research initiatives in areas complementary to their own endeavors.

Novartis (now part of Syngenta) has supported plant biology research at the University of California, Berkeley (Rausser 1999; Mena and Sanders 1998). Despite concerns over excessive corporate influence on university research, Novartis gets rights to first negotiation for only a portion of the patentable discoveries. It cannot control the research done with its support, beyond the appointment of two members of a five-person committee that determines allocation of the Novartis funds to individual projects. Knowledgeable observers conjecture that a major portion of the return envisioned by Novartis consists of the benefits of intimate access to the intellectual resources of the Berkeley campus.

Corporations thus appear willing to exchange access to technology for close contacts with expertise without demanding exclusive rights. Nonprofits should seek to expand such arrangements, while maintaining continued independence from undue private-sector influence. About half the $21 billion (1993 prices) of agricultural R&D in OECD countries is now done by private firms (see Chapter 5). This represents a wealth of expertise and technology to be tapped for Southern farmers. Yet public resources are seldom committed to privately performed research on agricultural problems and virtually none of the international aid dollars are so directed. Neither do nonprofit agencies directly fund much agricultural technology generation directed to LDCs (with the notable exception of the Rockefeller and McKnight Foundations). Commissioning research for LDCs may be a particularly effective way of directing private research toward poor peoples' food-security problems.

Revitalizing Nonprofit Research Private research will not do much to develop new varieties of staple foods for the world's poor, such as cassava, beans, yams, cooking bananas, and millet. Nor will it build a major part of ecologically specific research related to their cultivation and management. The case made above for increasing government funding for agricultural research conducted in or directed toward the problems of LDCs need not mean an increased role for government agencies. Properly directed university, nonprofit, and even contracted private for-profit research options are real possibilities. But there is also much governments can do to revitalize national programs of agricultural research. Taking advantage of research done elsewhere is an effective catch-up strategy for many countries.

Spillovers of agricultural research have been pervasive, but there are limits to the degree agricultural technologies developed elsewhere can be used locally (Alston 2002). Agricultural innovations are often site-specific, limiting the market in ways less common to other technologies (Alston and Pardey 1999). As a practical matter, this means countries must be outward looking, aware of what is being developed elsewhere, and effective in tapping it. This may involve doing only adaptive or screening research or giving up attempts to maintain full breeding programs. Maredia and Byerlee (2000) provide quite convincing evidence that 31 of the 71 national wheat breeding programs they studied could not justify their current levels of investment or efficiently sustain a full program of research, compared with the returns from smaller programs testing and screening technologies developed elsewhere. It makes little sense for countries to pursue a go-it-alone strategy for much of their research (Morris et al. 2001).

There are also many things that international funding agencies could do to help disseminate research, including support for Internet-based clearinghouses, attendance at international scientific gatherings, access to professional journals and study programs for LDC researchers. Aid agencies can also promote pooling of available talent among countries through research networks (Puckett, Smith, and Ozgediz 1990). Some networks are designed to stimulate information sharing. Despite divergent national interests, collective action drawing together individual researchers or small research programs across national boundaries is possible as a complement to expanded national research.

Preserving Agricultural Biodiversity The largest contribution agriculture can make to preserving the world's biodiversity is limiting its encroachment onto ever more marginal lands.[7] This means increasing crop yields and increasing biological specialization on farms. However, as these farms narrow their crop choice, both in terms of the types and number of different crops they grow and the genetic uniformity within each crop, concerns are raised over narrowing diversity within agriculture as scientifically bred varieties replace farmer selections (although farmers often hedge their bets by retaining some fields in traditional crops).[8] One option is to maintain diversity by monitoring and protecting the inventory of plants in an area (Wright 1997). This is known as in situ preservation (in the place of planting). It is costly and difficult. An alternative is to conserve genetic diversity ex situ (away from the place of planting), in facilities dedicated to the long-term conservation of crops in the form of seed samples or vegetative parts of plants.

Beginning in the early twentieth century (largely through the efforts of Russian biologist Nikolai Vavilov), samples of seeds from crops growing in fields, road ditches, or irrigation canals were collected and made available to breeders as a basis for improving crop varieties. The National Seed Storage Laboratory at Fort Collins, Colorado, created in 1958, was the first full ex situ facility (Pistorius 1997, 4). Since then, a significant investment has been made in collecting and conserving farmer-developed varieties and wild and weedy species of crops in long-term storage in genebanks around the world. By the mid-1990s, FAO (1998) estimated that more than 6 million seed samples were stored in over 1,300 genebanks worldwide. The 11 CGIAR genebanks now conserve more than 660,000 plant or seed samples of crops grown mainly by poor people (cassava, millet, sorghum, cowpeas, and others), staple food crops grown throughout the world (rice, wheat, and maize), and tree species used in agroforestry systems.

Because these conservation efforts are long term in nature, endowment or stewardship funds to support them makes sense. The earnings from such a fund would assure a funding stream to conserve this genetic material for future generations. A recent estimate of the annual cost of conserving and distributing the genetic material presently held in the CGIAR genebanks is $5.7 million per year (Koo, Pardey, and Wright 2002). Underwriting these services for future generations could be met by a fund of $148 million invested at a real rate of interest of 4 percent per year.[9] This would be sufficient to underwrite current core conservation activities in perpetuity as well as to maintain the distribution activities that provide germplasm to breeders, scientists, farmers, and others worldwide. Efforts to endow a Global Conservation Trust Fund have recently been launched by the CGIAR.

Without the types of scientific investments in food security that we have outlined, the future may reinforce an existing "scientific apartheid" in which the majority of humankind is locked out of advances of modern science (Serageldin 2001, 19). Although a handful of low-income countries like Argentina, Brazil, China, India, and South Africa seem capable of bridging the technological divide between North and South, most low-income countries are slipping behind scientifically, ending the convergence in agriculture evident in the late twentieth century. The gap is greatest in the poorest areas, especially Africa, as research dries up and regulatory and legal arrangements for patent protection remain undeveloped. The tightening legal requirements surrounding Northern research compounds the problem, making technology spillovers from Northern to Southern countries less likely. A world divided into technological haves and have-nots will result in the anti-poor scenarios outlined in Chapter 2. Closing the knowledge gap is key to ending hunger in a sustainable fashion, building the capacity to generate new scientific knowledge and to take advantage of technologies developed elsewhere.

INVESTING IN SUSTAINABILITY

Another area of needed investment, already touched on in the context of agricultural biodiversity, is the ecological integrity at the base of all agricultural systems. Three main types of environmental degradation dominate much of the developing world. The first is associated with intensification of agricultural production in irrigated and favorable rainfed environments and reinforced by policies that promote it. The second is a result of increased food demand resulting from continuing population growth, which has raised the value of cropland and forced cropping into forest and woodland and onto steeper slopes or otherwise less desirable areas for agriculture, increasing soil and species losses. A third results from damage caused by rapid growth in livestock production associated with diet changes induced by increasing incomes, leading to waste disposal and water-quality problems.

As noted in Chapter 3, the ecological consequences of intensive cropping—for example, rice in Asia—include buildups of soil salinity and waterlogging, declining soil nutrients, increased soil toxicities, and increased pest buildup, especially of soil pests. Many of these problems are also observed in the irrigated lowlands where wheat is grown after rice in rotation. The policies that encourage a narrow cropping range and excessive or unbalanced use of fertilizers and pesticides are a primary cause of lowland degradation. In much of Asia, for example, trade policies, output price policies, and input subsidies encourage monoculture by making rice, the staple food crop throughout the region, more profitable than other crops. Policies favoring rice self-sufficiency undervalue land and labor, pushing land beyond sustainable limits and labor toward subsistence. Eliminating preferential treatment of specific crops and cutting pesticide subsidies would arrest and possibly reverse these trends. Techniques for improving fertilizer use efficiency, for example, are available but will only be viable at the farm level when fertilizer subsidies are moderated. The same is the case with integrated pest management techniques or more judicious water management.

In less favorable areas, including large parts of Africa and Latin America, it is the pressure to expand area under production, rather than intensification, that is the major cause of degradation. These areas are frequently environmentally fragile and expanded cultivation has clear limits. Mining of soil fertility, soil erosion, deforestation, and loss of biodiversity impose high costs on those who depend on these areas for a living. Soil erosion contributes not only to lower yields on site, but also to siltation problems downstream, reducing the capacity and productivity of reservoir and irrigation schemes and thereby affecting an even broader area. Likewise, deforestation in upper watershed regions can contribute to flooding problems in lowland areas in wet seasons and to drought in dry ones.

Emerging evidence shows that the right kinds of investments can boost agricultural productivity in many less-favored lands, thereby reducing the pressure to expand onto increasingly fragile soils (Fan, Hazell, and Thorat 1999). Key investment strategies include improved technology and farming systems; more secure access to land and natural resources; effective risk management; rural infrastructure; a policy environment that does not discriminate against rainfed areas; and coordination among farmers, NGOs, and public institutions.

Increasing demand for meat and livestock products can also cause severe environmental degradation. Modernization of traditional livestock production systems will require huge investments to improve feeding potential, ensure a suitable animal environment, and provide other modern production and processing technology. This intensification poses potentially severe environmental problems, as waste by-products from high animal concentrations produce organic discharges beyond the carrying capacity of the environment. Livestock production also poses risks to animal and human health from endemic diseases, especially those that appear when animal concentrations are high or unconventional feeds are used. Discharges from feedlots may contain dangerous heavy metals such as copper, zinc, and cadmium. These industrial livestock systems require oversight and management skills to control waste that are often lacking in poor countries.

The Centrality of Water   As described in earlier chapters, the most severe environmental challenges facing many countries are water scarcity and quality. Water shortages result largely from rapidly growing demands for agricultural, industrial, and household use, but the potential for expanding supplies is also diminishing, aggravated by degraded irrigated land, insufficient levels of river flow for environmental and navigation purposes, upstream land degradation, and seasonal flooding. Water pollution from industrial waste, poorly treated sewage, and runoff of agricultural chemicals, combined with poor household and community sanitary conditions, is also a major factor in disease and malnutrition. New strategies for water development and management are urgently needed.

The water scenarios explored in Chapter 3 pointed to three broad strategies: (1) attacking the problem from outside the water sector—for example, through agricultural research to create more rapid crop yield growth in food crops; (2) increasing the supply of water; and (3) conserving water and improving water productivity through water management and policy reform, including water pricing. Agricultural research policy has already been discussed in this chapter. However, investments in water supplies and management and policy reforms merit further development.

Getting Water Where It's Needed Water requirements relate to food security in various ways, each of which poses different challenges. Water is needed especially for irrigation in order to expand food production. One way to achieve this is to move water from basin to basin with large water engineering projects. Another is to capture more rainwater by reducing runoff and waste. A third (and costly) method is to desalinate seawater. A fourth is to improve water recycling and the efficiency of water use.

Expanded irrigation has become an increasingly expensive alternative. In India and Indonesia, for example, the real costs of new irrigation have more than doubled since the late 1960s and early 1970s. Irrigation projects have absorbed more than half of all agricultural investment in China, Indonesia, and Pakistan and account for 30 percent of all public investment in Indian agriculture. National and international protests over the broad environmental and human effects of large irrigation projects have halted or delayed new ones, particularly when combined with evidence of relatively low returns to irrigation investment. Evidence from India (Evenson, Pray, and Rosegrant 1999) and China (Fan, Zhang, and Zhang 2002) shows very low rates of return to irrigation investment, compared with other public investment priorities.

In developing countries more generally, a number of problems have beset large irrigation systems, including low water use efficiencies at the field level; low cropping intensities, yields, and irrigated area; significant environmental impacts; and escalating costs (WCD 2000). Along with reduced funding levels, investments are being redirected toward support of existing irrigation infrastructure and building of mainly small-scale projects (WCD 2000). Even so, some huge projects are also under way, such as the Three Gorges Dam in China and Narmada in India. On balance, it is difficult to imagine expansion of irrigated area much in excess of the baseline scenario described in Chapter 3.

In the 1960s and 1970s, large transfers of water from adjacent basins or sub-basins were in vogue, particularly in arid regions anticipating growing urban and industrial use. Most of these schemes never got off the ground. Huge capital costs and increasing concerns over negative economic, environmental, and social impacts in the exporting basin halted them. But less grandiose, microlevel basin transfers over short distances have worked well in many regions. In arid regions or those with highly variable rainfall, water is lost to runoff and evapotranspiration. Water efficiency improvements under these conditions can make a big difference. Although successful strategies are very site-specific, water retention through conservation tillage, mulching, and other strategies can raise efficiency and reduce environmental damage (Oweis, Hatchum, and Kijne 1999).

Desalination is another potentially important source of water, but it is too expensive for all but the richest water-scarce countries. However, new methods of desalination offer potential cost advantages, although such technology will likely remain concentrated in the coastal regions of developed countries and water-scarce Persian Gulf countries. Desalination contributes only about 0.2 percent of global water withdrawals today (Martindale and Gleick 2001).

A final water source is recycling and reuse. This can occur in the factory and through wastewater collection, treatment, and redistribution to other locations. In developed countries, the most cost-effective way to meet specific water quality standards and pollution limits has been to recycle and reuse water a number of times before discharging it. In the United States, for example, total industrial water use fell 36 percent, while industrial output increased nearly fourfold between 1950 and 1990 (Postel 1992). Similar conservation efforts have also begun in the urban areas of some water-scarce developing countries. In Beijing, for example, the rate of water recycling increased from 61 percent in 1980 to 72 percent in 1985; and between 1977 and 1991, total industrial water use declined steadily while output increased by 44 percent in real terms (Nickum 1994).

Wastewater reuse is likely to play a smaller role. Israel has the largest wastewater reuse effort in the world: 65 percent of its treated sewage is used for crop production, accounting for 30 percent of the nation's agricultural water supply, thus freeing up significant freshwater for non-agricultural uses (Postel 1999). Worldwide, however, wastewater irrigates only about 500,000 hectares of cropland, two-tenths of 1 percent of the world's irrigated area. Like desalinization, wastewater reuse is most likely in wealthy, arid regions where cheaper conservation techniques are lacking.

Reforming Water Policies Because supply expansion can meet only part of growing demands for water, most will have to come by reforming policies and creating incentives to conserve. Such reforms will not come easily. In most societies, water has been a free good, and entrenched interests benefit from the existing arrangements and allocations. The key to these reforms will be to reward water savings, generating more "crop per drop." In addition, water used in river basins must be channeled more efficiently and polluted less severely. On the farm, the true value or price of water needs to be reflected. The result will be to use less water on a given crop, a shift to more water-efficient crops and crops that have higher value per unit of water. Realizing the true cost of water will also encourage farmers to adopt more efficient irrigation technology. Such a strategy will conserve and protect not only surface water but valuable stores of sub-surface groundwater, which are often depleted beyond the limits of natural recharge.

While agriculture is often the most wasteful user of water, urban areas can also conserve much more effectively. In urban areas within 50 kilometers of a coastline, where 30 percent of the world's population lives, most water drains directly to the ocean without reuse. Here, reduced wastage will translate directly into real water savings. In noncoastal cities, reuse of drainage water is also minimal. In the early 1990s, Cairo, Jakarta, Lima, and Mexico City had unaccounted-for water levels as high as 60 percent, compared with 10–15 percent in well-managed systems. The average level of unaccounted-for water in World Bank–assisted urban water projects is about 36 percent. Although some of this UFW is unreported water use by public agencies or unauthorized private use, much of it is simply lost. In Jakarta, for example, water loss through leakage has been estimated at 41 percent of total supply. Perhaps half of these losses can be eliminated cost effectively (Bhatia and Falkenmark 1993). Service coverage is also poor. Only 44 percent of Jakarta's population, 70 percent of Manila's, and 75 percent of Bangkok's population receive municipal water services. Most of the people not receiving water from municipal services are among the poorest of the urban population.

The inefficiency of urban water systems in most developing countries is mainly the result of policies that encourage waste of water and discourage adequate capital investment in water supplies. Urban water rates are highly subsidized relative to the cost of providing the service, and these subsidies go disproportionately to industries and urban households that are con-nected to the public system. The urban poor, who often must rely on water vendors, pay many times more for water than the residents who receive subsidized water from the public system. Low water rates also make it impossible for urban water companies to obtain financing to upgrade and expand services. The removal of general subsidies on urban water and im-plementation of realistic water charges that generate the revenues to cover the long-term costs of service would reduce the waste of water and make it feasible to obtain financing for service expansion and improvement.

A recent innovation in water policies has centered on the transfer of irrigation systems to decentralized user groups. While short of full-scale privatization (which has met with mixed success), irrigation management transfer can provide a sense of ownership, which improves performance and financial accountability while adapting to local needs. However, to convince farmers that expected benefits from participation outweigh costs, user groups must improve water control and farm profitability. A policy and legal environment that provides and adjudicates secure water rights, monitors the third-party impacts of irrigation, and provides technical and organizational support is necessary for effective operation (Meinzen-Dick and Sullins 1994).

Some have advocated the development of markets in tradable water rights. In theory, by overcoming the "free good" idea of water, such markets would encourage investments in water-saving technologies. Yet establishing such markets is complicated, costly, and largely untried in developing countries, making them a longer-term solution. However, innovative approaches combining water markets and user groups can often create the right incentives (Easter, Rosegrant, and Dinar 1998). User groups would be responsible for the internal allocation of the water, and they could re-sell water saved through efficient use. The price charged for water under this allocation method would have to be high enough to improve cost recovery for irrigation and encourage water conservation.

In summary, new investments in irrigation and water supply systems and some expansion of nontraditional sources can supply only a portion of growing future water needs. In most regions, only new conservation efforts, and new policies promoting it, can send the signal that water is scarce. The appropriate combination of new investments and reforms of policies will vary. Water-policy reforms should include a balance of improved management at the river-basin level, with decentralization to the private sector or community-based water-user groups at the sub-basin level. The types of policies needed to improve water management are applicable to other environmental problems. In the broadest sense, these policies improve the flexibility of resource allocation by removing subsidies that distort incentives and encourage misuse of resources; by establishing property rights; and by investing in research, education, and public infrastructure.

Climate Change and Agriculture   In coming decades, global agriculture is likely to face the prospect of a changing climate, which may adversely affect the goal of meeting global food needs. The prospective climate change consists of global warming and associated changes in other climatic variables. The impact on agriculture remains unclear because of uncertainty over the regional changes in temperature and precipitation, the possible positive effect of greater CO_2 on plant growth, and the adaptability of farming practices. In order to help mitigate the impacts felt by developing countries, policies that increase the flexibility of adjustment and reduce adaptation costs are crucial (Reilly 1999a, 1999b). Several adaptations related to planting and crop variety can lessen impacts: changing crop varieties, introducing new species and adjusting planting times. Because of increasing problems related to water quantity and quality, economic incentives to increase irrigation and water use efficiency are critical. Additional approaches include education to improve farmers' capacity to understand adaptation options and research into new crop varieties that will better withstand the changing climate. Overall, it is widely believed that slowing climate change will require more efficient energy use and greater reliance on alternative energy sources.

NEW INSTITUTIONAL FORMS

The institutional reforms transforming the international scene after World War II were possible because of the power vacuum left by the defeat of Germany and Japan and the commanding position of the Western Allies. While the situation at the dawn of the twenty-first century is not comparable, it is fair to say that the collapse of the former Soviet Union has left the Western democracies, especially the United States, in a position of near hegemony. Before the terrorist attacks of September 11, 2001, the United States and its allies seemed uncertain whether this power should be used to create new international institutions to respond to global needs such as food security. In the wake of the terrorist attacks, both conservatives and liberals have muted some of their criticisms of international institutions, especially the UN system and multilateral financial institutions, although recent discouraging developments in U.S. trade policies do not augur well for the trading system.

We believe that the global nature of food security requires a new multilateral response, built on the institutional foundations of the postwar order, but extending them in several important directions to create new institutional forms. First, national governments should reform their agricultural and trade policies in ways that reflect growing interdependencies among nations. Second, they should coordinate their responses to transnational global challenges, including a secure supply of food. The most important elements of this response are reforms to existing institutions, including the World Bank, FAO, and WHO. But innovations are also needed in international trade policy at the WTO, and through a new organization to respond to the global environmental challenges tied to future food production and beyond agriculture. Finally, we propose the creation of a consolidated group or network of NGOs, and a body devoted to private foundation assistance for poor nations ("private aid") targeted at improving food security.

Identity Crisis at the World Bank   The World Bank has been condemned by both NGOs and conservative critics, who argue that it has failed to promote the welfare of the world's poorest people, that its loans have been badly targeted, and that its own bureaucracy is bloated, cosseted, and self-absorbed. While we agree with many of these criticisms, we also feel that a newly revitalized bank, focusing on a variety of global public goods, can perform important services for the world's poor. Unfortunately, there is strong evidence that food-insecure countries are receiving only a small share of World Bank resources. One of the public goods a reformed World Bank could provide is technical support and grants to improve food security. However, before it can effectively address global public issues such as food security, the Bank requires a thorough reorganization.

A U.S. congressional commission concluded in 2000 that much of the World Bank's current lending could be done better by the private sector. The International Financial Institution Advisory Commission, led by economist Allan Meltzer, recommended that the Bank withdraw from middle-income countries with access to private capital in Asia and Latin America and replace much of its lending with grants to those countries that are most capital-starved. While these recommendations were viewed in some quarters as extreme (prompting numerous dissenting opinions inside the Commission), they pointed to a crisis in both the confidence in and the identity of the Bank (*Los Angeles Times* 2000, 3).

In 2000 the Bank, together with its regional counterparts—the African, Asian, and Inter-American Development Banks—employed 17,000 people and obtained $500 billion in government-sponsored financial support. It held a loan portfolio of $300 billion, and each year extended $50 billion in total loans to developing countries (International Financial Institution Advisory Commission 2000, 34–35). Yet even its own reviews reveal that 55–60 percent of its projects failed to achieve sustainable results, leading the Commission to a stark conclusion:

> The past decade has seen large changes in the global economy affect-ing the development banks. The Cold War is over and, with its end, any rationale disappeared for aid to corrupt or unstable regimes that once had strategic importance. Private capital flows now dwarf any foreseeable value of future annual flows from the four multilateral banks.
>
> The banks have been slow to adapt to these changes by redrawing the line between public and private activities, by identifying their comparative advantage under the new circumstances, by increasing their effectiveness, and by exploiting their individual strengths in a global effort to assure that every dollar of aid carries with it incentives that encourage performance and achieve results that can be moni-tored by independent reviewers. (International Financial Institution Advisory Commission 2000, 35)

Arguing that it had begun to restructure its mission and organize its resources more effectively, the Bank reacted defensively to the Commis-sion report. In particular, it responded to proposals for reduced aid to middle-income countries by pointing out that these countries still con-tain 60 percent of the world's poor.

From the perspective of food security, the question is, does the Bank need to continue its lending in these countries as a food security strategy of pro-poor growth? Commission Chairman Meltzer argued persuasively that the "decisive factor should not be the number of poor people . . . , but poor people who lack alternative financing" (Meltzer and Lerrick 2000, A23). China, for example, has a quarter of the developing world's popula-tion, receives World Bank loans of $1 billion per year, yet retains more than $150 billion in foreign exchange reserves and attracts in excess of $60 billion per year in private foreign investment. While some have argued that World Bank assistance helps leverage a more "open" China, the Bank's $1 billion in annual loans, if redirected as grants to food-insecure countries (such as Bangladesh) could be crucial. Moreover, the World

Bank could continue to offer ample technical assistance to countries such as China, creating other opportunities for openness, while enabling them to meet not only the food needs of their own population but to export surplus production. The Bank has continued to argue that without the inducement of loans, countries such as China will not listen to its advice, to which Meltzer responded pointedly that international institutions such as the Bank "are the only consultants that pay clients to take advice" (Meltzer and Lerrick 2000, A23).

The underlying issue in the proposed shift of resources—from loans to middle-income countries to grants to the poorest countries—is what the Bank calls "additionality," or the net addition to the pool of capital available to LDCs. Even the internal auditor of the Bank has questioned whether it is merely offering low-interest subsidized loans to countries that would otherwise seek (and get) the money from private banks. The effect is no net addition to available capital, and less capital available to those countries who need it most but whose credit rating falls well below investment grade. Indeed, from 1993 to 1999, the share of nonrated recipients of Bank loans (the highest risk category of countries) fell dramatically from 40 percent of total lending to less than 1 percent—averaging only about 20 percent. Conversely, 80 percent of resources excluding aid transfers went to countries with an international bond rating of B or higher, equal to or greater than many public agencies and municipalities in the United States (International Financial Institution Advisory Commission 2000, 37).

A second argument made by World Bank representatives is that the private sector will not lend for social purposes, and that the poorest segments of the middle-income countries would therefore be left behind. It is unclear how concerned the Bank itself has been over whether its borrowers have pursued pro-poor strategies. Few, if any, of the 70 percent of World Bank nonaid resources that go to countries that enjoy substantial access to private capital are to countries that are food insecure, and many are major net food exporters (International Financial Institutional Advisory Commission 2000, 7, 38).[10] If private lenders, like the Bank, insist on repayment guarantees, then pro-poor growth and food security will remain the responsibility of the borrower, just as under the terms of the Bank's loans. As we shall argue below, some of the multilateral aid funds of the Bank can be substantially augmented not only by private bank loans, but through new mechanisms of private aid, organized through NGOs with the huge capital accumulations in foundations resulting from the economic growth of the 1990s.

While we share many of the critical views of the Commission, we also believe that the Bank should retain a leading role in technical assistance and food security strategies, focused primarily on the poor countries, and the poorest segments of the middle-income countries. The Commission recommended that primary responsibility for national and regional programs in Asia and Latin America be shifted to the Asian Development Bank and Inter-American Development Bank, reserving public benefits best undertaken at a global level for the World Bank. These include the sustainable development of natural resources, improvements in legal and public infrastructure, health, and—we would argue—nutrition and food security. Because we believe food security is inherently a global public good, it requires a multilateral response for which the World Bank is uniquely equipped.

It is important to emphasize that as the private sector assumes a greater role in bank lending, and as the grant component of its portfolio expands, it will require more rather than fewer resources because repayment is not expected; hence, governments (and private foundations) committed to expanding the role of the private sector will also need to expand the public sector role. Further, such a shift should not imply any relaxation of compliance requirements for grant recipients.[11]

FAO—Troubled Transition   One of the most crucial aspects of a global food system is the capacity to organize and access information. Like food security itself, information is increasingly a global public good. Acting as a key and unbiased source of such information may be the most fundamental role of FAO. Established in 1945 to confront problems of world hunger, the FAO is a bureaucracy of about 4,000, of which about 2,200 are headquartered in Rome. It is separate from but works closely with the WFP, which focuses on emergency relief for war-ravaged or disaster-prone regions such as Kosovo, North Korea, or Eastern Timor and provides some food aid in support of development projects.[12]

However, FAO has been heavily burdened by political infighting and struggles over the type of emphasis it should give to information sharing and project activities (Stanley 1999, 7). At the center of this internal dissension is the emphasis given by FAO to food security itself. Although championed by FAO's Director General Jacques Diouf of Senegal, food security has also been attacked as simply a vehicle for his ambitions. Opposition was especially vocal from Great Britain, which has threatened to withdraw from FAO if reforms in the organization's strategy and management are not forthcoming. The bitter criticism by developed countries such as Britain of FAO's management style has to undermine support for technical assistance directed specifically to food security, with especially negative implications for Africa (FAO 1997; *The Economist* 1998a, 48).

British Member of Parliament Georges Foulkes, speaking to the 30th General Conference of FAO in November 1999 noted that FAO's target was to reduce the number of hungry people in the world by 20 million a year (the target set by the 1996 World Food Summit); the actual rate achieved was only 8 million a year. In order to reach the more ambitious target, Foulkes argued that FAO should concentrate on its role as a promulgator of "international standards and global indicators," such as those of the Codex Alimentarius. In addition, it should sharpen the focus of its strategy by carefully monitoring and measuring impacts, recruiting top staff, and making its governance simple and transparent (Foulkes 1999). As a model, Foulkes pointed to recent reforms in WHO, to be discussed below.

Regardless of the serious reservations raised by FAO's critics, it retains the strong support of most developing countries. FAO has also responded to at least some of its critics by recommitting itself to greater transparency and efficiency (FAO 2000b). And food security remains central, reflected by the Special Programme for Food Security, to help "low-income, food-deficit countries increase food production and improve access to food." Also targeted are pest prevention and control, environmental sustainability, and international standard setting, a particular emphasis of FAO's British critics.

If these statements, and the added emphasis FAO proposes to give to a number of other areas, are translated into reality, they should receive the support and blessings of the developed countries. The agreement to restore full U.S. funding for the UN agencies can, it is hoped, lead to a similar reestablishment of support for multilateralism in Great Britain and elsewhere. Another area targeted for emphasis by FAO is expanded cooperation with the private sector, which fits well with the proposed shifts in emphasis needed at the World Bank. Another is expanding use of Internet technologies in order to better inform those seeking access to FAO data and technical expertise on food, agriculture, fisheries, forestry, and rural development (although cuts in country-level data gathering and training to assist in it have hurt severely). Finally, of special significance to developing countries, is a new emphasis on links to NGOs and civil society, which is reinforced by the aforementioned information technology enhancements (FAO 1999b, 2000e).

Together, these reforms and areas of emphasis involve three basic themes: information, efficiency, and distribution. Information plays the central role, in terms of data, standard setting, technical advice, and expanded use of the Internet. Efficiency is enhanced both by information sharing and the internal efforts at transparency and reduced bureaucracy. Finally, distribution is a focus of relations with NGOs and civil society and in defining national priorities. An interesting example of FAO's programs on food security is a Philippine project designed to support 14 provinces, especially in communities of Mindanao formerly controlled by the Moro National Liberation Front, which signed a peace agreement with the Philippine government in 1996 (*Business World* 2000). Under the program, special emphasis is given to local household-level food production by paying as little as $5,000–10,000 per village for seeds, fertilizers, and farming tools. At the national level, production growth is targeted to achieve more equal income distribution, consistent with the pro-poor growth themes noted above.

The 1996 World Food Summit proposed a goal of reducing the hungry from 816 million in 1990-92 (the base period) to 408 million by 2015. However, far too little is being done to reach this objective. According to FAO (2002b), the number of hungry would have to be reduced by 22 million per year to reach this goal, compared with the average decline of only 6 million annually in the late 1990s. Unfortunately, developments during 2002 did not reflect well on the OECD countries commitment to ending hunger or supporting a revitalized FAO. In June 2002—five years after the 1996 summit—FAO's Diouf and the United Nations' Annan, in addressing the second World Food Summit, both pointedly criticized the U.S. farm bill and the negative impacts of rich countries' agricultural subsidies on farmers in the developing world. Most of the top officials from the developed countries skipped the summit altogether. The OECD, meanwhile, in a report issued in mid-2002, noted that one-third of the value of everything farmed in the European Union during 2001 was accounted for by subsidies or artificially inflated consumer prices; 21 percent was the corresponding figure for the United States. As Jacques Diouf noted, "If Western countries want to fight hunger in the world, let them start with what is essential: bringing their farm policies into line with global trading rules which they themselves have installed" (*The Guardian* 2002, 2).

WHO—The Nutrition Connection   Among the UN agencies, none has experienced more dramatic or comprehensive changes in the past decade than WHO. International cooperation on health issues has a long history, dating to the first meeting of international health experts in Paris in 1851. WHO was created after World War II (1948) to coordinate and assist national governments in strengthening health services. Today it functions from a headquarters in Geneva with a staff of about 2,000, with regional offices in Europe, the Americas, Africa, the Eastern Mediterranean, Southeast Asia, and the Western Pacific. While the regular budget is contributed by member states, WHO has maintained funds for voluntary contributions to malaria eradication and health promotion, as well as the UN Fund for Technical Assistance to Underdeveloped Countries, a major share of which is dedicated to health.

In the late 1990s, recognition that health was yet another in a set of global public goods led to calls for a reorganization of WHO and recommitment by its 191 member countries.[13] In 1998, a new director general assumed control: redoubtable Gro Harlem Brundtland, the former prime minister of Norway, is a medical doctor and famous for her work on sustainable development issues. Recognizing the need for a fresh start, Brundtland enlarged the focus of WHO to include chronic and noncommunicable diseases as well as infectious diseases such as malaria and tuberculosis, and she began to sort out WHO's linkages to development. In 1993, when the World Bank devoted its World Development Report to health, it launched what became a specialist network on health, nutrition, and population, which soon resulted in a loan portfolio nearly 10 times greater than WHO's budget (*The Economist* 1998b, 79–82). However, cooperation between the WHO and Bank initiatives was poor, as were its linkages to the private sector. Brundtland has focused especially on improving these cooperative linkages.

Under Brundtland, the number of program directors was cut from 50 to 36. In 1999, WHO reduced its administrative costs by 15 percent. In a move prefiguring that of Diouf at FAO, Brundtland emphasized WHO's role as a source of data and information, creating a cluster of activities called Evidence and Information for Policy and establishing new initiatives on bioethics and a multilateral framework convention on tobacco control (Brown 1999a, 1999b). Extra funds were dedicated to Africa, and a multi-sectoral approach to health policy was initiated based on poverty and its linkages to health. As Brundtland remarked, "All government ministers, not only the health minister, must know that alleviating poverty is vital to improving health" (Mach 1998, 302).

In response to these initiatives, supporters in the United States and elsewhere began calling for the United States to reverse its arrearage of $35 million in funding, noting that it compromises "America's vital interest in global health, violates the spirit of American generosity, and represents the antithesis of global leadership" (Bloom et al. 1999, 911). Brundtland's leadership also helped stimulate the decision of the Gates Foundation to provide hundreds of millions of dollars in private foundation funds for a global program of childhood vaccinations. In short, thorough reform at the WHO brought attention to the key role of multilateral institutions in an era of globalization, making global health a clear example of "a new era of public policy which is defined by increasing overlaps between domestic and foreign policy, multilateral and bilateral strategies, and national and international interest" (Kickbusch 2000, 11).

As a consequence of the transformation of WHO, the organization is attracting additional financial support for special projects. Such contributions increased by 40 percent between 1999 and 2001. The head of the Institute for Global Health noted in 2001 that the revitalized WHO has moved health from the sidelines and into the center of the global debate on development. *The Economist* wrote that "AIDS, malaria, and tuberculosis are now the stuff of 6–8 summits [and] special sessions at the United Nations" (*The Economist* 2001c, 79).

While the new leadership at WHO is clearly sensitive to the health–poverty nexus, there is an even more compelling connection between health and nutrition and thus food security in poor nations. Indeed, it is precisely the more food-insecure countries—where lack of adequate nutrition is most widespread—that are most likely to exhibit the full range of health problems. Inadequate nutrition, while not a disease as such, is a chronic condition highly correlated with both chronic illness and reduced immunity to infection. Just as vaccination efforts, led by WHO and private-sector collaborators such as the Gates Foundation, have ushered in a new emphasis on preventive health care, so nutrition and food security should be thought of as preventive responses to human disease.

While WHO cannot become a food or nutrition agency, it can build much more explicitly on health-to-nutrition linkages, in terms of both data collection and information dissemination and in its strategies for institutional infrastructure at the country level. Many health care workers in the poorest countries know that food distribution (such as child feeding centers) are opportune places to give vaccinations or disburse needed medicines. It is now vital to think of adequate food and nutrition as part of a regime of health care. This view will be especially reinforced in the years to come, as the line between pharmaceutical interventions and nutrition itself is blurred by biotechnological innovations such as beta-carotene enhanced *Golden*Rice™, one in a long list of emerging "nutra-ceuticals." Such a preventive health care view of food security and nutrition can also be a basis for additional efforts by private foundations, in collaboration with NGOs, in the same spirit as the Gates-financed vaccination campaign.

WTO—Trade and Food Security   In redefining the role of existing insti-tutions to promote food security, we have focused thus far on the World Bank, FAO, and WHO. Another leading postwar institution, the World Trade Organization (WTO), is also in the process of redefinition amid crisis (Díaz-Bonilla, Thomas, and Robinson 2002; Díaz-Bonilla et al. 2002). In discussing the WTO, however, we will focus not only on its changing role—especially in relation to developing countries—but also on the potential for a major new multilateral agency parallel to but separate from the WTO and devoted to sustainable growth and development: a global environment organization (GEO).

The failure in Seattle in late 1999 to launch a new round of multilateral trade negotiations was a debacle but probably tolerable in a then-booming U.S. economy, which despite larger trade deficits was capable of hauling the weakened economies of Asia out of their 1990s recessions. But the slowing global economy of 2001–02 raised the stakes for the global trading system, especially the developing countries. The successful outcome of the 2001 Doha meeting and the launch of the Doha Development Round was predicated on new promises by the OECD countries to fully integrate the developing countries' needs in a new round of trade talks.

Yet developments in trade policy after Doha were deeply discouraging, especially a new wave of protectionist steel tariffs, textile measures, and the 2002 U.S. farm bill mentioned earlier. The LDCs are especially critical of the new top-heavy agricultural subsidies and the exclusion of the developing world in global trade rule making as a matter of global injustice. They noted OECD statistics showing that every year roughly $280 billion is transferred in rich countries to agricultural producers, while LDCs are lectured on the distorting effects of agricultural subsidies, a situation that is "just not fair" (Schiff 1999, 1). As Kofi Annan noted gravely in Rome during the 2002 World Food Summit, "Put yourself in the shoes of a small developing country, which cannot export agricultural products because of restrictions and tariffs, a developing country that cannot export and compete on world markets because its richer partners are heavily subsidized" (*The Guardian* 2002, 2).

The clear message of the LDCs is that because large subsidies to farmers in poor countries are infeasible, only expanded market access to rich countries' markets can level the playing field. Global justice—as fairness—demands expanded market access. This theme was effectively disseminated to LDC interests through FAO's expanded linkages to NGOs and others via the Internet. The fact that it was clearly not on the rich countries' list of priorities may doom the new trade round.

If the new round of global trade negotiations under WTO is to survive, it is inconceivable that food security—linked to market access issues in agriculture—can be treated as a marginal concern. We would argue that the agricultural negotiations should be renamed the Food Security Negotiations and brought front and center. This does not imply, as many might imagine, a new set of excuses for trade protectionism, especially by the United States and Europe. Rather, as suggested in preceding chapters, it means that trade liberalization in agriculture should be pursued with specific attention to the needs of LDCs, including market access, technical assistance, and emergency food relief, so as to assure them that a system based on freer trade is indeed secure and fair.

Food Security and Environment: Toward a GEO   If the Doha Round can be retrieved from U.S. and European protectionism, LDCs should consider an additional set of reforms related to environmental protection: the creation of a GEO.[14] The argument for a GEO originally arose primarily from trade policy participants who felt that the WTO system was ill-equipped to respond when trade questions intersected with environmental issues. While sympathetic to stronger national environmental safeguards, they recognized that governments required coordinated multilateral responses to transnational environmental issues, not only when trade conflicts were apparent but also where trade was largely unaffected. While some argued for a beefed up UNEP, others suggested the need for an organization beyond UNEP, functioning at essentially the same level as the WTO. Even if the WTO system could be "greened," they felt that international environmental challenges required their own multilateral responses. Just as the General Agreement on Tariffs and Trade (GATT)—precursor of WTO—had evolved out of growing commercial interdependence following World War II and had helped to foster a set of rules by which the trade game should be played, so growing ecological interconnections now create the need for a set of global environmental rules.[15] The parallelism of trading rules and environmental rules arises from the fact that interdependent states could not cope with commercial or environmental challenges through unilateral or ad hoc solutions. A more stable and predictable system must be rule based, although the coexistence of a set of multilateral trade and environmental rules would give rise to questions of priority and consistency (Jackson 1992).

The basic design of a GEO advanced by Runge, Ortalo-Magne, and Vande Kamp (1994) was composed of a Secretariat and a Multilateral Commission on Environment. The Secretariat would be the formal, ministerial-level body of government representatives, meeting periodically to affirm certain policies. The Commission would be a policy-oriented group of environmental experts drawn from NGOs, academia, business, and government. While the representatives to the GEO Secretariat would, like WTO representatives, be government officials, expert environmental and business involvement was also proposed, similar to the International Labor Organization (ILO), via the Commission. The Commission would thus be composed of a standing group of environmental experts and government and business representatives from all member counties. Its meetings, open to the public, would allow worldwide access to the data and analysis underlying its work.

The primary focus of this work would be to propose ways to harmonize national environmental standards where transboundary environmental problems were clear, while carefully considering the technical issues and problems of this process for developing countries. The GEO Commission would issue regular reports and related documents proposing improved policies, identify environmental "hot spots," and recommend special projects for national governments. This process would allow for public comments from any group, governmental or nongovernmental. The effect would be transparency, an opening of the GEO Commission to full public participation and review.

The GEO and its commission would work closely with the World Bank and other multilateral lending agencies, such as the regional development banks, as well as the IMF, to develop funding for environmental projects to upgrade national infrastructure, especially for waste water treatment, sanitation, and hazardous waste disposal. It would also aggressively support expanded research and development to monitor changes in key environmental factors. National governments would be encouraged to establish an initial tranche of $10 billion for these purposes to operate on a revolving basis, possibly through the Global Environmental Facility.[16] This funding would focus primarily on projects in developing countries in Africa, Asia, Africa, Latin America, and in the Newly Independent Countries (Eastern Europe and the former Soviet Union), where national resources for environmental improvements are most scarce.

The GEO would also work jointly with the WTO and OECD to identify trade measures that threaten environmental quality and to develop environmental policies that are least burdensome to trade expansion. It could also serve as a general umbrella for the growing number of multilateral environmental agreements, such as the Montreal Protocol, just as the ILO serves as an umbrella over a large number of special labor agreements and arrangements. The overall effect would be to relieve the WTO of major institutional demands to accommodate a "green agenda." Since the WTO is not an environmental organization and should not become one, a well-engineered GEO would reduce pressure to "reform GATT," which would be diverted constructively into the development of instruments directly aimed at environmental targets. In cases where trade burdens resulting from environmental policies come before WTO dispute settlement panels, the GEO commission would utilize its expertise to offer evidence, analysis, and proposed alternatives to the policies in dispute. In addition the GEO could have its own dispute resolution procedures.

Unfortunately, the developing countries are among the most ardent opponents of a GEO. Many are convinced that a GEO would force Northern priorities on Southern interests, including environmental goals (regarded as of lower priority in LDCs) and trade protection in "green" disguise. As Juma notes, "many developing countries are concerned that a new environmental agency would only become another source of conditions and sanctions" (2000, 15). These concerns were amply revealed when the WTO's Committee on Trade and Environment was formed. In opposing even its formation, spokesmen for countries such as Egypt, Morocco, Tanzania, and Thailand all questioned the need for it. When the Committee's agenda was finally settled, it reflected a variety of issues of direct concern to LDCs, notably a cluster of issues that linked LDC environmental initiatives to the achievement of expanded access to Northern markets (Shaffer 2001).

One of the most pressing and unmet needs to which a GEO could contribute is thus to provide help and technical support to developing countries in the formulation and preparation of trade, development, and environmental initiatives. If a GEO is to succeed, it must treat these needs as of paramount importance, working with the Trade Policy Center to be discussed in the next section. In particular, a GEO should take responsibility for the implementation of the primary principles emerging from the 1992 Rio Declaration on Environment and Development (ostensibly the current responsibility of the Commission on Sustainable Development), which states that

- developing and developed countries have differing responsibilities to enact domestic measures to protect the environment,

- international transfers are necessary to assist developing countries to upgrade their environmental protection measures, and

- unilateral measures are to be avoided (Shaffer 2001).

In the context of a GEO, these three principles imply that a form of "special and differential treatment" in environmental policies is to be expected as part of an international body of multilateral environmental rules, in which the differing capacities of the North and South to mount programs of environmental protection are realistically acknowledged.

From the perspective of food security, the most important linkage to a GEO may be a recognized payoff to LDCs willing to promote environmental protection in the form of expanded market access to developed-country markets. This issue will be taken up in greater detail below. Unilateralism in trade policy is ultimately self-defeating, just as it is in environmental policy, at least where transborder issues are concerned. Naturally, a GEO would not require all national environmental measures to be subjected to oversight, but where these measures affect the "global commons," multilateralism should provide a foundation principle.

Finally, the GEO–WTO interface will be all important. Perhaps, paradoxically, if it is to take environmental pressures off of the WTO, a GEO should be located in Geneva. There, it could assist the WTO and would be situated to work in cooperation with the WHO and the growing number of environmental NGOs who have found it useful to use Geneva as a base.

Private Aid and Food Security   As noted in Chapter 5, the expanded presence of NGOs on the international scene has created, in Sylvia Ostry's phrase, a "virtual secretariat" devoted to issues of development in a globalized world (Ostry 2000). Yet it is arguable that NGOs would benefit from a more centralized effort focused on the interfaces of trade, food security, and the environment. This is a large part of the rationale for a Trade Policy Center. The Center would build on existing efforts such as the South Center, located in Geneva. Together with the WTO, WHO, and a newly formed GEO, it would provide technical expertise and guidance on a wide range of LDC issues, notably agricultural market access and food security. Its staff of legal, economic, and trade policy experts would be complemented by scholars from the world's universities and research centers, and it would function as a regular forum for LDC issues and concerns.

Unlike the UN agencies, however, we would argue that the Trade Policy Center should be funded from private foundation sources through an endowment capable of generating annual income on the order of $50 million per year, offering governments and NGOs assistance on a fee for service based on ability to pay. The Center would undergird the activities of LDC delegations by performing at least three vital functions. First, it would provide technical expertise and guidance to delegations on a wide range of developing-country issues and options, prominently including agriculture, food security, and intellectual property, by maintaining a permanent staff of legal, economic, and trade policy experts conversant in these issues. Second, it would serve as a host and magnet for scholars, NGOs, and practitioners from around the world wishing to conduct and disseminate applied research and to assist in advising LDCs. Third, it would serve as a forum for airing proposals, alternatives and ideas of special concern to LDCs, holding regular meetings. Only by creating such a substantial center of expertise can LDC interests be properly represented in the complex, skill-intensive process of trade reform.

The concept underlying such support for work on trade, food security, and environmental issues is what we shall call private aid, a new form of development assistance drawn, like the Gates Foundation's grant for childhood vaccines, from the resources of those whose fortunes globalization has helped create. This aid could create funding assistance not only to endow entities such as the Trade Policy Center but also to support expansions in the capabilities of the UN institutions. The WHO, for example, maintains funds for voluntary contributions to malaria eradication and health promotion, which could be expanded or augmented for nutrition-related programs of food security.

The issue of private aid leads us naturally to a larger question, the subject of the next chapter: Where might the necessary funds to invest in ending hunger be obtained? It is to this question that we now turn.

7 • INVESTING FOR A HUNGER-FREE WORLD

For those who live above subsistence, economic decisions involve trade-offs: "How much of what I want today will I forgo to invest to raise my income in the future?" For the poorest of the poor, where sheer survival is at stake, the question is only finding enough to survive until tomorrow. Hunger is ever present. Little is left for individual or collective investment. In the jargon of economists poor people are "capital constrained."

Providing the investment capital to break through these constraints and gain access to affordable personal credit or public support for services like health, schooling, agricultural technology, legal services, and transport and communication infrastructure is the way to raise and sustain poor peoples' productivity and welfare. But how much will it cost? Where will the funds come from? Individuals and local institutions must help foot most of the bill, but poor people, and especially those in poor countries, have few funds to spare. Rich people and rich countries must help find the additional funds.

In this chapter we identify the scale of the investments required and discuss how increased foreign development assistance, private business investment, and global philanthropy can each play a role. But first, to anchor the discussion, we lay out why rich countries and rich people should invest in the efforts to eliminate hunger.

The most compelling argument for eliminating hunger is that it is the right and fair thing to do. That hundreds of millions of people are chronically hungry in a world with unprecedented wealth is unconscionable. World income inequality, according to Milanovic (2002), is such that the combined income of the 50 million richest people in the world equaled the total income of the 2.7 billion poorest in 1993; 84 percent of the world's population received just 16 percent of world income; and an American with average income in the *bottom* 10 percent of the U.S. population is better off than two-thirds of the world's population.

THE NEED FOR PUBLIC FUNDING

The world over, citizens pool and collectively spend a portion of their individual incomes by granting their governments the coercive power of taxation. These tax revenues are then redistributed, as a reflection of government priorities, with economic self-interest playing a large role. Such public funds pay for defense, policing, education and research, transportation infrastructure, and whatever regulatory oversight a country prefers and can afford. Markets alone would fail to provide many of these public goods and services. Socially profitable opportunities would go unfunded or underfunded because they are privately unprofitable. Absent national and international collective commitments to provide these types of goods, countries acting in isolation will underinvest.[1]

In addition to national examples of public goods, there are many examples at the international level. By lowering the risk of contagion, vaccinations in one country benefit its citizens, but also citizens elsewhere in the world. Reducing air and water pollution in one location can be of direct benefit to people in far distant countries. Similarly, new knowledge from scientific research, such as new crop varieties of rice and wheat, can be planted in other areas, raising yields there too. Studies of agricultural productivity show that such spillovers might account for half or more of the total productivity growth (Alston 2002). And as global travel increases and modern communication technologies spread worldwide, the magnitude and spatial reach of these international public goods continue to grow.

Variations in the types of international public goods suggest differences in the best means to pay for them (Sandler 2002). Where everyone in the world gains from provision of the good (or exclusion of nonpayers is not feasible) some form of supranational structure is needed to raise the revenues required, either by fees, taxes, or some other means. Where only some countries or particular groups within countries gain or where exclusion of nonpayers is feasible (such as the development of new crop varieties that only grow in certain agroecologies, or a vaccine for a disease that only occurs in limited locales), then only those countries or groups need to pay for the good. If the benefits to a single country are large relative to the total benefits, then only a little financial coaxing from the international community is called for.

Most national taxation schemes strike a balance between efficiency and fairness when paying for national public goods; structuring the payments to reflect individuals' ability to pay as well as the benefits they receive for the collective good. Ability to pay and benefits criteria would also be a fair way of deciding the rich versus poor country shares of the costs of providing international public goods.[2]

WHAT MIGHT IT TAKE?

The World Bank recently estimated that reaching the United Nations' Millennium Development Goals, which call for reducing extreme poverty by half and substantial improvements in education and health in the developing world by 2015, would require a $40–60 billion increase in development assistance annually (World Bank 2002b). This would basically represent a doubling of the current level of aid, which totaled $57 billion in 1999. Substantially reducing malnutrition among children as a specific goal is estimated to require some $10 billion annually in additional public investment in human capital and agricultural research and development (Rosegrant et al. 2001). This investment, combined with faster economic and slower population growth, could reduce the estimated number of malnourished children by more than 65 percent by 2025. Separately, FAO has estimated that additional investments of US$24 billion annually will be needed to meet the 1996 World Food Summit goal of reducing by half the total number of hungry by 2015. The FAO figure includes both increased international assistance and spending by developing-country governments themselves, and is based on reducing overall hunger, not just child malnutrition (FAO 2002a).

The recently released *Report of the Commission on Macroeconomics and Health,* headed by economist Jeffery Sachs, graphically illustrates the dimensions of the infectious disease and general health problems worldwide, with special reference to the state of health in LDCs (WHO 2002). HIV/AIDS, tuberculosis, and malaria are the world's great killers: collectively these infectious diseases cause about 25 percent of all deaths worldwide. Three million people died of AIDS in 2001. There were an estimated 8.4 million new cases of tuberculosis in 1999, an increase from 8 million in

1997; 3 million of those cases were in Southeast Asia, and nearly 1.6 million in Sub-Saharan Africa. The disease kills about 2 million people per year. Malaria is a public health problem in more than 90 countries (inhabited by 2.4 billion people, 40 percent of the world's population); there are an estimated 300–500 million clinical cases of these diseases each year. Ninety percent of these are in Sub-Saharan Africa, where an estimated 1 million people (mostly young children under five and pregnant women) die each year. The WHO report estimates the amounts necessary to achieve basic health and nutrition at $6 per capita in public health spending in least-developed countries and $11 in total health spending, and $13 and $23 respectively in other low-income countries in 1997. The total cost of these essential interventions is $34 per capita annually.

These basic interventions would save an estimated 8 million lives annually by 2010. Total annual health and nutrition spending in developing countries would need to rise by $57 billion by 2007 and $94 billion by 2015. If an additional $35 billion by 2007 and $63 billion by 2015 came from the countries themselves, the remaining $22 billion by 2007 and $31 billion by 2015 could be financed by grants from donors, international organizations, industrial countries, and foundations. These investments would produce economic benefits estimated at $186 billion annually in reduced illness and lives saved, boosting economic growth (WHO 2002).

While any particular cost estimate is best taken with a grain of salt, taken as a group, they indicate that increased development assistance of at least $24 billion per year is needed to make clear progress. Closer to $50 billion seems appropriate to make substantial progress toward reducing poverty and hunger and achieving other important improvements in the lives of people in the South.

FUNDING OPTIONS

The investments needed to end hunger are clear: education, health, agricultural research, irrigation and water management, rural infrastructure such as roads, and key institutional innovations will be required. The most productive mix of these investments varies from country to country, and most of the funds will have to come from the developing countries themselves. Still, it is possible to think through the respective roles of foreign development assistance, private capital flows (especially foreign direct investment), and global philanthropy, as complements to developing-country governments.

LDC Governments   A sizable share of the financial burden for infrastructural, educational and other public goods investments in poor countries will be borne by poor people, either as individuals or collectively through the taxes they pay to their local and national governments. So how do LDC governments fare in terms of funding these types of investments compared with other countries and other funding priorities?

Table 7.1 compares the public expenditures in 1990 and 1998 among low-, middle-, and high-income countries for health, education, and military purposes and provides an estimate of overall spending by central governments (including debt repayment). Taking expenditure shares as indicative of government spending priorities, poor countries placed much more weight on military spending (17.7 percent of their respective public expenditure budgets in 1998) than did rich countries (9.6 percent). Notably, rich countries scaled back their military spending during the 1990s as the Cold War wound down, while poor countries as a group continued spending at ever higher levels. Correspondingly, low-income countries gave less priority to health (7.9 percent of public spending) but put about the same emphasis on education (19 percent) as did rich countries in 1998, where public spending on health was 25.2 percent of all public spending, and education accounted for 20 percent. Put another way, only $4.90 of public funds was spent on health-related goods and services for every man, woman, and child in poor countries, compared with $1,616 per capita in rich ones. Clearly poor countries as a group continue to give insufficient attention to public goods types of investments.

But with only $1.8 trillion (6.2 percent) of the world's $28.86 trillion in output in 1998, low-income countries had limited funds to invest in their futures. Overall, public expenditures by governments in low-income countries were only 2 percent of the world's public-sector expenditures. This partly reflects rich versus poor country shares of global output, but it is also because governments in rich countries typically account for more of their respective GDPs (29 percent on average in 1998) than do poor-country governments (17.3 percent). Wealthier countries tend to have more extensive and more effective tax collection systems than do poorer ones. Thus the limited budgets facing poor-country governments mean that even shifting their priorities away from guns and toward more butter types of spending will fall far short of what is necessary to end hunger in our lifetime. The figures in Table 7.1 underscore the immensity of the geographical asymmetries in public spending. For every dollar of public spending on

TABLE 7.1 · Structure of government spending worldwide, 1990 and 1998

Expenditure/income level of country	Number of countries		Total spending (millions of current US$)		Per capita spending (current US$)		Share of GDP (%)	
	1990	1998	1990	1998	1990	1998	1990	1998
Health expenditures								
Low income	48	52	11,745	10,718	6.4	4.9	1.4	1.2
Lower-middle income	47	45	38,381	55,565	21.3	28.3	2.3	2.6
Upper-middle income	28	31	49,011	91,647	91.7	147.5	2.8	3.1
High income	32	32	907,307	1,386,810	1,110.2	1,615.7	5.3	6.0
World	155	160	1,006,444	1,544,740	201.6	273.9	4.7	5.3
Education expenditures								
Low income	42	50	27,731	25,919	15	13	3.5	3.1
Lower-middle income	40	37	35,451	56,682	22	32	3.4	3.2
Upper-middle income	24	26	48,331	102,820	136	236	3.8	4.7
High income	38	33	729,645	1,101,314	986	6,279	4.7	4.8
World	144	146	841,158	1,286,735	186	252	4.5	4.6
Military expenditures								
Low income	44	54	20,100	24,151	11	11	3.0	2.7
Lower-middle income	33	43	50,663	58,689	31	30	5.0	2.7
Upper-middle income	23	25	67,230	75,215	125	122	3.8	2.6
High income	32	33	575,061	530,060	709	617	3.4	2.3
World	132	155	713,054	688,114	150	121	3.5	2.4

Total debt service								
Low income	50	58	31,681	47,041	17	21	4.6	5.2
Lower-middle income	38	46	55,968	81,646	32	41	3.6	3.8
Upper-middle income	25	28	63,571	180,013	128	300	4.0	6.4
World	*113*	*132*	*151,219*	*308,700*	*37*	*64*	*4.0*	*5.3*
Total public expenditures								
Low income	27	30	105,611	136,370	70	73	17.9	17.3
Lower-middle income	27	31	155,216	365,078	100	191	17.5	17.7
Upper-middle income	24	23	393,607	675,017	820	1,130	24.4	24.2
High income	31	31	4,761,255	5,505,722	5,876	7,518	27.8	29.0
World	*31*	*115*	*5,415,689*	*6,682,186*	*1,247*	*1,310*	*26.8*	*27.1*

SOURCE: Constructed by authors using data from World Bank 2002c.

NOTES: Annual health, education, and total public expenditures are reported on a country basis as a percentage of gross domestic product (GDP) and are estimated using corresponding GDP figures; military spending is reported as a percentage of gross net income (GNI) and is estimated using the corresponding GNI figures; missing expenditure data for some countries for some years (especially 1998) were estimated using percentages for the nearest available year. Health, education, and military data ostensibly represent total (recurrent and capital) spending by all branches of government; data for military spending for some countries are based on partial or uncertain data or rough estimates. Total public expenditures include current or capital spending by central government only. Debt service is the sum of principal repayments and interest actually paid in foreign currency, goods, or services, plus repayments to the International Monetary Fund (IMF). Countries are grouped into income classes using World Bank (2002c) designations. Grouped per capita and share of GDP data are weighted averages using population and national income as weights.

health in low-income countries, $129 is spent in the rich counties; for every dollar of spending on education in poor countries, $42 is spent in rich ones. In addition, the poorest countries collectively spent $47 billion in servicing their publicly held debt in 1998, which at $21 per capita is more than they spent on health and education per capita combined. Relying solely on their own economies, poor-country governments and the people they serve will make only limited headway in ending hunger, additional funds are needed from elsewhere to do the job.

Foreign Assistance   There is a widespread impression that foreign assistance has been ineffective and the money largely wasted. While true of some projects and programs, the consensus emerging from a group of new studies is that foreign aid has added to economic growth in developing countries with sound governments and prudent economic and trade policies, but it has done little for countries with poor governance (Burnside and Dollar 2000). Unfortunately, there is no pattern of total assistance or bilateral aid favoring countries with sound policies. In contrast, multilateral aid by the World Bank and other institutions (accounting for about a third of the total) has tended to be directed toward countries that the Bank deems to have favorable policy environments.

The real problem with development aid is its paucity, especially from the United States. In fiscal 2001, the U.S. Congress allocated $10.7 billion to international development assistance, of which $1.3 billion went to multilateral and $8.4 billion to bilateral assistance, plus $835 million for Public Law (P.L.) 480, the Food-for-Peace Program (USAID 2001). This represented about six-tenths of 1 percent of the federal budget of some $1.8 trillion, and only about one-tenth of 1 percent of U.S. GDP. By way of comparison, the United States poured $13 billion into the Marshall Plan to help rebuild Europe after World War II, amounting to 4.5 percent of U.S. GDP, albeit spread over a number of years.

The United States commitment to foreign aid after World War II was motivated by the global struggle of the Cold War, as the United States and the Soviet Union competed to attract developing world countries to their side. The Cold War is no longer a motivation, and moral obligation has been afflicted by "donor fatigue," reflecting the perceived ineffectiveness of much previous development assistance (Anderson 1998). In the aftermath of September 11, 2001, U.S. engagement in global problems is needed to shape the world in ways conducive to American interests. Narrow domes-

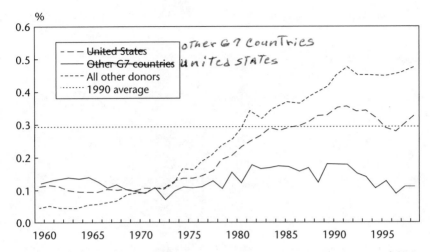

FIGURE 7.1   •   Net overseas development assistance as a percentage of GDP, 1960–99

SOURCE: Compiled by authors from OECD n.d.

tic special interest groups, such as U.S. textile manufacturers and sugar producers and the U.S. steel industry have all too often thwarted the larger national interest in foreign and trade policy.[3]

Figure 7.1 shows that U.S. overseas development assistance has remained at about one-tenth of 1 percent of GDP in recent years. Other Group of Seven (G7) countries—Canada, France, Germany, Great Britain, Italy, and Japan—now contribute three times as much in relation to GDP. Other donors, including the Scandinavian countries, allocate almost half of 1 percent of GDP to foreign aid—five times that of the United States.

Looked at on a per capita basis (Figure 7.2), U.S. foreign assistance amounted to $82 (in 1997 prices) per capita annually in the period 1960–66, whereas the other G7 countries and donors were providing about $26. U.S. per capita aid, however, has declined steadily since then and now is far below the others. The level of overseas development assistance per person by the United States actually fell from 1966 to 1999, while it increased in other G7 countries and other donor nations (Figure 7.3). Figure 7.4 shows the regional breakdown for recipients of foreign assistance. The Middle East/North Africa foreign assistance per capita specifically reflects assistance to Israel by the United States and to Egypt after the Camp David Accords peace agreement.

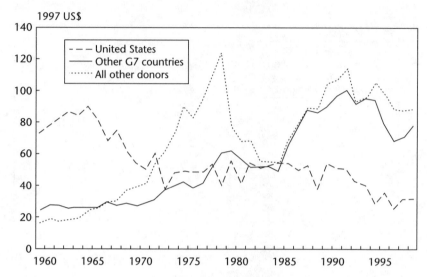

FIGURE 7.2 • Net overseas development assistance per capita, 1960–99

SOURCE: OECD n.d.

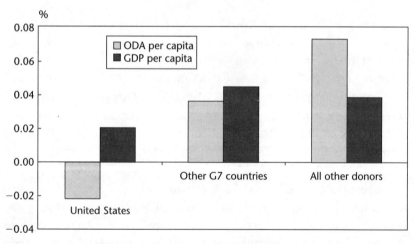

FIGURE 7.3 • Overseas development assistance (ODA) and GDP per capita annual growth rate, 1960–99

SOURCE: OECD n.d.

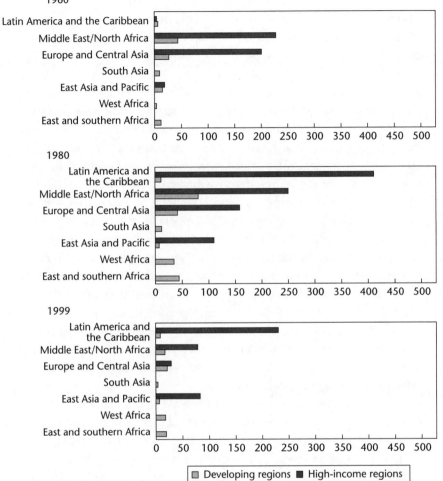

FIGURE 7.4 • Overseas development assistance per capita for all recipients, 1960, 1980, and 1999

SOURCE: Compiled by authors from OECD n.d.

NOTE: Categorization of high-income regions follows World Bank country classification, World Bank 2001.

There is a disjuncture between much of the rhetoric and the reality of development aid. The declining funding for foreign assistance does not square with the attitudes of average Americans. A recent national survey by the University of Maryland found that most Americans support government assistance to fight hunger in poor countries—and would be willing to pay more taxes to do it. Eighty-three percent agreed that the United States should work with other industrial nations to reduce world hunger, and 75 percent would be willing to pay an additional $50 per person in taxes to do so if other industrial countries paid a like amount. The same group grossly overestimated the amount currently spent on foreign aid, guessing that 20 percent of the federal budget went to fund it. Most thought it got more money than Medicare or even national defense, when in fact it receives only a fraction (Program on International Policy Attitudes 2001). Americans were more supportive of foreign aid to fight hunger than to achieve strategic goals. A majority believe that substantially more should be spent. Some 87 percent favored food and medical assistance to people in poor countries and 73 percent favored aid to help these countries develop economically. When told that Africa has the highest percentage of undernourished people and that hunger is growing fastest there, more than 70 percent felt the United States should give special attention to Africa. Only 25 percent see military aid to countries that are friendly to the United States as a good use of tax dollars (Program on International Policy Attitudes 2001).

With the announcement in March 2002 of the U.S. Millennium Challenge Account, there is reason to believe that U.S. commitments to development aid are turning around. In the fall of 2002, the U.S. government committed to increasing its funding by 25 percent for an "initiative to cut hunger in Africa," with a focus on boosting agricultural productivity and increasing trade (USAID 2003). Yet such increases must make up for years of underfunding, and must be sustained over decades to be effective.

Private International Capital Flows   Table 7.2 documents the enormous increase in private-sector investment in developing countries in the 1990s and also the marked regional disparities in the flow of that capital. East Asia (in this case including China) Latin America, and the Newly Independent States of Eastern Europe and Central Asia account for the lion's share of private investment. The lack of investment in Sub-Saharan Africa, South Asia, and the Middle East/North Africa shows their lagging position

TABLE 7.2 • Net private capital flows and foreign direct investment by region, 1990 and 1998

Region	Net private capital flows (US $ million)		Foreign direct investment (US $ million)	
	1990	1998	1990	1998
Sub-Saharan Africa	1,283	3,452	834	4,364
East Asia	18,720	67,249	11,135	64,162
South Asia	2,174	7,581	464	3,659
Latin America and Caribbean	12,412	126,854	8,188	69,323
Middle East/North Africa	369	9,223	2,458	5,054
Newly Independent States	7,649	53,342	1,051	24,350

SOURCES: World Bank 2001, 315; Paarlberg 2002, 10.
NOTE: The Newly Independent States include countries of the former Soviet Union and Eastern Europe.

in the process of globalization. These countries' business climates are too risky to attract private capital because of political instability, civil unrest, and institutionalized graft and corruption.[4] It is not a coincidence that the problems of hunger and poverty are most serious in these same areas of the world. As Paarlberg (2002, 10–11) notes, "globalization's impact has been relatively weak in the two regions (Sub-Saharan Africa and South Asia) of the world where food security problems remain most conspicuous."

In particular, foreign direct investment in developing countries by companies based in industrial countries has increased substantially with globalization and now dwarfs foreign aid. Foreign private investment was five times greater in 1998 than in 1968, in constant 1997 U.S. dollars, as shown in Figure 7.5. Such direct investment in industrial plants and operations can contribute significantly to the development process. In contrast, short-term capital flows invested in financial instruments can be destabilizing, as demonstrated during the 1998 Asian financial crisis. However, the impact of even large amounts of foreign direct investment on hunger and poverty may be limited.

Little of this investment is in agriculture or rural areas. Because they are largely public goods, agricultural research and education do not attract sufficient private investment. Despite its growth, what foreign direct investment there is, is largely concentrated in just a few countries. Only 5 countries accounted for more than half of all foreign direct investment in 1998 and just 12 for all but a small amount (Figure 7.6). Only $4.36 billion of foreign direct investment was made in Sub-Saharan Africa in 1998 and

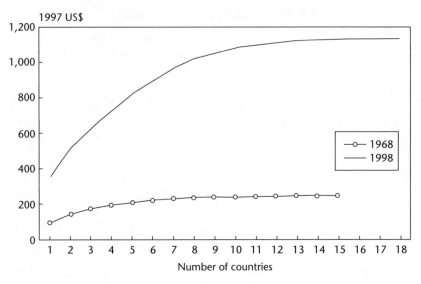

FIGURE 7.5 • Recipients' share of foreign direct investment, 1968 and 1998
SOURCE: OECD n.d.

$3.66 billion in South Asia, including India, whereas $69.32 billion was invested in Latin America and $64.16 billion in East Asia, including China (Table 7.2).

Remittances by workers to their families, friends, and more distant relatives are another way funds flow to developing countries. Throughout poor countries (and in some richer ones as well), many husbands, sons, and increasingly daughters leave rural homes and villages for employment in the cities and other countries, sending whatever surplus they can scrape together back to their families. There are large expatriate populations of Filipinos working in the United States and Middle East, several million nonresident Mexicans working in North America, and Bangladeshis working in the United Kingdom, for example, who send sizable shares of their income to their families left behind. Migrants send money to reimburse others for past spending on schooling, or for the costs of migration, or out of concern for their inheritance, or as a way of maintaining status so that they can return home with dignity. Funds may also be sent to invest in building or improving a house or to buy land, as well as to smooth out shortfalls in family income at home due to crop failures, job layoffs, or ill health.[5] Migrants sent back an estimated $75 billion in remittances to

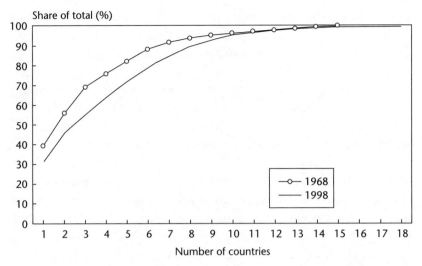

FIGURE 7.6 • Foreign direct investment by companies based in industrial
countries, 1968 and 1998

SOURCE: OECD n.d.

poor countries in 2000 (Yusuf 2001), more than all development assistance
from foreign governments.

Global Philanthropy   Because governments usually put domestic before
global interests, private philanthropy has a vital role in redefining the
global economic system. Just as the large accumulations and concentrations of capital in the late nineteenth and early twentieth centuries by the
Ford, Rockefeller, and Carnegie families were used to advance U.S. public
interests in an era of more limited government, so the new wealth of the
late twentieth and early twenty-first centuries can be put to work for global
public goods such as food security and human health, promoting the
assumption of greater responsibility for these issues by multilateral institutions and rich country governments. Andrew Carnegie spoke of the "gospel
of wealth": the need to match extraordinary affluence with generosity
and social responsibility. John D. Rockefeller said that "anybody who dies
rich dies disgraced" (Abelson 2000b, C1). The charitable work of the super-
rich can unquestionably burnish their public image, but can also have a
profound impact on global problems.

Philanthropy is beginning to reflect the accumulation of wealth by a
new generation of entrepreneurs that has reshaped the American economy.

In 1998, before the final dramatic rise and then decline in the U.S. stock market, there were some 170 billionaires, 250,000 decamillionaires and 4.8 million millionaires in the United States (Abelson 2000b). There are more than 7 million individuals worldwide with a million dollars or more of investable assets, who together control about one-third of the world's wealth (*The Economist* 2001a). Many Americans and other wealthy individuals, attuned to global concerns because many of their businesses are international, have increasing concerns over the global divide between haves and have-nots.

The Ford and Rockefeller Foundations took the lead in investing in developing countries starting in the 1950s and 1960s. Rockefeller, in fact, started the wheat and maize improvement program in Mexico, which became CIMMYT and ultimately expanded into the worldwide CGIAR agricultural research system. The Green Revolution of the 1960s, largely financed by the Rockefeller and Ford Foundations, is one of the most successful examples of high-impact global philanthropy. Under the leadership of Gordon Conway, the Rockefeller Foundation has indicated a refocusing of its mission to concentrate on the world's poor. The Foundation, which had already directed some 70 percent of its funding overseas, plans to concentrate its resources in four key areas: food, health care, the environment, and culture and creativity (Abelson 1999).

We would propose that the recent leadership already shown by the Gates and Turner Foundations be expanded to a wider range of foundations. The role of the Turner Foundation's major contribution to the United Nations, and its further role in breaking the impasse over U.S. funding for UN agencies, suggests the capacity of private aid to support international institution-building. Consider the magnitude of these funds. Foundation assets in the United States at the end of 1999 were US$448.6 billion, although they declined with the fall in the stock market (U.S. Bureau of Census 2001, 361). Total foundation giving was $24.5 billion in 2000 (Lewin 2001a). Bill Gates has stated on numerous occasions that he intends to give virtually all his money away during his lifetime, which will provide the Bill and Melinda Gates Foundation an endowment several times its current level of some $24 billion, already the world's wealthiest. The Gates Foundation is focusing on improving the health and education of children worldwide. The Foundation, which has a basic goal of helping to bridge the gap between the haves and the have-nots, directed 48 percent of its grants to global health problems in 2000 ($685.5 million) and committed a total of US$750 million over five years to childhood vaccina-tion efforts in the developing world (Bill and Melinda Gates Foundation 2001; Abelson 2000a).

George Soros, one of the world's wealthiest men, has been giving sub-stantial sums to international causes, particularly in the transition coun-tries of Eastern Europe. Warren Buffet, the famous investor, and Larry Ellison, CEO of the software company Oracle, have said they plan to give most of their billions away. Buffet has said that his money will go to his foundation, a major focus of which is global population issues (Bianco 1999). It is not just wealthy Americans who are involved in international philanthropy. The Sasakawa Foundation, founded by the late Japanese businessman Ryoichi Sasakawa, has focused on improving agriculture in Sub-Saharan Africa, with the help of Nobel Prize Laureate Norman Borlaug and former President Jimmy Carter.

Charitable contributions in the United States doubled since 1990 to total US$203.5 billion in 2000 (of which religious organizations received the largest share, 36.5 percent of the total). Three-quarters ($152.1 billion) of the total philanthropic funding was donated by individuals; much more than the already mentioned $24.5 billion provided by foundations and the $10.9 billion by private corporations (U.S. Bureau of Census 2001, 360). However, just $2.7 billion (about 1.3 percent) of those funds were directed to international initiatives (Lewin 2001b). In addition to founda-tions many individuals give to groups such as CARE, Oxfam, and Médecins Sans Frontières (Doctors Without Borders), as well as other international causes. If only 10 percent or so of the more than $200 billion in charitable giving could be directed to international food, health, and environmental issues, the impact could be immense. Of course, despite this discussion of the roles of private foundations, donor governments' assistance, together with direct investment from private businesses, are the twin pillars of poverty and hunger alleviation. Even so, the large sums of accumulated wealth controlled by a small number of individuals could play an impor-tant role in ending poverty and hunger. A major challenge will be to channel and target such funds appropriately.

The desire for a direct involvement in their charities pertains not just to the super rich, such as Bill Gates, but also to many of the wealthy. Since many of their fortunes are self-made, they bring an entrepreneurial per-spective to philanthropy. A survey of wealthy Americans found 60 percent interested in education and half in issues of poverty, inequality, hunger, and health care (Abelson 2000b). Many have an international perspective, and want to be actively engaged in their charitable efforts. They place more reliance on the marketplace and less on government, are "outcome oriented" and want to act as "social entrepreneurs," which may explain the appeal of approaches such as microcredit projects (Abelson 2000b, C1, C23; *The Economist* 1998a).

INSTITUTIONAL INNOVATION AND FUNDING

Alliances and partnerships that bring together various institutions involved in development assistance are growing in importance. They recognize that governments and international organizations have been joined in the development arena by NGOs, foundations, universities, and private philanthropists. Both the United Nations and USAID are emphasizing building alliances and partnerships with the private sector and civil society (Annan 2001). The Global Compact initiated by UN Secretary-General Kofi Annan asks companies to enact certain human rights, labor, and environmental standards in their global business operations, with a goal of enlisting a thousand companies by 2002. The Compact also seeks to promote investment in the poorest countries; by helping to ensure that the benefits of the global economy are widely shared, corporations are not just being generous but are furthering their own vested interests if they want to expand their overseas markets and reduce the backlash against globalization. Annan considers one of the top goals of the Compact to make poor countries more attractive for both domestic and foreign private investment.

In May 2001, Secretary of State Colin Powell announced the Global Development Alliance, which would play a central role in U.S. development efforts and form the foundation of USAID's future operations (USAID 2000). The Global Alliance is meant to serve as a fundamental realignment of how USAID operates. Strategic partnerships will be used to leverage its resources. USAID literally hopes to act as a venture capital operator, trying to use relatively small sums of start-up funds to attract much larger investments. U.S. development assistance would also be directed to areas that are not attractive to the private sector, particularly institutional and policy changes necessary for development, including agriculture.

In March 2002, President Bush announced the Millennium Challenge Account, a 50 percent increase in basic assistance to developing countries through 2006 (Bush 2002b). The account would increase overseas development assistance in 2004, 2005, and 2006, ending with $5 billion in increased funding by 2006. The "challenge" comes in the form of explicit attention to recipient nations' stances toward corruption, human rights, education, health care, and liberal economic policies. In this sense, the aid is conditional, but the conditions are precisely those advocated by nearly all those involved in ending hunger and poverty in the developing world.

Another important new institutional innovation for attracting additional funds to development is the dedicated trust fund. One of the most well known is the global fund to combat HIV/AIDS in Africa established by the United Nations under Kofi Annan. The ultimate goal of the trust fund is to attract US$7–10 billion from governments, businesses, foundations, and individual philanthropists (Perlez 2001). If such dedicated funds are to become a major mechanism for addressing developing-country problems, they must prove both effective at addressing the specific issue and efficient at using the funds. Donors want to be confident that their contributions will not be subject to the widespread waste and corruption that has eroded much development assistance in the past.

Another trust fund is the aforementioned billion-dollar Global Alliance for Vaccines and Immunizations, started with major funding by the Gates Foundation, which focuses on making basic immunizations for preventable diseases available to children in poor countries. The fund reflects Bill Gates' private-sector perspective of tight accountability and making funding contingent on demonstrated performance. The Immunization Fund actually sends auditors into developing-country health clinics. However, the Fund may find that it is quite unreasonable to expect developed-country record-keeping and accounting practices in the world's poorest countries (Zimmerman 2001).

Gates has also backed the International AIDS Vaccine Initiative, which provides funds to pharmaceutical companies (Zimmerman 2001). The stipulation is that although pharmaceutical companies may keep the patent and licensing rights to any vaccine developed with donated funds for sale at profitable prices in developed industrial countries, the vaccine must be made available at affordable prices in poor countries. However, the question of what is an affordable price is likely to be open to very different interpretations by drug companies and developing countries. FAO, under Director-General Jaques Diouf, has launched a Trust Fund for Food Security and for Emergency Prevention of Transboundary Pests and Diseases of Animals and Plants to try to augment the support for fighting hunger. The initial goal is to raise $500 million from voluntary contributions (FAO 2001a).

Overall, revitalizing and substantially increasing the financial resources of key United Nations agencies, particularly FAO and WHO, could play a crucial role in the fight against world hunger and poverty. The World Bank should accelerate the realignment of its support away from projects that can attract private financing, toward investments in human capital, especially education, health, nutrition, and agricultural research.[6] Some of the most critical actions to fight hunger will require little direct funding but will necessitate enormous commitment and political will by the industrial countries to overcome powerful vested interests. One of the most important steps the rich countries can take to speed the development of poor countries is to drop the barriers to trade for the products in which they are likely to have a comparative advantage, such as textiles and certain agricultural products, like sugar.

The very sizable investments necessary for a pro-poor growth strategy will largely have to come from the reallocation of public spending by poor countries themselves, especially from military budgets and other unproductive government expenditures. Debt forgiveness for the poorest countries needs to be accelerated, since 45 of the poorest countries—30 of which are in Africa—have external debts (totaling some $235 billion) that will be impossible to repay. These indebted countries are forced to reduce investments in schools, health clinics, and agricultural research to meet their debt repayments. In fact, African countries currently spend about four times more on debt service than on government expenditures for education, health, and nutrition (IFPRI 2001b).

The strong system of international agricultural research centers, which is currently significantly underfunded, provides an institutional base for raising food output in the South and stimulating rural development. Agricultural universities in the industrial countries can make substantial contributions to developing-country agricultural research and development, given the availability of expanded funding. In the end, although the role of businesses, foundations, and private philanthropists is growing, there is no substitute for a much greater political and financial commitment by the governments of the rich countries, led by the United States, to the fight against poverty and hunger.

There are some hopeful signs that development funding may be about to substantially improve. In the 1990s a political consensus by conservatives and liberals was formed that led to the major reform of U.S. domestic welfare policy. Something similar may now be happening in terms of global poverty and hunger. The emerging consensus on aid can be summed up in four points of agreement: (1) increased funding and enlarged debt forgiveness are needed; (2) aid cannot be effective when local conditions lead to its being stolen or misspent; (3) donors must be more flexible and less bureaucratic; and (4) geopolitical expediency should not dominate the distribution of aid. Another component of the "new middle ground" is the widespread understanding that trade is as important as aid (Keller 2002). The March 2002 Millennium Challenge Account put forward by President Bush, promising a $5 billion increase in American foreign aid by 2006, is properly focused on nations that "govern justly, invest in their people, and encourage economic freedom" (Bush 2002a, 3). This is mirrored in a proposal by the Europeans to substantially increase their funding for development assistance. All told, the governments of the six to eight leading economies have promised to increase development assistance focused on poverty reduction by $12 billion a year. The budget proposed by the Bush administration for 2004 calls for a $2 billion increase in foreign aid with a total of $18 billion. This would represent the largest increase in foreign aid in two decades, much of it directed toward the new Millennium Challenge Account. The Challenge Account will require greater accountability by the recipients. Countries would sign "contracts," which would be cancelled if they failed to use the funds effectively, and there would be financial audits. A bipartisan consensus in Congress, which has not existed since the Cold War, could develop to support foreign aid. There is a strong argument that foreign assistance enhances American security and is in the U.S. national interest (Dao 2003). Delivering on these financial promises will be an essential and large step forward on the high road toward ending hunger in our lifetimes. However, to put the United States on a par as a percentage of GDP with the other G-7 nations, the group of the world's wealthiest countries, would require boosting development assistance to $27 billion annually.

8 • CONCLUSION

Look 25 years into the future and consider two possible fates for the Hassans' sons and their granddaughter. In the first, Bangladesh has benefited from sustained economic growth stimulated by greater access to rich country markets for products such as textiles and clothing. Business investment, both domestic and foreign, has created new jobs. Real wages have risen along with productivity. With the assistance of international organizations, NGOs, development aid, and private philanthropy, Bangladesh has substantially improved education, health, and the nutrition of its people.

Investments in agriculture have shifted to focus on small peasant farmers, improved irrigation, rural roads, and electricity, as well as agricultural research and extension. Rice yields are up as farmers adopt new seeds developed through agricultural research, together with a more nutritional array of secondary crops. Genetic modification has activated genes in rice DNA with beneficial effects, which were not previously expressed. Less fertilizer is needed because the new varieties can fix their own nitrogen, as soybeans currently do. They are also more tolerant of saline water and inundation. Genetic modification has bred in natural resistance to diseases and pests prevalent in rice, so less pesticide is needed. Successful reforestation programs in the foothills of the Himalayas have reduced severe flooding. Simple improvements like power rototillers have replaced water buffaloes for field cultivation, so that farming takes less time and is more efficient. The road to the nearest main town has been upgraded, paved, and a bridge built, making access much easier and reducing the cost of getting goods to market.

As farmers have become more prosperous, new businesses and jobs throughout the countryside have flourished. Farm numbers are down, as former farmers are drawn to other jobs. One of the Hassans' sons completed technical school and is now a computer programmer in the city. The other is operating a successful electronics shop in the nearest large town, selling products such as cell phones. He also operates a small Internet café that lets customers pay to log on. Both sons are married and have two children.

The Hassans' granddaughter has finished teachers' college and now teaches fourth and fifth grades in the local village school. As the status of women has improved, marriage no longer requires a dowry, and she has been able to keep working. She has one child. All three families eat much better than their parents did. Rice is still the main staple, but many more vegetables, fruits, fish, dairy products, and poultry are affordable. Their diet contains adequate calories and nutrients; in fact, the adults worry about gaining weight. Their children are healthy and well nourished.

So might it be, if the investments, innovations, and institutions on which food security depends are realized. But another fate may lie in store if they are not. Destitution may await the Hassan children and grandchildren. If the world economy fails to sustain robust economic growth and stagnates for long periods, if terrorism and war plague the world, or if trade reform comes to a standstill due to protectionist barriers in the rich countries, Bangladesh will slide backward. Poorer, more crowded, and ecologically ravaged, racked by increasing political instability and civil unrest, the Hassans' village will be an even more desperate island in the storm than it is now.

The Hassans' sons will not pursue an education. They will eke out a living as rickshaw pullers, like their father. After he dies, they will fight over his meager plots. With no dowry, the granddaughter will make a poor marriage to an older man in the next village who will not let her work outside the home. Her youngest child will die as an infant from pneumonia, but malnutrition will be the real cause of death because the mother will be so poorly nourished that her breast milk will dry up.

Farming methods will stay the same. Villagers will own little of their own land, and their parcels will shrink. Flooding will be rampant as upstream watersheds are denuded. Sea levels will rise as polar ice fields begin to melt, inundating millions of acres of low-lying coastal areas. Many coastal areas will not be cropped because of saltwater encroachment. Bangladeshis will try desperately to get to Europe or the United States. One of the sons will manage to be smuggled into Europe, but he will be caught and sent back.

Which of these futures will be the fate of the Hassans depends largely on the choices and efforts made by the people and government of Bangladesh. However, the decisions made by rich nations to invest, innovate, and institutionalize progress in food security also play an important role. If these choices are made in the Hassans' favor, a much better future for their children and grandchildren can be achieved in our lifetime. The number of hungry can fall dramatically, and chronic hunger can be ended by mid-century. The choice is collectively ours, rich and poor, to make.

These choices are not only about the poor but the world that we will give to all of our children and grandchildren. Ever greater divisions between haves and have-nots will foster neither peace nor stability. The rich cannot simply wall themselves off from deprivation at home or from the poor countries of the developing world. Speaking at the World Economic Forum in New York City in early February 2002, UN Secretary General Kofi Annan said, "The forces of envy, despair, and terror in today's world are stronger than many of us realized. But they are not invincible. Against them, we must bring a message of solidarity, of mutual respect and, above all, of hope" (Schmemann 2002, A14).

Without major changes, progress against poverty and hunger will be too slow to win this fight. The Hassan children and granddaughter, emblematic of the world's poor, will have little hope of leading better lives than their parents. We have detailed what needs to be done—increase investments in poor people, pursue new innovations in agricultural science and environmental sustainability, and create new institutional remedies to global dilemmas. Robust economic growth is the sine qua non for generating the funds for this process. Trade must play a crucial role as an engine of this growth. For this to happen, rich countries must open access to their markets for products in which developing countries have a comparative advantage—in agriculture, textiles, and clothing. And while necessary, economic growth is not sufficient. For the poor to share broadly in the economic gains, major investments in their education, nutrition, and health care are also required. Countries like Thailand, which have pursued such a strategy, have been able to make remarkably rapid progress in reducing the number of poor and hungry.

Progress against world hunger will also require more and better science and substantial investments in agricultural research. More research should focus on the needs of farmers in tropical areas, especially small peasant farmers. Increases in agricultural productivity can propel the whole rural sector forward. Much of the research required will not be done if left to the private sector. Public international and national research must be reinvigorated, incentives designed to direct private research toward the needs of poor farmers, and greater public/private cooperation fostered. A major reason for the increasing poverty and hunger in Sub-Saharan Africa is the neglect of these issues.

The science underlying agricultural research has become increasingly complex. Part of this complexity revolves around intellectual property rights. Intellectual property issues require protection of incentives without locking out those who need access to new technologies. Biotechnology is part of the answer. If its critics succeed in slowing its application, the poor may suffer more than the privileged rich, who have generated most of the criticism.

The environmental base of agriculture must be protected and sustained. Environmental degradation is caused mainly by the intensification of production, the cultivation of marginal land, and the consequences of increasing livestock concentration. Widespread agricultural policies that distort incentives and discourage farmers from caring for the environment must be reformed. With the right technology and investment, yields can be maintained and even boosted, not only on the best land but also on less-favored lands, helping to keep the most fragile lands out of production. Industrial animal systems also pose major environmental threats, which must be controlled and closely managed.

Water resources will need to be more carefully and efficiently used. The worldwide demand for water is rapidly increasing, yet affordable supplies are limited. Incentives to conserve water, improved recycling, and more efficient use hold great potential. Large-scale water projects, with major economic, social, and environmental costs, are being replaced by more efficient small-scale efforts. Irrigation can provide the greatest gains, but there is also room for much greater efficiency in industrial and urban uses. Water markets and user groups can encourage more efficient use, but their successful establishment is complicated. Improvements in rural communications and transportation infrastructure are also essential to improving market access and expanding opportunities for rural people.

International organizations need to be reformed, as do many national agricultural policies, including those of the United States and the European Union. International trade policy should be redirected toward the needs of the developing countries. The Doha Round of WTO trade negotiations for agriculture should be renamed the "Food Security Negotiations," augmented by offers of greater technical support and guidance on trade issues to developing-country trade delegations.

The primary responsibility for the welfare of citizens, including food security, rests with national governments. However, given the growing interdependencies among nations, food security has taken on characteristics of a global public good, necessitating a multilateral response. The denial of this interdependence and the pursuit of nationalistic self-sufficiency policies have created inefficient distortions and left unresolved problems of poverty and hunger.

The means of improving poverty, health, and food security are closely interconnected, and so must cooperation be among the various international agencies involved. Reforms are needed in the World Bank to support pro-poor growth strategies, a direction in which the Bank has begun to move. Its resources should shift toward grants to the poorest countries and the poorest segments in middle-income LDCs. There are also expanded roles for FAO and WHO, requiring commensurate increases in funding. A GEO is needed to address directly transboundary environmental issues, rather than forcing existing organizations such as the WTO to respond to issues for which they are ill suited. NGOs have done much to bring the perspective of civil society into the debate on the environment, trade, and development, but they should expect to be held to the same standards of accountability, transparency, and legitimacy that they impose on international organizations.

Much of the criticism of globalization is fundamentally related to concerns about distributive equity and social justice. International institutions and the rich countries of the North must not only increase the efficiency of the global food distribution system, but they must assure LDCs that the international market economy is both fair and just, if these countries are to become full players in the system and increase their reliance on it for their national food security.

The investments necessary for widespread progress against food insecurity and hunger will not be possible without adequate funding. As detailed in the previous chapter, foreign private investment is playing an increasingly important role in economic development, along with domestic investment. However, most foreign direct investment is concentrated in only a handful of developing countries. The poorest countries receive little. Moreover, much of the social investment in public goods, such as education and scientific research, will not attract private investment. There is an opportunity for a new generation of philanthropists to follow the example of Bill and Melinda Gates, George Soros, and Ted Turner and serve as catalysts in addressing global problems. However, even the substantial accumulation of wealth of the current foundations and most successful entrepreneurs is limited in comparison to the task. In the final analysis, if the rich countries of the North are going to take seriously the goal of sharply cutting global poverty and hunger in our lifetime, a much greater financial commitment to foreign assistance will be required.

As Amartya Sen, winner of the 1998 Nobel Prize in Economics, eloquently stated:

> The contemporary age is not short of terrible and nasty happenings, but the persistence of extensive hunger in a world of unprecedented prosperity is surely one of the worst. . . . Massive endemic hunger causes great misery in many parts of the world . . . debilitating hundreds of millions and killing a sizable proportion of them with statistical regularity. What makes this widespread hunger even more of a tragedy is the way we have come to accept and tolerate it as an integral part of the modern world, as if it is essentially unpreventable. (Sen 1999, 204)

The persistence of widespread hunger is unacceptable in a world of prosperity. Ending hunger is an achievable goal. With appropriate investments, innovations, and institutions, we can end chronic hunger in our lifetimes. Making the case for these investments and innovations cannot be left to books such as this one, but must include active participation and involvement by citizens around the world. In Appendix C, we have listed some of the organizations and NGOs dedicated to the task of overcoming indifference and building political will.

This book began with a quotation from a young Ghanian woman who presciently observed that ending hunger will not come quickly or easily. Yet, the greatest obstacle may not come from economic, resource, or scientific constraints, but from complacency, indifference, and a lack of political commitment. The battle against hunger and poverty will require broad cooperation among rich and poor nations and their peoples.

APPENDIX A • THE METHODOLOGY

USED FOR HUNGER PROJECTIONS

A simple but structured method was used to estimate the number of chronically hungry and food insecure people (see Senauer and Sur 2001 for greater detail). First, we statistically estimated the link between income and calorie consumption (a "calorie-income curve" as shown in the top panel of Figure A.1), using data for 55 low- and low-middle–income countries during the period 1992–96. Second, we calculated how income is distributed within the population of each country used in our study based on a division of the population into fifths, or "quintiles," with the highest quintile representing the top 20 percent in terms of GDP per capita, the next the second 20 percent, and so on. Data on average per capita calorie consumption by country were obtained from FAO. Data on average GDP per capita by country and the distribution of income by quintile were taken from the World Bank database. The income data for each country was converted into 1993 U.S. dollar equivalents, using the purchasing power parity (PPP) approach, which accounts for differences among countries in the cost of buying a similar bundle of goods.

Using FAO's minimum energy requirement of 1,800 calories per day, the income level at which this amount would be reached can be read off the calorie-income curve in Figure A.1. Reaching 1,800 calories a day would require an average annual per capita GDP of US$565 in this example. This figure is higher than the minimum cost of buying a diet of 1,800 calories per day. Although poor households typically spend the majority of their income on food; there are other things they must buy. In addition, average GDP per capita estimates are frequently higher than actual per capita income levels. The percentage of the population with

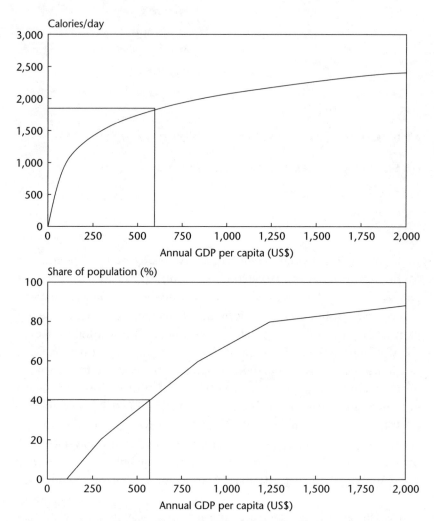

FIGURE A.I • Calorie-income and income distribution curves
SOURCE: Senauer and Sur 2001.

incomes below $565 can be read from the income distribution curve. In the hypothetical curve shown, this is 40 percent. This approach allows the necessary income level to vary across countries and lets us project the effect on hunger of changes in average per capita income, the distribution of income, and food prices for each region.

The minimum per capita energy requirements (Table A.I) vary somewhat by region, reflecting the age and body stature of the population (FAO

TABLE A.1 • Minimum energy requirements

Country/region	Current	2025 (calories/capita)	2050
Sub-Saharan Africa	1,800	1,850	1,900
East Asia	1,880	1,950	2,000
China	1,880	1,950	2,000
South Asia	1,790	1,890	1,940
Latin America	1,870	1,950	2,000
Middle East/North Africa	1,840	1,890	1,940
Newly Independent States	1,900	1,950	2,000

SOURCES: Current requirements are from FAO 1996b; 2020 and 2050 requirements are authors' estimates.
NOTE: The Newly Independent States include countries of the former Soviet Union and Eastern Europe.

1996b, 53). Where population growth is rapid, as in Sub-Saharan Africa, the share of children is larger, which lowers the average minimum calorie requirement. Similarly, where individuals are smaller in stature, as in South Asia, the average minimum calorie requirement is less. These requirements were raised for 2025 and 2050 to reflect slowing population growth and increases in the average age. People who are under the minimum requirement are undernourished. Once above it, they are counted as food secure. This approach obviously represents a simplification of the situation.

For every country where data were available, the methodology yielded an estimate of the proportion of the population that is undernourished and lacks food security. The weighted average of the proportion of food insecure in individual countries within a region was multiplied by the total regional population to arrive at the estimates of food insecurity for the seven regions and the global aggregate, shown in Table 2.4 in Chapter 2. The populations of each country were used as weights.

A different approach using household food consumption survey data had to be used to estimate the current number of undernourished people in India, because of the substantial discrepancy between India's GDP estimates and the data for income and its distribution. The most recent evidence on the incidence of poverty and food insecurity for India was used to generate the results presented in this book. For this analysis, 28 percent of India's population is assumed to be undernourished versus 33 percent previously in Senauer and Sur (2001). This revision reflects the difference between household responses for 7- and 30-day food consumption surveys in India. Respondents may significantly understate their consumption in the longer period surveys because they cannot remember that far back (Dugger 2000).

Our estimate for 1996–98 of the number of hungry people globally was 1.1 billion, which is higher than the FAO's 1996–98 figure of 826 million. Our estimates are substantially higher than FAO for Sub-Saharan Africa and South Asia. As discussed, many experts believe FAO underestimates hunger in these regions. Our figures are somewhat higher for other regions than FAO, except for East Asia, which is slightly lower. The USDA derived an estimate of 1.1 billion food-insecure people for 1998 and 865 million for 1999 with a methodology similar to this analysis (Shapouri and Rosen 1999, 3; USDA, ERS 1999, 5). Shane et al. (2000) estimated that approximately 1 billion people were food insecure.

The various projections for 2025 involve upward shifts in the income distribution curve (bottom panel, Figure A.1) to reflect growth in per capita income (GDP), plus changes in its distribution to represent pro-poor or anti-poor growth and shifts in the calorie-income curve to reflect changes in the real price of food. The population and income growth rates on which the 2025 baseline projections are based were the ones used in IFPRI's supply and demand forecasts using the IMPACT model at the time of this analysis in 1999. They are basically the same as those currently used and discussed in Appendix B. The population and income growth rates averaged for the regions and over the time period are shown in Table 2.3, along with the resulting per capita income growth rates. The forecast growth rates used by IFPRI and in this analysis were from the World Bank for GDP and from the United Nations for population (UN, Population Division 1998). For the latter, the medium scenario projections were used.

In Table 2.4 the estimates for various scenarios have been converted into percent changes, which can be applied to FAO's 1996–98 estimates as a baseline to obtain numbers of hungry people. FAO base figures are used to avoid a confusing array of numbers. Moreover, although there may be room to improve the FAO methodology, its estimates serve as a widely accepted measure of the status of global hunger.

The forecasts in Table 2.4 can be compared with projections from other studies. FAO predicts a decline of 30 percent in the number of hungry people by 2015 and 52 percent by 2030 (FAO 2000a, 2000f, 3). FAO projections of future undernourishment assume a more equitable distribution in countries with highly unequal access to calories (FAO 2000a). Therefore, the FAO projections should probably be compared with the 43 percent reduction forecast in column 4 (pro-poor growth) in Table 2.4, which assumes a more equal distribution of income, and hence calories. Shane et al. (2000) forecast an 18 percent decrease in the number of food-insecure persons by 2015.

APPENDIX B • INTERNATIONAL MODEL FOR POLICY ANALYSIS OF AGRICULTURAL COMMODITIES AND TRADE (IMPACT)—MODEL DESCRIPTION

The analysis of future trends in global food supply and demand in Chapter 3 uses two linked models, IMPACT and IMPACT-WATER.[1] IMPACT is recognized as a leading agricultural sector model for assessing the global food situation. It has been applied in a wide variety of contexts for medium- and long-term policy analysis of global food markets. IMPACT-WATER extends the model to incorporate a detailed treatment of water resources and water-agriculture interactions.

THE IMPACT MODEL: AN OVERVIEW

IFPRI's IMPACT model offers a methodology for analyzing baseline and alternative scenarios for global food demand, supply, trade, income, and population. IMPACT covers 36 countries and regions, accounting for virtually all world food production and consumption (Table B.1), and 16 commodities (Table B.2), including all cereals, soybeans, roots and tubers, meats, milk, eggs, and oils, oilcakes, and meals. IMPACT is a representation of a competitive world agricultural market for crops and livestock. It is specified as a set of country or regional submodels, within each of which supply, demand, and prices for agricultural commodities are determined. The country and regional agricultural submodels are linked through trade, a specification that highlights the interdependence of countries and commodities in the global agricultural markets. The model uses a system of supply and demand elasticities incorporated into a series of linear and nonlinear equations to approximate the underlying production and demand functions (Figure B.1). World agricultural commodity prices are determined annually at levels that clear international markets. Demand is

TABLE B.1 • Definitions of IMPACT countries and regions

Regions	Subregions	Countries
Developed countries and regions		
Western world	Australia	Australia
	European Union (EU 15)	Austria, Belgium, Denmark, Finland, France, Germany, Greece, Ireland, Italy, Luxembourg, the Netherlands, Portugal, Spain, Sweden, and the United Kingdom
	Japan	Japan
	United States	United States
	Other developed countries	Canada, Iceland, Israel, Malta, New Zealand, Norway, South Africa, and Switzerland
	Eastern Europe	Albania, Bosnia-Herzegovina, Bulgaria, Croatia, Czech Republic, Hungary, Macedonia, Poland, Romania, Slovakia, Slovenia, and Yugoslavia
	Central Asia	Kazakhstan, Kyrgyzstan, Tajikistan, Turkmenistan, Uzbekistan
Former Soviet Union (FSU)	Other Former Soviet Union	Armenia, Azerbaijan, Belarus, Estonia, Georgia, Latvia, Lithuania, Moldova, Russian Federation, and Ukraine
Developing countries and regions		
Central and Latin America	Argentina	Argentina
	Brazil	Brazil
	Colombia	Colombia
	Mexico	Mexico
	Other Latin America	Antigua and Barbuda, Bahamas, Barbados, Belize, Bolivia, Chile, Costa Rica, Cuba, Dominica, Dominican Republic, Ecuador, El Salvador, French Guiana, Grenada, Guadeloupe, Guatemala, Guyana, Haiti, Honduras, Jamaica, Martinique, Netherlands Antilles, Nicaragua, Panama, Paraguay, Peru, Saint Kitts and Nevis, Saint Lucia, Saint Vincent, Suriname, Trinidad and Tobago, Uruguay and Venezuela
Sub-Saharan Africa	Central and Western Sub-Saharan Africa	Benin, Cameroon, Central African Republic, Comoros Island, Congo Democratic Republic, Congo Republic, Gabon, Gambia, Ghana, Guinea, Guinea-Bissau, Ivory Coast, Liberia, Sao Tome and Principe, Senegal, Sierra Leone, and Togo
	Eastern Sub-Saharan Africa	Burundi, Kenya, Rwanda, Tanzania, and Uganda

	Nigeria
Nigeria	Burkina Faso, Chad, Djibouti, Eritrea, Ethiopia, Mali, Mauritania, Niger, Somalia, and Sudan
Northern Sub-Saharan Africa	Angola, Botswana, Lesotho, Madagascar, Malawi, Mauritius, Mozambique, Namibia, Reunion, Swaziland, Zambia, and Zimbabwe
Southern Sub-Saharan Africa	Egypt
West Asia/North Africa (WANA)[a]	Turkey
	Algeria, Cyprus, Iran, Iraq, Jordan, Kuwait, Lebanon, Libya, Morocco, Saudi Arabia, Syria, Tunisia, United Arab Emirates, and Yemen
Egypt	Bangladesh
Turkey	India
Other West Asian and North African countries	Pakistan
South Asia	Afghanistan, Maldives, Nepal, and Sri Lanka
Bangladesh	Indonesia
India	Malaysia
Pakistan	Myanmar
Afghanistan, Maldives, Nepal, and Sri Lanka	Philippines
	Thailand
	Viet Nam
Other South Asian countries	Brunei, Cambodia, and Laos
Southeast Asia	China includes Taiwan and Hong Kong
Indonesia	Republic of Korea
Malaysia	Democratic People's Republic of Korea, Macao, and Mongolia
Myanmar	
Philippines	
Thailand	
Vietnam	
Other Southeast Asian countries	
East Asia	
China	
Republic of Korea	
Other East Asian countries	
Rest of the world	Cape Verde, Fiji, French Polynesia, Kiribati, New Guinea, Papua New Guinea, Seychelles, and Vanuatu

SOURCE: Compiled by the authors.
[a]The classification West Asia/North Africa, used here and in Chapter 3, includes Cyprus and Turkey, whereas Middle East/North Africa, used elsewhere in the book, does not.

TABLE B.2 • Definitions of IMPACT commodities

Commodity group	Commodity name	Details
Livestock		
Meat	Beef	Beef and veal (meat of bovine animals, fresh, chilled or frozen, with bone in) and buffalo meat (fresh, chilled, or frozen, with bone in or boneless)
	Pork	Pig meat (meat, with the bone in, of domestic or wild pigs, whether fresh, chilled, or frozen)
	Poultry	Chicken meat (fresh, chilled, or frozen). May include all types of poultry meat like duck, goose, and turkey if national statistics do not report separate data.
	Sheep and goat	Meat of sheep and lamb, whether fresh, chilled, or frozen, with bone in or boneless, and meat of goats and kids, whether fresh, chilled, or frozen, with bone in or boneless
Other livestock products	Eggs	Weight in shell
	Milk	Cow, sheep, goat, buffalo, and camel milk. (Production data refer to raw milk containing all its constituents. Trade data normally cover milk from any animal, and refer to milk that is not concentrated, pasteurized, sterilized, or otherwise preserved, homogenized, or peptonized.)
Crops		
Grains	Maize	Used largely for animal feed and commercial starch production
	Other coarse grains	Barley (varieties include with husk and without; used as a livestock feed, for malt, and for preparing foods), millet (used locally, both as a food and as a livestock feed), oats (used primarily in breakfast foods; makes excellent fodder for horses), rye (mainly used in making bread, whisky, and beer; when fed to livestock, it is generally mixed with other grains), and sorghum (a cereal that has both food and feed uses)

	Rice	Rice milled equivalent (white rice milled from locally grown paddy; includes semi-milled, whole-milled, and parboiled rice)
	Wheat	Used mainly for human food
Roots and tubers	Cassava and others	Cassava and other tubers, roots, or rhizomes (cassava is the staple food in many tropical countries; it is not traded internationally in its fresh state because tubers deteriorate very rapidly)
	Potatoes	Mainly used for human food
	Sweet potatoes and yams	Sweet potatoes (used mainly for human food; trade data cover fresh and dried tubers, whether or not sliced or in the form of pellets) and yams (a starchy staple foodstuff, normally eaten as a vegetable, boiled, baked, or fried)
Other	Meals	Copra cake, cottonseed cake, groundnut cake, other oilseed cakes, palm kernel cake, rape and mustard seed cake, sesame seed cake, soybean cake, sunflower seed cake, fish meal, meat, and blood meal (residue from oil extraction, mainly used for feed)
	Oils	Vegetable oils and products, animal fats and products (obtained by pressure or solvent extraction; used mainly for food)
	Soybeans	The most important oil crop (oil of soybeans under oils) but also widely consumed as a bean and in the form of various derived products because of its high protein content, for example, soya milk, meal, and so forth

SOURCE: FAO 2000a.

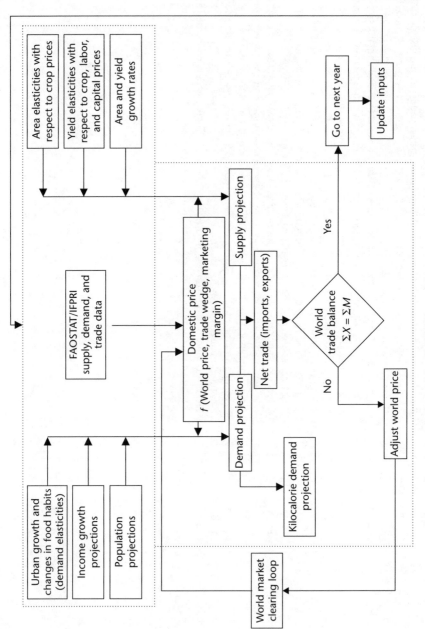

FIGURE B.1 • Schematic representation of the IMPACT model

a function of prices, income, and population growth. Growth in crop production in each country is determined by crop prices and the rate of productivity growth. Future productivity growth is estimated by its component sources, including crop management research, conventional plant breeding, wide-crossing and hybridization breeding, and biotechnology and transgenic breeding. Other sources of growth considered include private-sector agricultural research and development, agricultural extension and education, markets, infrastructure, and irrigation.

A wide range of factors with potentially significant impacts on future developments in the world food situation can be modeled based on IMPACT. They include population and income growth, the rate of growth in crop and livestock yield and production, feed ratios for livestock, agricultural research, irrigation and other investment, price policies for commodities, and elasticities of supply and demand. For any specification of these underlying factors, IMPACT generates projections for crop area, yield, and production; demand for food, feed, and other uses; prices; and trade. It also projects livestock numbers, yield, production, demand, prices, and trade. A base year of 1997 (a three-year average of 1996–98) is used because this was the most recent data available from the FAOSTAT database at the time of the 2001 update of the projections. Projections are made to the year 2020.

TECHNICAL DETAILS OF THE IMPACT MODEL

Crop Production   Domestic crop production is determined by the area and yield response functions. Harvested area is specified as a response to the crop's own price, the prices of other competing crops, and the projected rate of exogenous (nonprice) growth trend in harvested area. The projected exogenous trend in harvested area captures changes in area as a result of factors other than direct crop price effects, such as expansion due to population pressure and contraction due to soil degradation or conversion of land to nonagricultural uses. Yield is a function of the commodity price, the prices of labor and capital, and a projected nonprice exogenous trend factor reflecting technology improvements. The nonprice yield trend projections are central to projecting yield. The sources of growth considered in these projected trend factors include (1) public research by international and national agricultural research centers including management research, conventional plant breeding, wide-crossing and hybridization breeding, and biotechnology (transgenic) breeding; (2) private-sector research and development related to agriculture; (3) agricultural extension and farmers' schooling; (4) markets; (5) infrastructure; and (6) irrigation. The growth contribution of modern inputs such as fertilizers is accounted for by price effects in the yield response function and as a complementary input with irrigation and the modern varieties generated by research. To generate the projected time path of yield growth, the methodology makes use of before-the-fact and after-the-fact studies of agricultural research priority setting, studies of the sources of agricultural productivity growth, an examination of the role of industrialization in growth, and expert opinion (Evenson and Rosegrant 1995). Annual production of a commodity in a specific country is then estimated as the product of its area and yield in that country.

Livestock Production Livestock production is modeled similarly to crop production, except that livestock yield reflects only the effects of expected developments in technology. Total livestock population is a function of the livestock's own price and the price of competing commodities, the prices of intermediate (feed) inputs, and a trend variable reflecting growth in the number of livestock slaughtered. Total production is calculated by multiplying the slaughtered number of animals by the yield per head.

Demand Functions Domestic demand for a commodity is the sum of its demand for food, feed, and other uses. Food demand is a function of the price of the commodity and the prices of other competing commodities, per capita income, and total population. Per capita income and population increase annually according to country-specific population and income growth rates. Feed demand is a derived demand determined by the changes in livestock production, feed ratios, and own- and cross-price effects of feed crops. The feed demand equation also incorporates a technology parameter that indicates improvements in feeding efficiencies. The demand for other uses is estimated as a proportion of food and feed demand. Note that total demand for that livestock consists only of food demand. The source of supply and demand data is the FAOSTAT database (FAO 2000c); UN, Population Division (1998) was used for the population data; and elasticities and growth rates were obtained from relevant literature and expert estimates.

Prices Prices are endogenous in the model. Domestic prices are a function of world prices, adjusted by the effects of price policies, expressed in terms of the producer subsidy equivalent (PSE), consumer subsidy equivalent (CSE), and the marketing margin (MI). The PSE and CSE measure the implicit level of taxation or subsidy borne by producers or consumers relative to world prices and account for the wedge between domestic and world prices. The MI reflects other factors such as transport and marketing costs. In the model, PSE, CSE, and MI are expressed as percentages of the world price. In order to calculate producer prices, the world price is reduced by the MI value and increased by the PSE value. Consumer prices are obtained by adding the MI value to the world price and reducing it by the CSE value. The MI of the intermediate prices is smaller because wholesale instead of retail prices are used, but intermediate prices (reflecting feed prices) are otherwise calculated the same way as consumer prices. Most prices are obtained from the World Bank's *Global Commodity Markets: A Comprehensive Review and Price Forecast* (World Bank 2000c). Prices that were not available in this report were collected from FAO (2000c, 2000d) and USDA's National Agricultural Statistics Service (USDA, NASS 2001).

International Linkage: Trade The country and regional submodels are linked to each other through trade. Commodity trade by country is the difference between domestic production and demand. Countries with positive trade are net exporters, while those with negative values are net importers. This specification does not permit a separate identification of countries that are both importers and exporters of a particular commodity. In the 1997 base year, changes in stocks are computed at the 1996–98 average levels. Therefore, production and demand values are not equal in the base year. Stock changes in the base year are phased out during the first three years of the projection period to achieve long-run equilibrium, that is, a supply–demand balance is achieved with no annual changes in stocks.

Algorithm for Solving the Equilibrium Condition The model is written in the General Algebraic Modeling System (GAMS) programming language. The solution of the system of equations is achieved by using the Gauss-Seidel method algorithm. This procedure minimizes the sum of net trade at the international level and seeks a world market price for a commodity that satisfies the market-clearing condition.

The world price (PW) of a commodity is the equilibrating mechanism such that when an exogenous shock is introduced in the model, PW will adjust and each adjustment is passed back to the effective producer (PS) and consumer (PD) prices via the price transmission equations, as discussed in the "Prices" section above. Changes in domestic prices subsequently affect commodity supply and demand, necessitating iterative readjustments until world supply and demand are balanced, and world net trade is again equal to zero.

Determination of Malnutrition   In order to explore food security effects, IMPACT projects the percentage and number of malnourished preschool children (0 to 5 years old) in developing countries. A malnourished child is defined as a child whose weight-for-age is more than two standard deviations below the weight-for-age standard set by the U.S. National Center for Health Statistics/World Health Organization. This standard is adopted by many UN agencies in assessing the nutritional status of persons in developing countries. The projected numbers of malnourished children are derived from an estimate (Smith and Haddad 2000) of the functional relationship between the percentage of malnourished children and several factors: average per capita calorie consumption, nonfood determinants of child malnutrition such as the quality of maternal and child care (proxied for by the percentage of females undertaking secondary schooling as well as by females' status relative to males' as captured by the ratio of female to male life expectancy at birth), and health and sanitation (proxied for by the percentage of the population with access to treated surface water or untreated but uncontaminated water from another source).

Calorie consumption is projected directly from the IMPACT food demand projections. Projected life expectancy ratios, female enrollment rates, and percentage of population with access to safe water are based on recent trends at the country level, with projected investment levels, as well as diminishing returns as prevalence rates improve, taken into consideration. The percentage of malnourished children is then applied to the projected population of children 0 to 5 years of age to compute the number of malnourished children.

THE IMPACT-WATER MODEL

In projecting crop production, IMPACT assumes a "normal" climate condition for the base year as well as for all subsequent years. Effects of year-to-year climate variability on food production, demand, and trade are therefore not captured in the primary IMPACT model. In reality, however, food production, demand, and trade are significantly affected by climate variability and particularly by water availability. More important, water demand is increasing rapidly, but water supply may decline or may not fully satisfy the increased demand due to water quality degradation, high costs of new supply, and physical limits to infrastructure development. Therefore future water availability, particularly for irrigation, may differ from water availability today. Both the long-term change in water demand and water availability and the year-to-year variability in rainfall and run-off will affect food production, demand, and trade in the future. In order to explore the impacts of water availability on food production, water demand and water availability must thus be projected over the period and then incorporated into food production simulation. This motivates an extension of IMPACT by development of a Water Simulation Model (WSM) at the global scale.

The WSM simulates water availability for crops, taking into account total renewable water, nonagricultural water demand, water supply infra-structure, and economic and environmental policies related to water development and management at the river basin, country, and regional levels. Crop-specific water demand and supply are calculated for the nine crops modeled in IMPACT (namely rice, wheat, maize, other coarse grains, soybean, potato, sweet potato, cassava, and other roots and tubers) as well as for crops that are not considered in IMPACT (which are aggregated into a single crop for water demand assessment). Water supply in irrigated agri-culture is linked with irrigation infrastructure, permitting estimation of the impact of investment on expansion of potential crop area and improve-ment of irrigation systems.

IMPACT-WATER, an integration of IMPACT and WSM, thus incorporates water availability as a stochastic variable with observable probability dis-tributions in order to examine the impact of water availability on food supply, demand, and prices. This modeling framework allows explo-ration of the relationships between water availability and food production, demand, and trade at various spatial scales—from river basins, countries, or regions, to the global level—over a 30-year time horizon.

APPENDIX C • ORGANIZATIONS

STRIVING TO END HUNGER

To learn how to make a personal commitment to ending hunger, you might contact the following organizations.

ACDI/VOCA

ACDI/VOCA is a private, nonprofit organization that promotes broad-based economic growth and the development of civil society in emerging democracies and developing countries. The organization offers a comprehensive range of technical assistance services, and since 1989 has administered USAID and USDA food aid programs. ACDI/VOCA directly distributes food aid to vulnerable populations in low-income, food-deficit countries or sells the food to local buyers, the proceeds from which are used to fund development projects designed to stimulate local economies and increase food security.

ACDI/VOCA
50 F Street, NW
Suite 1100
Washington, DC 20001
202-383-4961
www.acdivoca.org

ACTION AGAINST HUNGER—USA

Action Against Hunger directly delivers emergency aid and longer-term assistance to people suffering from the dire consequences of natural disaster or man-made crisis. The agency's mission is to save lives by combating hunger, disease, and the crises threatening the lives of helpless men, women, and children.

Action Against Hunger–USA
247 West 37th Street, Suite 1201
New York, NY 10018
212-967-7800
www.aah-usa.org

AMERICA'S SECOND HARVEST

America's Second Harvest is the largest domestic hunger relief organization in the United States. Through a network of over 200 food banks and food-rescue programs, they provide emergency food assistance to more than 23 million hungry Americans each year, of whom 8 million are children.

America's Second Harvest
35 E. Wacker Dr., #2000
Chicago, IL 60601
1-800-771-2303
312-263-2303
www.secondharvest.org

AMNESTY INTERNATIONAL

Amnesty International is a worldwide campaigning movement founded in 1961 with a vision of a world in which every person enjoys all of the human rights enshrined in the Universal Declaration of Human Rights and other international human rights standards. They undertake research and action focused on preventing and ending grave abuses of the rights to physical and mental integrity, freedom of conscience and expression, and freedom from discrimination, within the context of work to promote all human rights.

Amnesty International,
  United Kingdom
99-119 Rosebery Avenue
London EC1R 4RE
020-7814-6200
www.amnesty.org.uk/

Amnesty International,
  United States
322 8th Avenue
New York, NY 10001
212-807-8400
www.amnestyusa.org

BREAD FOR THE WORLD

Bread for the World is an advocacy organization founded in 1973 that directly and via its 46,000 members contacts members of the U.S. Congress and other government representatives about legislation that affects hungry people in the United States and worldwide. They do not provide direct relief or development assistance, but rather focus on using their power as citizens in a democracy to support policies that address the root causes of hunger and poverty.

Bread for the World
50 F Street, NW, Suite 500
Washington, DC 20001
202-639-9400
www.bread.org

CARE INTERNATIONAL

CARE International is a confederation of 11 national CARE organizations that constitute one of the world's largest private international humanitarian organizations, committed to helping families in poor communities improve their lives. CARE USA was founded in 1945 to provide relief for survivors of World War II. Its mission has expanded greatly to include humanitarian work designed to find lasting solutions to poverty for poor communities in over 60 countries.

CARE International Secretariat
Boulevard du Regent, 58/10
B-1000 Brussels
Belgium
32-2-502-43-33
www.care.org

CARE USA, Headquarters
Atlanta
151 Ellis Street
Atlanta, GA 30303
404-681-2552
www.careusa.org

DOCTORS WITHOUT BORDERS (MÉDECINS SANS FRONTIÈRES)

Médecins Sans Frontières (MSF), founded in 1971 by a small group of French doctors, is an international humanitarian aid organization that provides emergency medical assistance to populations in danger in more than 80 countries. MSF is an international network that brings together 2,500 volunteer doctors, nurses, and other medical professionals, logistics experts, water and sanitation engineers, and administrators to work with 15,000 locally hired staff to provide medical aid in more than 80 countries.

MSF International Office
Rue de la Tourelle, 39
Brussels, Belgium
32-2-280-1881
www.msf.org

Doctors Without Borders
6 E. 39th St., 8th floor
New York, NY 10016
212-679-6800
www.doctorswithoutborders.org

FOOD AND AGRICULTURE ORGANIZATION OF THE UNITED NATIONS

The Food and Agriculture Organization of the United Nations (FAO) was founded in 1945 with a mandate to raise levels of nutrition and standards of living, to improve agricultural productivity, and to better the condition of rural populations. Today, FAO is one of the largest specialized agencies in the United Nations system and the lead agency for agriculture, forestry, fisheries and rural development. An intergovernmental organization, FAO has 183 member countries plus one member organization, the European Community.

Food and Agriculture Organization of the United Nations (FAO)
Viale delle Terme di Caracalla, 00100
Rome, Italy
39-06-5705-1
www.fao.org

THE HUNGER SITE

On average more than 220,000 individuals from around the world visit the site each day to click the "give free food" button and help feed the hungry. Founded in June 1999, The Hunger Site was the first online activism site on the Web. To date more that 101 million visitors have given more than 198 million cups of staple food.

The Hunger Site
One Union Square
600 University Street, Suite 1000
Seattle, WA 98101-4107
206-268-5400
www.thehungersite.com

(Clicking the "free food button" on this site provides the hungry with a value of 1.1 cups of staple foods provided by the listed daily sponsors of the Web site.)

INTERNATIONAL FOOD POLICY RESEARCH INSTITUTE

The International Food Policy Research Institute (IFPRI) was established in 1975 and is one of 16 Future Harvest Centers that receive funding from governments, private foundations, and international and regional organizations, most of whom are members of the Consultative Group on International Agricultural Research. IFPRI's mission is to identify and analyze policies for sustainably meeting the food needs of the developing world. Research at IFPRI concentrates on economic growth and poverty alleviation in low-income countries, improvement of the well-being of poor people, and sound management of the natural resource base that supports agriculture. IFPRI seeks to make its research results available to all those in a position to use them and to strengthen institutions in developing countries that conduct research relevant to its mandate.

International Food Policy Research Institute
2033 K Street, NW
Washington, DC 20006-1002
202-862-5600
www.ifpri.org

OXFAM INTERNATIONAL

Oxfam International is a confederation of 12 organizations working together in more than 100 countries to find lasting solutions to poverty, suffering, and injustice. With many of the causes of poverty global in nature, members of Oxfam International believe they can achieve greater impact in addressing issues of poverty by their collective efforts. To achieve the maximum impact on poverty, Oxfams link up their work on development programs, humanitarian response, and lobbying for policy changes at national and global levels. The organization conducts campaigns and communication work aimed at mobilizing public opinion for change.

Oxfam International
Oxfam International Secretariat, Oxford
266 Banbury Road, Suite 20
Oxford, OX2 7DL, UK
44-1865-31-39-39
www.oxfam.org

Oxfam America
Headquarters
26 West Street
Boston, MA 02111
1-800-77-Oxfamusa
www.oxfamamerica.org

PEACE CORPS

The Peace Corps, founded in 1961 at the instigation of President John F. Kennedy, is an agency of the U.S. government designed to facilitate volunteer service by U.S. citizens in countries around the world. Presently 7,000 Peace Corps volunteers are serving in 70 countries. The mission of the Peace Corps is to help the people of interested countries meet their need for trained men and women; to help promote a better understanding of Americans on the part of the peoples served; and to help promote a better understanding of other peoples on the part of Americans.

Peace Corps
The Paul D. Coverdell Peace Corps Headquarters
1111 20th Street NW
Washington, DC 20526
1-800-424-8580
www.peacecorps.gov

UNITED STATES AGENCY FOR INTERNATIONAL DEVELOPMENT (USAID)

USAID's history goes back to the Marshall Plan reconstruction of Europe after World War II and the Truman administration's Point Four Program. In 1961, President John F. Kennedy signed the Foreign Assistance Act into law and created USAID by executive order. Since that time, USAID has been the principal U.S. agency to extend assistance to countries recovering from disaster, trying to escape poverty, and engaging in democratic reforms. USAID is an independent federal government agency that receives overall foreign policy guidance from the Secretary of State. Many other developed-country governments maintain similar agencies with similar poverty alleviation and economic development objectives. See the Development Cooperation Directorate section of the Organization for Economic Cooperation and Development (OECD) Web site for further details (www.oecd.org).

U.S. Agency for International Development Information Center
Ronald Reagan Building
Washington, DC 20523-1000
202-712-4810
www.usaid.gov

WORLD BANK

Founded in 1944, the World Bank Group is one of the world's largest sources of development assistance. The Bank, which provided US$19.5 billion in loans to its client countries in fiscal year 2002, is now working in more than 100 developing economies, bringing a mix of finance and ideas to improve living standards and eliminate the worst forms of poverty. For each of its clients, the Bank works with government agencies, nongovernmental organizations, and the private sector to formulate assistance strategies. Its country offices worldwide deliver the Bank's program in countries, liaise with government and civil society, and work to increase understanding of development issues. Several regional development banks undertake similar activities including the African Development Bank (www.afdb.org), Asian Development Bank (www.adb.org), InterAmerican Development Bank (www.iadb.org), and the European Bank for Reconstruction and Development (www.ebrd.org).

The World Bank
Headquarters
1818 H Street, N.W.
Washington, DC 20433
202-473-1000
www.worldbank.org

WORLD FOOD PRIZE

The World Food Prize was created in 1986 as the brainchild of Dr. Norman Borlaug (winner of the Nobel Peace Prize in 1970 for his work in world agriculture). It is the foremost international award recognizing—without regard to race, religion, nationality, or political beliefs—the achievements of individuals who have advanced human development by improving the quality, quantity, or availability of food in the world.

The World Food Prize Foundation
666 Grand Ave
Suite 1700
Des Moines, IA 50309
515-245-3783
www.worldfoodprize.org

WORLD FOOD PROGRAMME OF THE UNITED NATIONS

Set up in 1963, the World Food Programme (WFP) is the United Nation's frontline agency in the fight against global hunger. In 2001, WFP fed 77 million people in 82 countries, including most of the world's refugees and internally displaced people.

World Food Programme
Via C.G.Viola 68
Parco dei Medici
00148 Rome, Italy
06-65131
www.wfp.org

WORLD HEALTH ORGANIZATION OF THE UNITED NATIONS

The World Health Organization (WHO), the United Nations specialized agency for health, was established in 1948. WHO's objective, as set out in its constitution, is the attainment by all peoples of the highest possible level of health. Health is defined in WHO's constitution as a state of complete physical, mental, and social well-being and not merely the absence of disease or infirmity.

WHO Headquarters
Avenue Appia 20
1211 Geneva 27
Switzerland
41-22-791-21-11
www.who.int/en/

APPENDIX D · ACRONYMS

BMI	body mass index
Bt	*Bacillus thuringiensis*
CGIAR	Consultative Group on International Agricultural Research
CIMMYT	Centro Internacional de Mejoramiento de Maiz y Trigo [International Maize and Wheat Improvement Center]
Codex	Codex Alimentarius Commission
CSE	consumer subsidy equivalent
FAO	Food and Agriculture Organization of the United Nations
G7	Group of Seven countries (Canada, France, Germany, Great Britain, Italy, Japan, and United States)
GATT	General Agreement on Tariffs and Trade
GDP	gross domestic product
GEO	global environment organization
GM	genetically modified
HIV/AIDS	human immunodeficiency virus/acquired immune deficiency syndrome
IFAD	International Fund for Agricultural Development
IFPRI	International Food Policy Research Institute
ILO	International Labour Organisation
IMF	International Monetary Fund
INGO	international nongovernmental organization
LDCs	less-developed countries
MI	marketing margin
MSF	Médecins Sans Frontières [Doctors Without Borders]
NGO	nongovernmental organization

NIS	Newly Independent States
NRC	National Research Council (of the United States)
ODA	overseas development assistance
OECD	Organisation for Economic Co-operation and Development (30 member nations: Australia, Austria, Belgium, Canada, Czech Republic, Denmark, Finland, France, Germany, Greece, Hungary, Iceland, Ireland, Italy, Japan, Korea [South], Luxemburg, Mexico, New Zealand, Norway, Poland, Portugal, Slovak Republic, Spain, Sweden, Switzerland, Turkey, United Kingdom, and the United States)
PBRs	plant breeding rights
PPP	purchasing power parity
PSE	producer subsidy equivalent
RDA	recommended daily allowance
R&D	research and development
UN	United Nations
UNCTAD	United Nations Commission on Trade and Development
UNDP	United Nations Development Programme
UNEP	United Nations Environment Programme
USAID	United States Agency for International Development
USDA	United States Department of Agriculture
WFP	World Food Programme
WHO	World Health Organization
WIPO	World Intellectual Property Organization
WRI	World Resources Institute
WSM	water simulation model
WTO	World Trade Organization

NOTES

CHAPTER 1 · INTRODUCTION

1. The Hassans' name is fictitious, but the family is real. This narrative is based on the detailed responses of one family to a statistically representative survey of 956 households collected by the International Food Policy Research Institute (IFPRI), the Bangladesh Institute of Development Studies, and the Institute of Nutrition and Food Science at Dhaka University in 1996–97 in rural villages in Bangladesh.

2. See Wahid (1999) and Zeller et al. (2001) for a discussion of microcredit institutions.

3. Davis, Thomas, and Amponsah (2001, 718) define food security to include (1) food availability, (2) stability, (3) accessibility, (4) sufficiency, (5) autonomy, (6) reliability, (7) equitability, and (8) sustainability. In their view, globalization has had mixed effects in assuring these aspects of food security.

4. The developing countries are variously referred to as the South, poor countries, developing countries, and less-developed countries (LDCs). The developed countries are referred to as the North, rich countries, developed countries, industrial countries, and OECD countries (referring to the Organisation of Economic Co-operation and Development, of which the industrial countries are members). These terms are used interchangeably throughout this book.

5. Human capital relates to improvements in people's education, health, nutrition, and skills that raise their productive capacity.

CHAPTER 2 · HUNGER IN A PROSPEROUS WORLD

1. In fiscal year 2001, for example, the U.S. government shipped $1.28 billion in food aid to countries the world over (USDA, FAS 2002).

2. See Haddad, Hoddinott, and Alderman 1997, for an excellent review of the issue of intrahousehold resource allocation; Senauer, Garcia, and Jacinto 1988 for an empirical analysis; and Smith and Haddad (2000) on the implications for child malnutrition.

3. Countries' currencies were converted to dollars using purchasing power parity, a method that allows a dollar to have the same purchasing power in different countries.

4. FAO's methodology obviously relies on the accuracy of the underlying data, which are quite poor for some countries. Only calories are accounted for and deficiencies in other nutrients are not considered. Seasonal variations in food availability are ignored. A person who consumed only one calorie below the minimum energy requirement would be counted as undernourished. Some argue that the methodology is inherently biased. The estimated number of food insecure is predominantly determined by the adequacy of calorie availability in the national food supply and does not fully reflect the distributional impact on calorie consumption of poverty, which may cause a substantial underestimate of hunger, especially in South Asia (Hopper 1999; Smith 1998; and Svedberg 1998).

5. Child malnutrition is further discussed in Chapter 3. The number of underweight children has been included as an outcome variable in the model used as the basis for much of the discussion in that chapter.

6. In a study by Milanovic (2002), based on household survey data for a common sample of 91 countries, the Gini coefficient, a widely used measure of inequality, shifts from 62.8 in 1988 to 66.0 in 1993, when incomes are adjusted for differences in countries purchasing power. A value of zero would represent perfect equality and 100 complete inequality, in which one household would receive all the income. The increase in world income inequality is driven more by differences in average incomes between countries than by inequalities within countries. In a study by Dikhanov and West using a different methodology, the Gini coefficient increases by about 6 percent (Wade 2001). It should be noted that the period 1988–93 may not be indicative of longer-term trends in income distribution.

7. Bhalla (2002) derives a Gini coefficient for world inequality of 65 for 1998, down from a peak of 72 in 1968 and 69 in the early 1960s and 1980s.

8. Such a large increase in hunger in Sub-Saharan Africa is consistent with other studies. The U.S. Department of Agriculture (USDA) (USDA, ERS 1999) also projects a substantial increase in food insecurity in Africa by 2009, and Shane et al. (2000) forecast an increase of 71 percent to a total of 413 million food-insecure people in Sub-Saharan Africa by 2015.

9. A review of a number of analyses of food consumption disaggregated by income level for various developing countries suggests the elasticity of total calorie consumption related to a change in the price of the primary staple food is in the range of 0.5 for low-income households (Dawson and Tiffin 1998; Waterfield 1985). Therefore, a 10 percent increase in calories purchased would require a 20 percent decline in price.

CHAPTER 3 · ENDING HUNGER SUSTAINABLY

1. Area is a function of crop price, investment in irrigation, and estimated rates of loss of land to urbanization and land degradation. Crop yield is a function of crop price, input prices, investments in irrigation, and yield growth due to technological change.

2. These are results from the IMPACT WATER model, which is calibrated for consistency with the basic IMPACT model, but also explicitly incorporates water availability into the crop area and yield functions (Rosegrant and Cai 2000).

3. Investment expenditures under each scenario are computed as the sum between 1997 and 2025 of the annual flows of investment required to increase the stock of services to projected 2025 levels. For example, investments in rural roads under each scenario are calculated by multiplying the incremental road length projected in 1997–2025 by investment costs per kilometer. Operations and maintenance costs and depreciation on the stock of roads existing in 1997 are not included in the estimate.

4. See Delgado et al. (1999) for more discussion and analysis of the global livestock markets, using a similar but earlier (and here updated and extended) set of projections.

5. This leaves some 83 percent of the world's cropland (and 95 percent of all agricultural land) reliant on rainfall as the sole source of water. The amount and variability of rain (or more meaningfully the length of growing period [LGP], which measures the number of days per year in which moisture and temperature conditions support plant growth) play a major role in determining the productivity of agriculture. Regions with low and erratic rainfall (that is, short and variable LGPs) often support pastoral systems; those with longer and more stable LGPs support improved pastures and annual and permanent crops. About one-fifth of the world's land in agriculture receives less than 400 millimeters (16 inches of rainfall in an average year, but few years are average).

6. The trade liberalization scenario examines the impact of removing all trade-distorting agricultural subsidies and all international agricultural trade barriers, including tariffs and quotas, for the commodities covered in the IMPACT model.

7. The positive, pro-poor scenario modeled here does not simulate direct redistribution of income or wealth to the poor nor liberalize trade policies, but it does postulate dramatic increases in investment in pro-poor social capital, including education and health, as well as substantial increases in agricultural research spending, which benefits the rural areas where most of the poor live.

CHAPTER 4 · SCIENCE AND FOOD SECURITY

1. Smith (1995) provides a fascinating account of the origins of agriculture. Smith et al. (1992) provide an equally entertaining and insightful account of the discovery and geographical spread of crops such as coffee, cacao, mango, citrus, cloves, cashews, and many other beverage, spice, fruit, nut, and oil crops from tropical locales throughout the world.

2. An examination of industry and experimental yield data has been used to substantiate these views. See, for example, Cassman, Olk, and Dobermann (1997), Conway (1997), and Pingali and Heisey (2001).

3. See relevant chapters on plant breeding and genetics in Chrispeels and Sadava (2002).

4. At present, no entirely satisfactory method exists for comparing consumption or expenditure among countries at different (or even the same) points in time. We express research expenditure figures in "international dollars" (where

an international dollar is set equal to one U.S. dollar in the benchmark year) using a procedure described by Pardey, Roseboom, and Craig (1992). Research expenditures in current local currency units are first deflated to a base year set of prices (in our case 1993), using a local price deflator and then converting to a common currency unit (specifically international dollars), using purchasing power parity indexes (PPPs) for 1993 obtained from the World Bank (2000d). This technique is preferable to using official exchange rates to perform the currency conversions, for they do not properly account for the sometimes substantial differences in price levels among countries. In this instance, the tendency would be to understate the quantity of research resources used in economies with relatively low prices and to overstate the quantity of resources used in countries with high prices. This is particularly a problem when valuing something like agricultural R&D expenditures, where typically 60–70 percent of the expenditures are on local scientists and support staff, not capital and other goods and services that are commonly traded internationally.

5. An exception to the general pattern of a slowdown was China, where spending during the 1990s rebounded from a period of stagnation during the last half of the 1980s. Signs of recovery were evident in parts of Latin America too, where Pardey and Beintema (2001) estimate overall growth of 2.8 percent per year from 1991 to 1996, compared with little or no growth during the previous decade. However, since the mid-1990s, public spending in Brazil (accounting for half of Latin America's public spending on agricultural research) may once again be on the decline. In inflation-adjusted terms, funding for Embrapa, a nonprofit statutory authority accounting for around 62 percent of Brazil's public agricultural R&D spending, was more than 10 percent lower in 1999 than it was in the mid-1990s.

6. If instead we classify countries as developed or developing, there is almost as close a match: in 1997, 59 percent ($935 billion) of the world's $1.3 trillion worth of agricultural output came from developing countries, quite close to the 54 percent of global R&D spending on agriculture that occurred in these countries.

7. Complementing the work of the CG are two large French institutions, the Centre de Coopération Internationale en Recherche Agronomique pour le Développement and the Institut de Recherche pour le Développement. They focus on tropical countries and spend about half as much as the CGIAR.

8. Although the tomatoes achieved the delayed-softening and taste-retention objectives of its developers, yields were poor, mechanical handling equipment turned most of them into mush before they got to market, and consumers weren't willing to pay enough of a premium over conventional fresh tomatoes to cover costs. The seeds of the biotechnology protests started with the Flavr-Savr™ too, when Jeremy Rifkin managed to persuade Campbell's Soup not to use biotech tomatoes in its products (Kasler and Lau 2000).

9. Herbicide-tolerant technologies enable farmers to adjust the time of application of weed-controlling herbicides to have maximum effect without damaging the crop itself. Plants genetically engineered to incorporate *Bacillus thuringiensis* (*Bt*) are systemically resistant to some key pests like bollworm in cotton and stem borer in maize, thereby reducing or eradicating the need for pest-controlling

insecticide sprays. Valuing these effects with any precision is still problematic (Marra 2001), but the available empirical evidence, in conjunction with the rapid uptake of these technologies in markets where they are approved for planting, indicates that farmers' production costs per unit of output are lowered. These technologies also appear to significantly reduce the amount of chemicals used in agriculture or their toxicity (at least in areas where the rate of chemical use was substantial), with consequent reductions in the amount of chemicals that leach into groundwater and surface waterways or persist as residues on crops. China reports fewer pesticide poisonings with *Bt* cotton (Pray et al. 2001).

10. This relative measure helps to capture the complementary nature of different types of research investment, much as labor productivity measured as output per unit of labor carries with it returns to the use of complementary land, capital, and other purchased inputs. By analogy, research produces new know-how and new and improved techniques that act like additional inputs and raise productivity. For example, a farmer working just half a hectare of land is likely to produce more if she has a whole hectare to farm (so that the productivity of labor increases as the intensity of land use relative to labor increases). Similarly, the amount of rice harvested from a quarter of a hectare is likely to be higher if nitrogen fertilizer is applied than if it is not used (so that land productivity increases as the intensity of fertilizer use relative to land increases).

11. Likewise, R&D can improve the quality of an existing amount of output (such as enhancing the vitamin A status of rice), which can be seen as increasing the amount of a bundle of outputs (that includes both rice and vitamin A) and thus raising productivity in this fashion.

12. Agricultural GDP is a "value added" measure of agricultural output that represents the gross value of output minus the value of purchased inputs such as fertilizer, pesticides, and machinery. Hence, these research intensity ratios are higher than, and not directly comparable with, other research intensity ratios that divide agricultural research spending by the *gross* value of output.

13. We estimate a research intensity of 5.43 percent for rich countries in 1994–96, when the total of public and private spending is used to form the measure, compared with 0.66 percent for poor countries.

14. Pioneer 2375 was the leading variety in Minnesota during the 1990s and was planted on nearly half the state's wheat acreage by the middle of the decade.

15. These same problems constrain the generation as well as the accumulation of knowledge. The effectiveness of science spending in developing new knowledge is also affected by the composition of funding (too many LDCs give scientists insufficient funds to plant or maintain field trials, properly stock laboratories, and so on), and the downtime doing research is often higher than in rich countries because of poorer communications and transport infrastructure and such. Lower (and many times "lost" or late) salaries also lower the quality of scientific staff that can be hired or retained.

16. Funding from aid agencies is subject to similar problems of myopia. Often grants are made on a project basis with funding cycles usually less than five years in duration (and often only two or three years).

17. These represent rapid, but, contrary to some claims, not entirely unprecedented rates of uptake of new genetic technologies. Double-cross hybrid maize

seed varieties are obtained by crossing two lines that have been "in-bred," or self-pollinated, for several generations. These in-bred lines are not especially productive, but when crossed to restore their hybrid vigor, some lines are produced that are markedly superior to the original varieties. Hybrids were first released for commercial use in the United States in the early 1930s. By 1940 more than 40 percent of the U.S. maize acreage was sown to hybrids, and by 1960 around 96 percent of the acreage was so planted (USDA, NASS 2001). Like the current crop of transgenic technologies, hybrid varieties are bred for and perform differently in different locations. Iowa's maize crop was 90 percent hybrid by 1940, but it took until 1951 for 90 percent of Kentucky's maize crop to be sown to hybrids (Griliches 1957).

18. According to data presented in James (2001), just four countries (Argentina, Canada, China, and the United States) and two transgenic technologies (*Bt*-induced insect resistance and herbicide tolerance) accounted for 99 percent of the world's transgenic cropping acreage in 2001, 68 percent of which was in the United States and 22 percent in Argentina. Of this global total, transgenic soybean varieties account for 63 percent, followed by maize (18 percent), cotton (13 percent), and canola (5 percent).

19. Marra (2001) reviews the evidence and discusses the difficulty of assessing the "with" and "without" technology situations, without including variations in other factors that also affect farmers' costs of production.

20. Indeed these technologies can address health concerns that have not been solved through conventional breeding.

21. The inadvertent use of genetically modified Starlink™ maize, which had been approved for use in animal feeds but not for human consumption, in some food products such as taco shells caused a considerable ruckus in 2000. However, the Centers for Disease Control and Prevention (CDC 2001) could not confirm the reported illnesses were a food-related reaction. Moreover, in follow-up tests, the Food and Drug Administration (FDA) determined that virtually none of the food samples obtained from people who complained of an allergic reaction actually contained any Starlink™ maize (Pollack 2001).

22. With pesticide-inherent crops, some pests with resistance may survive. By providing a portion of the field where susceptible pests can survive and mate with the resistant pests, the rate of resistance build-up is slowed.

23. There are other relevant forms of property protection that have an impact on biotechnology, most notably plant breeders' rights (PBRs), copyrights, and trade secrets (Binenbaum et al. 2003). PBRs are becoming increasingly prevalent. To be granted a PBR, an applicant must demonstrate that the variety is new, distinct from other varieties, and genetically uniform and stable through successive generations. The holders of a PBR have a legal monopoly over commercialization of their varieties for a prescribed length of time. Although the details of protection vary from country to country, in general, the sale, reproduction, and importation of new varieties of plants are encompassed. Under this scheme, use of plants for further breeding is unrestricted, and the progeny are eligible for PBR protection provided they are distinct from the parents (where distinctiveness may be, for example, a difference in flower color in a soybean, where flower color is irrelevant commercially). Thus, in contrast to a patent, utility or usefulness is not required for a PBR.

24. The crops include rice, wheat, maize, soybeans, cassava, coconut, ground-nuts, bananas, beans, potatoes, sorghum, lentils, millet, barley, and chickpeas.

CHAPTER 5 · HUNGER AND INSTITUTIONAL CHANGE

1. On local self-reliance see, for example, Lappé et al. (1998); on civil society concerns, see Salamon et al. (1999) and Bruyn (2000); and on globalization gen-erally, see Friedman (1999) and Barkin (2000). One of the most interesting debates relating to civil society concerns whether individuals have standing in relation to international trade rules, or whether their relationship to these rules must necessarily be mediated by their governments, many of which are not dem-ocratic. NGOs have sought to broaden recognition of individual rights, while strict "statists" have sought to limit these claims (Charnovitz 2001).

2. See Appendix D for a list of acronyms for a list of countries that are OECD members.

3. The expression was coined by A. K. Sen, whose arguments will be taken up in the sections below.

4. The effects of expanding product choices on consumer welfare in LDCs are more ambiguous (see James 2000).

5. See Kaul, Grunberg, and Stern (1999), Chen, Evans, and Cash (1999). Three recent treatments of international public goods related to food security also emphasize the challenges they pose. Kanbur and Sandler (1999), in an evaluation of development assistance policy, note that global public goods, including food security, cannot simply be supplied by charging individual nations for their "share," because problems of free riding on the actions of oth-ers abound, especially when the "spillovers" of benefits or costs across national boundaries are substantial. In an explicit treatment of food security issues, Paarlberg (2002) argues that only if national governments supply their own countries with needed public goods will global public goods dilemmas be resolved. Third, the 2002 State of Food and Agriculture report from FAO is devoted to "Agriculture and Global Public Goods Ten Years After the Earth Summit" (FAO 2002b).

6. The "assurance problem" is a game-theoretic construction that captures the basic notion of tit-for-tat: if I expect you to contribute to a public good (such as improving the neighborhood), I will too; if you don't, then I won't. It is often contrasted with the "prisoners' dilemma," where no matter whether I expect you to contribute or not, I won't. For an exposition in the context of global or inter-national public goods, see Sandler (1997) and Ferroni and Mody (2002); for a dis-cussion of fairness and public goods, see Runge (1984).

7. Economists' behavior may be a result of either preselection or socialization. In a set of experiments testing the "free rider hypothesis," Maxwell and Ames (1981, 309) found that economists were not concerned with fairness (justice) in contributing to public goods or, when asked what was fair, gave "complex, uncodable responses."

8. Rawls' theoretical conception was motivated in part by a technical argu-ment made some years earlier by Harsanyi (1955) and is in the tradition of Hume and other classical contractarians. In Rawls' application, individuals are behind

a "veil of ignorance" when deciding on rules of distribution. They do not know, when the veil is lifted, whether they will be rich or poor, or even in which generation they will live. Given this uncertainty, Rawls argues that they would find a "reflective equilibrium" based on two rules or principles: (1) a rule of equal division, and, in the event of unequal shares, (2) a rule in which provision would be made first for those who were worst off (the "difference principle") (Rawls 1971, 75).

9. Rather than strict adherence to Rawls' two principles, this has elsewhere been termed "fair-mindedness" (Runge 1984). For an exposition in the context of food aid and trade, see Runge (1977).

10. See Maggi (1999). It may be argued that the GATT/WTO rules do not rise to the level of Rawls' two principles, but they do capture a sense of "fair-mindedness" in the same sense as a "tit-for-tat" strategy. See Runge (1984) and Axelrod (1984).

11. For a comprehensive analysis, see Jackson (1997b).

12. Sen refers to the denial of opportunities to gain access to the benefits of an economy or society as "capability deprivation" (Sen 1999).

13. UNDP (1999b) focuses mainly on an interpretation of Von Hayek's (1991) support of markets as an example of "unintended consequences."

14. See UNDP (1999b), especially Chapter 5, 97–114.

15. For a statistical overview of gender gaps by country, see UNDP (1999b, Tables 25–28, 229–41).

16. For an excellent account of the "debacle in Seattle," see Odell (2000). See also Runge and Senauer (2000).

17. Berlin (1958) clearly felt that of the two, negative freedom was more fundamental to the maintenance of democratic societies and that positive freedom was more likely to be exploited in the name of a "higher rationality." In partial defense of an expanded role for positive freedom see Macpherson (1973).

18. See Trebilcock and Soloway (2000) for a discussion in the context of GM organisms, and Runge, Bagnara, and Jackson (2001).

19. As detailed in a recent review by Ostry (2000), the Third World Network is a selective list of the leading Asian NGOs with affiliates and links to activist/advocacy groups in North America and Europe. Asian NGOs, such as those based in Thailand and India, have been connected since 1995 to the South Centre in Geneva. African NGOs include the International South Group Network, based in Zimbabwe, and Seatini, with three African offices, funded by UNCTAD and several African governments. Seatini was established after the Singapore WTO ministerial meeting to provide research and analysis for African countries. Linking Asian and African NGOs is the Consumer Unity and Trust Society and the Centre for International Trade Economics and Environment. European-based NGOs include WEED, based in Germany, which is dedicated to training and consultancy for Southern NGOs, and the 92 Group, based in Denmark, a North/South Coalition concerned with the environment. The International Centre for Trade and Sustainable Development, established in Geneva in 1996 and jointly funded by governments and foundations, publishes *Bridges Weekly Trade Digest,* which provides comprehensive coverage on trade and trade-related issues. The Centre for International Environmental Law, established in Washington, D.C., in 1989 and in Geneva in 1995, provides training for Southern NGOs. Other train-

ing and research institutions are RONGEAD of France; INTRAC, ACTION AID, and CHRISTIAN AID of the United Kingdom.

20. For an extensive theoretical description and model of such structural and systemic interrelationships, see Rosenau (1990). An examination of state and civil society interrelationships based upon relative strengths is provided by Migdal (1988). And an example of assent and rejection mechanisms can be found in Rothchild and Chazan (1988).

21. See Farer (1995); Clark (1995); Brown (1991); Princen and Finger (1994); and Sikkink (1993).

22. For a full description of assumption differences, see Elswick (1996).

23. On this dimension see Scitovsky (1992) and Schelling (1978).

CHAPTER 6 · POLICIES AND INSTITUTIONS

1. Fan, Hazell, and Thorat (1999), for example, found that additional government spending on rural roads had the largest impact on reducing poverty and increasing productivity in Indian agriculture of all the forms of public investment they analyzed. Spending on agricultural R&D, education, and irrigation had less significant but still sizable poverty-reducing effects.

2. The same concern is raised in terms of public funding crowding out private funding for R&D, especially in the context of offering R&D tax concessions to firms, for instance, through expensing current R&D costs at rates greater than 100 percent or accelerated depreciation of R&D capital costs (Alston and Pardey 1999).

3. Though administered by Embrapa, the fund is open to all relevant Brazilian R&D institutions. There were four calls for proposals from 1997 to the end of 2000, resulting in 392 submissions, of which 46 were approved. Embrapa is the executing agency for two-thirds of the projects; about 13 percent are led by universities and 9 percent by state government agencies. The private sector participation is negligible.

4. Similar criticisms were leveled against the semi-dwarf gene technologies in rice and wheat that gave rise to the Green Revolution beginning in the 1960s (Hayami and Ruttan 1985, 329–45). The technologies tended to be taken up early on by bigger, more commercially oriented farmers, causing critics to view them as intrinsically biased against smallholder, subsistence producers—some of whom even now have yet to adopt improved seed varieties (notwithstanding the fact that semi-dwarf seeds may well have become the most widely adopted technologies by poor people in the history of mankind). While the profitability of a technology is a critical element in its success, there is a mountain of evidence that farmer education, access to credit, and physical and market infrastructures are also important determinants of adoption (Feder, Just, and Zilberman 1985; Feder and Umali 1993). To be sure, technology can substitute for a lack of some other factors critical to development, but it is better seen as part of a package.

5. Increasing amounts of the seed that embody these technologies are also subject to "plant breeders' rights", which restrict the communication of protected crop varieties but not their use for breeding purposes.

6. In addition to the options broached here, Nottenburg, Pardey, and Wright (2002) also discuss patent pooling, cross licensing, and merger or joint-venture arrangements.

7. In this regard it is also important to limit the negative environmental externality effects of agriculture, like excessive fertilizer runoff into waterways leading to eutrophication, soil erosion leading to silting, and the effects of pesticide and herbicide treatments on nontargeted pests and diseases.

8. Concerns about "genetic erosion" (loosely, a narrowing of the genetic resource base used by farmers or breeders for improving crop varieties) were raised by NRC, Committee on Genetic Vulnerability of Major Crops (1972) and Harlan (1972), among others.

9. These annual and in perpetuity estimates are sensitive to a number of factors, including the crop composition and size of the holdings and the number of samples distributed annually from the gene banks, the technology of germplasm storage, the rate of interest used to calculate the present value of distant future costs, and various conservation protocols (especially the frequency with which aging seed samples are tested for viability and regenerated when necessary to maintain the vigor and size of the sample). The $148 million conservation fund represents Koo, Pardey, and Wright's best estimate, but with plausible variations in two key factors (specifically, interest rates and regeneration cycles), the fund ranges from between $100 to $323 million.

10. The share of these 11 countries grew from 63 to 74 percent between 1993 and 1999. The countries and their share were: China (12 percent); Argentina (10 percent); Russia (9 percent); Mexico, Indonesia, and Brazil (7 percent each); Korea (6 percent); India (4 percent); Thailand and Turkey (3 percent each); and the Philippines (2 percent).

11. Recognizing the recent slow and uneven progress in dealing with poverty and agricultural development issues, the World Bank (2002a) and Pehu (2002) have drafted new strategies for rural development and science for agriculture, with the intent of reinvigorating funding for many of the sustainable, growth-oriented public goods for which we have argued in this volume. The extent to which the Bank will back these initiatives with additional, well-targeted funding is not clear as this book was being written.

12. For a general discussion of FAO and World Food Programme activities see White (1999).

13. See, for example, Walt (1998); Lucas et al. (1997); Raymond (1997); Peabody (1995); and Ermakov (1996).

14. See Runge (2001).

15. See Maggi (1999) and Bagwell and Staiger (1999). For a longer history of trade–environment interactions, see Pearson (2000).

16. The Global Environmental Facility was launched in 1991 as a three-year pilot program to allow for actions where no international agreement had yet been negotiated. It is jointly managed by the World Bank, UNEP, and UNDP. Its role was further elaborated at the 1992 Rio Conference, and it has complex links to the Biodiveristy and Climate Conventions, as well as to the Montreal Protocol. Its further role is, however, still the subject of debate among all of the organizations involved (see Piddington 1992). On environmental monitoring, see Wood, Sebastian, and Scherr (2000).

CHAPTER 7 · INVESTING FOR A HUNGER-FREE WORLD

1. Markets alone will not work properly for public goods, which economists refer to as "market failure," and will lead to underinvestment. Unlike private goods, which are consumed individually, the benefit of public goods, such as clean air, can be shared and, in fact, if they are true public goods, people cannot be excluded from enjoying their benefits. Therefore, their value is not what people are willing to pay for them individually, but what they are willing to pay collectively, hence the need for public and not private funding. For example, the value of cleaner air in a city is equal to the *sum* of what all the city's residents would be willing to pay. If each person would pay $50 and there are 1 million residents, the real value of cleaner air is $50 million. Moreover, since residents cannot be excluded from enjoying the benefits of cleaner air, they might just as soon let everyone else pay and avoid paying themselves. This problem, which economists refer to as the "free rider" is another reason for the necessity of public funding mechanisms.

2. The "doing well while doing good" or enlightened self-interest rationale for international aid is developed in Ruttan (1989), Tribe (1991), and Patterson (2002).

3. Lancaster (2000) puts the case for some radical reforms in U.S. aid institutions and policies, in part to more efficiently and effectively deliver international public goods. See Kreuger, Michalopoulos, and Ruttan (1989) and the references therein for earlier perspectives on U.S. aid policies and programs.

4. There are international and rich-country efforts to tackle bribery problems wherever they may occur. American citizens and firms operating abroad are subject to the U.S. Foreign Corrupt Practices Act of 1997, and 35 countries are signatory to the OECD Convention on Bribery (*The Economist* 2002d).

5. The economics of remittances have been studied by Lucas and Stark (1985), Cox (1987), and Rosenzweig (1988a). Kingma (1989), Posnett and Sandler (1986), and Smith, Kehoe, and Cremer (1995) analyze charitable giving.

6. Foreign aid and the international institutions, particularly the World Bank, have been widely criticized by both the political left and the right. For an "insiders" critical review of the Bank, see Easterly (2001).

APPENDIX B · INTERNATIONAL MODEL FOR POLICY ANALYSIS OF AGRICULTURAL COMMODITIES AND TRADE (IMPACT)—MODEL DESCRIPTION

1. The forecasts reported in this book are to 2025, benchmarked on data that are a three-year average centered on 1997. Previous IMPACT forecasts to 2020 using earlier configurations of the model and data benchmarked in earlier years are reported by Agcaoili-Sombilla and Rosegrant (1994), Delgado et al. (1999), Pinstrup-Andersen, Pandya-Lorch, and Rosegrant (1997), Rosegrant and Ringler (1997, 2000), and Rosegrant, Agcaoili-Sombilla, and Perez (1995).

REFERENCES

Abelson, R. 1999. Foundation turns focus on the poor. *New York Times*. December 12.

———. 2000a. Foundation giving is at $23 billion high. *New York Times*. March 29.

———. 2000b. New philanthropists put donations to work. *New York Times*. July 6.

Adams, M. R., and B. H. Hurd. 1999. Climate change and agriculture: Some regional implications. *Choices* 14 (1): 22–23.

Ades, A. F., and E. L. Glaeser. 1999. Evidence on growth: Increasing returns and extent of the market. *Quarterly Journal of Economics* 114 (3): 1025–46.

Adusei, E. O., and G. W. Norton. 1990. The magnitude of agricultural maintenance research in the USA. *Journal of Production Agriculture* 3 (January–March): 1–6.

Agcaoili-Sombilla, M., and M. W. Rosegrant. 1994. World supply and demand projections for cereals, 2020. 2020 Brief No. 2. Washington, D.C.: International Food Policy Research Institute.

Alex, G. 1997. *USAID and agricultural research—Review of USAID support for agricultural research, 1952-96.* Special Report No 3. Environmentally Sustainable Development Agricultural Research and Extension Group. Washington D.C.: World Bank.

Alston, J. M. 2002. Spillovers. *Australian Journal of Agricultural and Resource Economics* 46 (3): 315–46.

Alston, J. M., and P. G. Pardey. 1996. Current policy in a contemporary context. Chapter 8 in *Making science pay: The economics of agricultural R&D policy,* ed. J. M. Alston and P. G. Pardey. Washington D.C.: American Enterprise Institute.

———. 1999. The economics of agricultural R&D policy. Chapter 2 in *Paying for agricultural productivity,* ed. J. M. Alston, P. G. Pardey, and V. H. Smith. Baltimore: Johns Hopkins University Press for the International Food Policy Research Institute.

Alston, J. M., M. C. Marra, P. G. Pardey, and T. J. Wyatt. 2000. *A meta analysis of rates of return to agricultural R&D: Ex pede Herculem?* Research Report No. 113. Washington D.C.: International Food Policy Research Institute.

Altman, L. K. 2000. UN warning AIDS imperils Africa's youth. *New York Times.* June 29.

Anderson, J. R. 1998. Selected policy issues in international agricultural research: On striving for international public goods in an era of donor fatigue. *World Development* 26 (6): 1149–62.

Anderson, K., C. P. Nielson, S. Robinson, and K. Thierfelder. 2001. Estimating the global effects of GMOs. Chapter 4 in *The future of food: Biotechnology markets and policies in an international setting,* ed. P. G. Pardey. Washington, D.C.: International Food Policy Research Institute.

Anderson, K., J. Francois, T. W. Hertel, B. Hoekman, and W. Martin. 2000. *World trade liberalization for the new millennium: An empirical study.* Washington, D.C.: Brookings Institution.

Annan, K. 2001. Address to world economic forum. Davos, Switzerland, January 28, 2001. <http://www.un.org> accessed December 7, 2001.

Atack, I. 1999. Four criteria of development NGO legitimacy. *World Development* 27 (5): 855–64.

Axelrod, R. 1984. *The evolution of cooperation.* New York: Basic Books.

Bagwell, K., and R. W. Staiger. 1999. An economic theory of GATT. *American Economic Review* 215 (48): 258–306.

Bailey, R. 2001. Dr. Strangelunch, or: Why we should learn to stop worrying and love genetically modified food. *Reason* 32 (8): 2129.

Bank, D. 2001. Oracle CEO Ellison will decide which school gets millions. *The Wall Street Journal.* June 11.

Barkin, D. 2000. Overcoming the neoliberal paradigm: Sustainable popular development. In *Critical perspectives on globalization and neoliberalism in the developing countries,* ed. R. L. Harris and M. J. Seid. Leiden, the Netherlands: Brill Publishers.

Baum, W. C. 1986. *Partners against hunger: The Consultative Group for International Agricultural Research.* Washington, D.C.: World Bank.

BEA (Bureau of Economic Analysis). 2001. Current-dollar and "real" gross domestic product. Bureau of Economic Analysis, United States Chamber of Commerce. <http://www.bea.doc.gov/bea/dn/gdplev.xls.> accessed August 23, 2001.

Becker, E. 2002. Raising farm subsidies, U.S. widens international rift. *New York Times.* June 15.

Behrman, J. R., and A. B. Deolalikar. 1988. Health and nutrition. In *Handbook of development economics,* Vol. 1, ed. H. Chenery and T. N. Srinivasan. New York: North Holland.

Beintema, N. M., and P. G. Pardey. 2001. Recent developments in the conduct of Latin American agricultural research. Paper prepared for the International Conference on Agricultural Science and Technology, Beijing, November. <http://www.asti.cgiar.org/pubs-lac.htm>.

Beintema, N. M., A. F. D. Avila, and P. G. Pardey. 2001. *Agricultural R&D in Brazil: Policy, investments, and institutional profile.* Washington, D.C.: IFPRI, Embrapa, and FONTAGRO.

Berlin, I. 1958. Two concepts of liberty. Inaugural lecture delivered before the University of Oxford, October 31. Oxford, U.K.: Clarendon Press.

Beyers, L., Y. Ismaël, J. Piesse, and C. Thirtle. 2001. Can GM-technologies help the poor? The efficiency of Bt cotton adopters in the Makhathini flats of KwaZulu-Natal. Paper presented at Biotechnology and Rural Livelihood— Enhancing the Benefits, a consultation at the International Service for National Agricultural Research, The Hague, June.

Bhagwati, J. 2002. Coping with antiglobalization: A trilogy of discontents. *Foreign Affairs* (January/February): 2–7.

Bhalla, S. S. 2002. *Imagine there's no country: Poverty, inequality, and growth in the era of globalization.* Washington, D.C.: Institute for International Economics.

Bhatia, R., and M. Falkenmark. 1993. Water resource policies and the urban poor: Innovative approaches and policy imperatives. *Water and Sanitation Currents.* Washington, D.C.: United Nations Development Programme, World Bank Water and Sanitation Program, World Bank.

Bianco, A. 1999. Charity, the Buffet way. *Business Week.* October 25: 84–87.

Bill and Melinda Gates Foundation. 2001. *Annual report 2000.* <http://www. gatesfoundation.org> accessed June 10, 2001.

Binenbaum, E., C. Nottenburg, P. G. Pardey, B. D. Wright, and P. Zambrano. 2003. South-North trade, intellectual property jurisdictions, and freedom to operate in agricultural research on staple crops. *Economic Development and Cultural Change* 51 (2): 309–36.

Binswanger, H. P., and P. Landell-Mills. 1995. *The World Bank's strategy for reducing poverty and hunger: A report to the development community.* Environmentally Sustainable Development Studies and Monographs Series No. 4. Washington, D.C.: World Bank.

Bloom, R., D. E. Bloom, J. E. Cohen, and J. D. Sachs. 1999. Investing in the World Health Organization. *Science* 284 (5416): 911.

Borlaug, N. E. 2001. Feeding the world in the 21st century: The role of agricultural science and technology. Speech given at Tuskegee University, Alabama, April. <http://www.agbioworld.org> accessed May 1, 2001.

Bread for the World Institute. 1997. *Hunger in a global economy. Hunger 1998: Eighth Annual Report on the State of World Hunger.* Silver Spring, Md., U.S.A.: Bread for the World Institute.

Bread for the World Institute and NASFAM (National Smallholder Farmers Association of Malawi). 2000. Smallholder farmer household food security in Malawi: Final Report. Washington, D.C.: Bread for the World Institute.

Bread for the World Institute and UNAC (*Uniao Nacinal de Camponeses*). 2001. *Food security survey report.* Washington, D.C.: Bread for the World.

Briscoe, J. 2001. Two decades of change in a Bangladesh village. *Economic and Political Weekly* 36 (40). October 6, archived. <http//:www.ipw.org.in>.

Brooks, D. 2002. Why the U.S. will always be rich. *New York Times Magazine.* June 9: 88, 90–91, 124.

Brown, L. D. 1991. Bridging organizations and sustainable development. *Human Relations* 44 (8): 807–30.

Brown, L. R. 1973. The next crisis? Food. *Foreign Policy* 13 (Winter): 3–33.

———. 1995. *Who will feed china? Wake-up call for a small planet.* London: W. W. Norton.

Brown, P. 1999a. Reform at WHO is too slow, say critics. *British Medical Journal.* May 8: 1231.

———. 1999b. WHO steps closer to its responsibilities. *Nature* (March 18): 175.

Bruyn, S. T. H. 2000. *A civil economy: Transforming the market in the twenty-first century.* Ann Arbor, Mich.: University of Michigan Press.

Burnside, C., and D. Dollar. 2000. Aid, policies, and growth. *American Economic Review* 90 (4): 847–67.

Bush, G. 2002a. Policy in focus: Aid to developing nations. Speech on global development, Inter-American Development Bank, Washington, D.C., March 14. <http://www.Whitehouse.gov>.

———. 2002b. President proposes $5 billion plan to help developing nations. Remarks by the President on global development. Inter-American Development Bank. Washington, D.C., March 14, 2002.

Business World (the Philippines). 2000. UN agency pushes for food security amid economic crisis. October 25: 24.

Byerlee, D. 1996. Modern varieties, productivity, and sustainability: Recent experience and emerging challenges. *World Development* 24 (4): 697–718.

Byerlee, D., and P. Moya. 1993. *Impacts of international wheat breeding research in the developing world, 1966–90.* Mexico City: Centro Internacional de Mejoramiento de Maiz y Trigo (CIMMYT).

Cassman, K. G., D. C. Olk, and A. Dobermann. 1997. Scientific evidence of yield and productivity declines in irrigated rice systems of tropical and sub-tropical Asia. FAO International Rice Commission Newsletter No. 46: 7–18.

CDC (Centers for Disease Control and Prevention). 2001. Investigation of human health effects associated with potential exposure to genetically modified corn. A report to the U.S. Food and Drug Administration. Centers for Disease Control and Prevention, Atlanta, Ga., U.S.A.

CGIAR (Consultative Group on International Agricultural Research). 2001. The challenge of climate change: Poor farmers at risk. *Annual report 2000.* Washington D.C.: CGIAR.

Charnovitz, S. 2001. Rethinking WTO trade sanctions. *American Journal of International Law* 95 (4): 792–833.

Chen, T. C., T. G. Evans, and R. A. Cash. 1999. Health as a global public good. In *Global public goods: International cooperation in the 21st century.* New York: Oxford University Press for the United Nations Development Programme (UNDP).

Chrispeels, M. J., and D. E. Sadava, eds. 2002. *Plants, genes, and crop biotechnology,* 2nd ed. Boston: Jones and Bartlett.

Clark, A. M. 1995. Non-governmental organizations and their influence on international society. *Journal of International Affairs* 48 (2): 507–25.

Clark, J. 1991. *Democratizing for development: The role of voluntary organizations.* West Hartford, Conn., U.S.A.: Kumarian Press.

Conway, G. 1997. *The doubly green revolution: Food for all in the 21st century.* Ithaca, N.Y., U.S.A.: Cornell University Press.

Cox, D. 1987. Motives for private income transfers. *Journal of Political Economy* 95 (3): 508–46.

Dalrymple, D. G. 2000. The role of public agricultural research in international development. In *Warren E. Kronstad Honarary Symposium,* ed. R. Karow and

B. Reed. Special Report 1017. Corvallis, Ore., U.S.A.: Oregon State University Extension Service.

Dao, J. 2002. Two top officials offer stern talk on U.S. policy. *New York Times*. February 2.

————. 2003. With rise in foreign aid, plans for new way to give it. *New York Times*. February 3.

Darwin, R., M. Tsigas, J. Lewandrowski, and A. Raneses. 1995. *World agriculture and climate change. Economic adaptations*. Agricultural Economic Report No. 703. Washington, D.C.: U.S. Department of Agriculture.

Davis, C. G., C. Y. Thomas, and W. A. Amponsah. 2001. Globalization and poverty: Lessons from the theory and practice of food security. *American Journal of Agricultural Economics* 83 (3): 714–21.

Dawson, P. J., and R. Tiffin. 1998. Estimating the demand for calories in India. *American Journal of Agricultural Economics* 80 (August): 474–81.

Delgado, C. L., M. W. Rosegrant, H. Steinfeld, S. Ehui, and C. Courbois. 1999. *Livestock to 2020. The next food revolution*. 2020 Vision for Food, Agriculture, and the Environment Discussion Paper No. 28. Washington, D.C.: International Food Policy Research Institute.

Diao, X., A. Somwaru, and T. Roe. 2001. A global analysis of agricultural reform in WTO member countries. Chapter 1 in *Agricultural policy reform and the WTO: The road ahead*. Economic Research Service Report 802. Washington, D.C.: U.S. Department of Agriculture.

Díaz-Bonilla, E., M. Thomas, and S. Robinson. 2002. Trade liberalization, WTO, and food security. TMD Discussion Paper No. 82. Washington, D.C.: International Food Policy Research Institute.

Díaz-Bonilla, E., S. Robinson, M. Thomas, and Y. Yanoma. 2002. WTO, agriculture, and developing countries: A survey of issues. Washington, D.C.: TMD Discussion Paper No. 81. International Food Policy Research Institute.

Dollar, D., and A. Kraay. 2002. Spreading the wealth. *Foreign Affairs* 81 (1): 120–33.

Downing, T. E. 1993. The effects of climate change on agriculture and food security. *Renewable Energy* 3 (4/5): 491–97.

Dugger, C. W. 2000. India tries to reassess its measure of poverty. *New York Times*. October 8: 5A.

Dyson, T. 1998. World food trends and prospects to 2025. Presented at the National Academy of Science Colloquium, Plants and Population: Is There Time? University of California at Irvine, December 5–6.

Easter, K. W., M. W. Rosegrant, and A. Dinar. 1998. The future of water markets: A realistic perspective. In *Markets for water: Potential and performance*, ed. K. Easter, M. W. Rosegrant, and A. Dinar. Boston: Kluwer Academic Publishers.

Easterly, W. 2001. *The elusive quest for growth*. Cambridge, Mass., U.S.A.: MIT Press.

The Economist. 1998a. Philanthropy in America: The gospel of wealth. May 30. <http://www.economist.com> accessed September 4, 1999.

————. 1998b. Repositioning the WHO: The World Health Organization is about to be given a much-needed kick in the backside. May 9: 79–82.

————. 1999a. FAO: Harvesting votes. May 15: 48.

————. 1999b. Why Greens should love trade. October 9: 18.

———. 2001a. The new wealth of nations (special survey supplement). June 16: 3–4.

———. 2001b. Patches of light. June 9: 69–72.

———. 2001c. A triumph of experience over hope. May 26: 79.

———. 2002a. Blowing hot and cold. Special supplement: How many planets? A survey of the global environment. July 6: 9–11.

———. 2002b. The great race. July 6: 3–5.

———. 2002c. Hunger: Always with us. June 15: 73–74.

———. 2002d. The short arm of the law. March 2: 63–65.

Edwards, M., and D. Hulme, eds. 1996. *Beyond the magic bullet.* Hartford, Conn., U.S.A.: Kumarian Press.

Ehrlich, P. R. 1968. *The population bomb.* New York: Ballantine Books.

Eicher, C. K. 2001. Africa's unfinished business: Building sustainable agricultural research systems. Department of Applied Economics Staff Paper 01-10. East Lansing: Michigan State University.

Elswick, L. 1996. The World Food Summit: Perspectives from civil society. *Development* 4: 62–69.

Epstein, P. R. 2000. Is global warming harmful to health? *Scientific American* 283 (2): 50–57.

Ermakov, V. 1996. Reform of the World Health Organization. *Lancet* 347 (9014): 1536–38.

Esty, D. C. 1994. *Greening the GATT: Trade environment and the future.* Washington, D.C.: Institute for International Economics.

Evans, L. T. 1998. *Feeding the ten billion: Plants and population growth.* Cambridge, U.K.: Cambridge University Press.

Evenson, R. E. 2000. *Crop genetic improvements and agricultural development.* Washington, D.C.: Consultative Group on International Agricultural Research.

Evenson, R. E., and M. W. Rosegrant. 1995. Productivity projections for commodity marketing modeling. Paper presented at the final workshop of the International Cooperative Research Project "Projections and Policy Implications of Medium and Long-Term Rice Supply and Demand," organized by IFPRI, International Rice Research Institute (IRRI), and the China Council on Economic Research; Beijing, China, April 23–26.

Evenson, R. E., C. E. Pray, and M. W. Rosegrant. 1999. *Agricultural research and productivity growth in India.* Research Report No. 109. Washington, D.C.: International Food Policy Research Institute.

Fan, S., P. Hazell, and S. Thorat. 1999. *Linkages between government spending, growth, and poverty in rural India.* IFPRI Research Report No. 110. Washington, D.C.: International Food Policy Research Institute.

Fan, S., L. Zhang, and X. Zhang. 2002. *Growth, inequality, and poverty in rural China: The role of public investments.* Research Report No. 125. Washington, D.C.: International Food Policy Research Institute.

FAO (Food and Agriculture Organization of the United Nations). 1996a. *Rome declaration on world food security and World Food Summit plan of action.* Rome: FAO.

———. 1996b. *The sixth world food survey.* Rome: FAO.

———. 1997. *Reforming FAO: The challenge of food security.* Rome: FAO.

————. 1998. *The state of the world's plant genetic resources for food and agriculture.* Rome: FAO.

————. 1999a. *The state of food insecurity in the world: 1999.* Rome: FAO.

————. 1999b. *The strategic framework for FAO 2000 2015.* Rome: FAO.

————. 2000a. *Agriculture: Towards 2015/30,* Technical Interim Report. Rome: FAO.

————. 2000b. FAO ready to face challenges of new millennium, says FAO director general. Press Release, July 7. Rome: FAO.

————. 2000c. *FAOSTAT database.* <http://www.apps.fao.org>.

————. 2000d. *Food Outlook.* Global information and early warning system on food and agriculture, Commodities and Trade Division (ESC), Rome: FAO.

————. 2000e. *Reforming FAO: Into the new millennium.* Rome: FAO.

————. 2000f. *The state of food insecurity in the world: 2000.* Rome: FAO.

————. 2001a. FAO sets up trust fund for food security. *News & Highlights,* Food and Agriculture Organization of the United Nations, July 17. <http://www.fao.org/News/2001/010704-e.htm> accessed July 2002.

————. 2001b. FAOSTAT database. <http://www.apps.fao.org> accessed July 2001, last updated by FAO May 2001.

————. 2001c. FAOSTAT database. <http://www.apps.fao.org> accessed April 2002, last updated by FAO December 2001.

————. 2002a. *Anti-hunger programme: Reducing hunger through agricultural and rural development and wider access to food.* Rome: FAO.

————. 2002b. *The state of food and agriculture: Agriculture and global public goods ten years after the earth summit.* Rome: FAO.

Farer, T. 1995. New players in the old game: The defacto expansion of standing to participate in global security negotiations. *American Behavioral Scientist* (38) 6: 843–54.

Feder, G., and D. L. Umali. 1993. The adoption of agricultural innovations: A review. *Technological Forecasting and Social Change* 43 (3/4): 215–39.

Feder, G., R. E. Just, and D. Zilberman. 1985. Adoption of agricultural innovations in developing countries: A survey. *Economic Development and Cultural Change* 33 (2): 255–98.

Ferroni, M., and A. Mody, eds. 2002. *International public goods: Incentives, measurements, and financing.* Dordrecht: Kluwer Academic Publishers for the World Bank.

Filmer, D., and L. Pritchett. 1999. The effects of wealth on education attainment: Evidence from 35 countries. *Population and Development Review* 25 (1): 85–120.

Finger, J. M., and P. Schuler. 2000. Implementation of Uruguay round commitment: The development challenge. *The World Economy* 23 (4): 511–25.

Fogel, R. W. 1994. Economic growth, population theory, and physiology: The bearing of long-term processes on the making of economic policy. *American Economic Review* 84 (3): 369–95.

Foulkes, G. (M.P.) Parliamentary Under Secretary of State, Department of International Development, United Kingdom. 1999. FAO into the twenty-first century. Address to the 30th General Conference of FAO. Rome. November.

Fowler, C. 1994. *Unnatural selection: Technology, politics, and plant evolution.* Yverdon, Switzerland: Gordon and Breach Scientific Publishers S.A.

Frankel, J. A., and D. Romer. 1999. Does trade growth cause growth? *American Economic Review* 89 (3): 379–99.

Friedman, T. L. 1999. *The Lexus and the olive tree.* New York: Farrar, Straus, and Coiroux.

Gopalan, C., B. V. Rama Sastri, and S. C. Bala Subramanian. 1971. *Tables of food composition of Indian Foods.* Hyderbad, India: National Institute of Nutrition.

Graff, G., A. Bennett, B. Wright, and D. Zilberman. 2001. *Intellectual property clearinghouse mechanisms for agriculture.* IP Strategy Today No. 3–2001. <http://www.bioDevelopments.org/ip>.

Griliches, Z. 1957. Hybrid corn: An exploration in the economics of technological change. *Econometrica* (25) 4: 501–22.

Gryseels G., and J. R. Anderson. 1991. International agricultural research. Chapter 9 in P. G. Pardey, J. Roseboom, and J. R. Anderson, eds., *Agricultural research policy: International quantitative perspectives.* Cambridge, U.K.: Cambridge University Press.

The Guardian. 2002. FAO asks rich nations to stop agriculture subsidies. June 11: 18.

Haddad, L., J. Hoddinott, and H. Alderman. 1997. *Intrahousehold resource allocation in developing countries: Models, methods, and policy.* Baltimore, Md., U.S.A.: Johns Hopkins University Press for the International Food Policy Research Institute.

Hardin, G. J. 1977. *The limits of altruism: An ecologist's view of survival.* Bloomington, Ind., U.S.A.: Indiana University Press.

Harlan, J. R. 1972. Genetics of disaster. *Journal of Environmental Quality* 1 (3): 212–15.

Harriss, B. 1991. The intrafamily distribution of hunger in South Asia. In *The political economy of hunger,* Vol. 1, ed. J. Dreze and A. K. Sen. New York: Oxford University Press.

Harsanyi, J. 1955. Cardinal welfare, individualistic ethics, and interpersonal comparisons of utility. *Journal of Political Economy* 63: 309–21.

Hayami, Y., and V. W. Ruttan. 1985. *Agricultural development: An international perspective.* Baltimore, Md., U.S.A.: Johns Hopkins University Press.

Hazell, P. B. R., and C. Ramasamy. 1991. *The Green Revolution reconsidered: The impact of high-yielding rice varieties in South India.* Baltimore, Md., U.S.A.: Johns Hopkins University Press for the International Food Policy Research Institute.

Heim, M. N., and L. L. Blackslee. 1986. Biological adaptations and research impacts on wheat yields in Washington. Paper presented at the American Agricultural Economics Association Annual Meetings, Reno, Nevada.

Heisey, P. W., M. Lantican, and H. J. Dubin. 1999. Assessing the benefits of international wheat breeding research: An overview of the global wheat impacts study. Part 2 in *CIMMYT 1998–99 world wheat facts and trends: Global wheat research in a changing world: Challenges and achievements,* ed. P. L. Pingali Mexico City: Centro Internacional de Mejoramiento de Maiz y Trigo (CIMMYT).

Herdt, R. 1999. Enclosing the global plant genetic commons. Paper presented to the China Center for Economic Research. Rockefeller Foundation. New York, May 24.

Hoekman, B., and K. Anderson. 1999. *Developing country agriculture and the new trade agenda.* Policy Research Working Paper 2125. Washington, D.C.: World Bank.

Hopper, G. R. 1999. Changing food production and quality of diet in India: 1947-98. *Population and Development Review* (25) 3: 443-77.

Hudec, R. E. 1987. *Developing countries in the GATT legal system.* London: Trade Policy Research Centre.

IFAD (International Fund for Agricultural Development). 2002. About IFAD. <http://www.ifad.org>.

IFPRI (International Food Policy Research Institute). 2000. AIDS mushrooms into a development crisis. *2020 Vision News and Views.* December.

———. 2001a. *A better world in 2020. Wake-up calls from the next generation.* Washington, D.C.: IFPRI.

———. 2001b. Vision document. Washington, D.C.: IFPRI.

International Financial Institution Advisory Commission. 2000. International financial institutions reform: Report of the International Financial Institution Advisory Commission, March 2000.

Jackson, J. H. 1992. World trade rules and environmental policies: Congruence or conflict? *Washington and Lee Law Review* 49 (4): 1227-78.

———. 1997a. The great sovereignty debate: United States' acceptance and implementation of the Uruguay Round results. *Columbia Journal of Transnational Law* 36: 157-88.

———. 1997b. *The world trading system: Law and policy of international economic relations,* 2nd ed. Cambridge, Mass.: MIT Press.

Jackson, L. 2000. Agricultural biotechnology and the privatization of genetic information: Implications for innovation and equity. Paper prepared for the 8th biennial conference of the International Association for the Study of Common Property, Bloomington, Ind., U.S.A. Indiana University, May 31–June 4.

James, C. 2001. *Global review of commercialized transgenic crops: 2000.* ISAAA Brief No. 23. Ithaca, N.Y., U.S.A.: International Service for the Acquisition of Agri-Biotech Applications.

James, J. 2000. *Consumption, globalization and development.* London: Macmillan.

Jefferson, R. A. 2001. Transcending transgenics: Are their babies in the bathwater or is that a dorsal fin? Chapter 5 in *The future of food: Biotechnology markets and policies in an international setting,* ed. P. G. Pardey. Washington, D.C.: International Food Policy Research Institute.

Johnson, D. G. 1975. *World food problems and prospects.* Foreign Affairs Study No. 20. Washington, D.C.: American Enterprise Institute.

———. 1998. The growth of demand will limit output growth for food over the next quarter century. Presented at the National Academy of Science Colloquium, Plants and Population: Is There Time?, at the University of California at Irvine, December 5-6.

Josling, T. 1999. The WTO and its potential role in GMO regulations. In *The economics and politics of genetically modified organisms in agriculture: Implications for WTO 2000.* Bulletin 809, November. Urbana-Champaign, Ill., U.S.A.: University of Illinois.

Juma, C. 2000. The perils of centralizing global environmental governance. *Environment Matters.* Annual Review. Washington, D.C.: World Bank.

Kanbur, R., and T. Sandler (with K. M. Morrison). 1999. *The future of development assistance: Common pools and international public goods.* Policy Essay No. 25. Washington, D.C.: Overseas Development Council.

Kasler, D., and E. Lau. 2000. At Calgene, a harvest of uncertainty. *Sacramento Bee,* May 7. <http://www.sacbee.com/news/projects/biotechnology/> accessed June 15, 2001.

Kassouf, A. L., and B. Senauer. 1996. Direct and indirect effects of parental education on malnutrition among children: A full income approach. *Economic Development and Cultural Change* 44 (4): 817–38.

Kaul, I., I. Grunberg, and M. A. Stern. 1999. Defining global public goods. In *Global public goods: International cooperation in the 21st century,* ed. I. Kaul, I. Grunberg, and M. A. Stern. New York: Oxford University Press for the United Nations Development Programme.

Keller, B. 2002. Pollyanna meets Cassandra. *New York Times.* June 1.

Kendall, H. W., and D. Pimentel. 1994. Constraints on the expansion of the global food supply. *Ambio* 23 (3): 198–205.

Kickbusch, I. 2000. The development of international health policies—Accountability intact? *Social Science and Medicine* 51 (6): 11.

Kingma, B. R. 1978. An accurate measurement of the crowd-out effect, income effect, and price effect for charitable contributions. *Journal of Political Economy* 97: 1197–1207.

———. 1989. An accurate measurement of the crowd-out effect, income effect, and price effect for charitable contributions. *Journal of Political Economy* 97: 1197–1207.

Koo, B., P. G. Pardey, and B. D. Wright. 2002. *Endowing future harvests: The long-term costs of conserving genetic resources at the CGIAR centers.* Rome: International Plant Genetic Resources Institute.

Korten, D. C. 1987. Third generation NGO strategies: A key to people-centered development. *World Development* 15 (supplement): 145–59.

———. 1990. *Getting to the 21st century: Voluntary action and the global agenda.* West Hartford, Conn., U.S.A.: Kumarian Press.

———. 1995. *When corporations rule the world.* West Hartford, Conn., U.S.A.: Kumerian Press.

Kreuger, A. O., C. Michalopoulos, and V. W. Ruttan. 1989. *Aid and development.* Baltimore, Md., U.S.A.: Johns Hopkins University Press.

Kryder, R. D., S. P. Kowalski, and A. F. Krattinger. 2000. *The intellectual and technical property components of pro-vitamin A rice (GoldenRice™): A preliminary freedom-to-operate review.* ISAAA Brief No. 20. Ithaca, N.Y., U.S.A.: International Service for the Acquisition of Agri-Biotech Applications.

Kuchinsky, M. 2000. Increasing food security equity—The case for NGOs. Bread for the World, Washington, D.C. (mimeo).

Lancaster, C. 2000. *Transforming foreign aid: United States assistance in the 21st century.* Washington D.C.: Institute for International Economics.

Lanjouw, J. O. 2001. A patent proposal for global diseases. In *Annual World Bank conference on development economics,* ed. B. Pleskovic and N. Stern. Washington, D.C.: World Bank.

Lappé, F. M., J. Collins, and P. Rosset, with L. Esparza. 1998. *World hunger: 12 myths.* New York: Grove Press.

Lewin, T. 2001a. Foundation grants surged last year despite slow economy. *New York Times*. March 27.

———. 2001b. U.S. gifts to charity topped $203 billion in 2000, study says. *New York Times*. May 24.

Lindert, P. 2000. *Shifting ground: The changing agricultural soils of China and Indonesia*. Cambridge, Mass., U.S.A.: MIT Press.

Lipton, M. L., with R. Longhurst. 1989. *New seeds and poor people*. Baltimore: Johns Hopkins University Press.

Los Angeles Times. 2000. Panel recommends curbs on IMF, World Bank; Report: Congressional Commission seeks end to long term lending. Critics call proposals "devastating." March 9.

Lucas A., S. Mogedal, G. Walt, S. Hodne Steen, S. E. Kruse, K. Lee, and L. Hawken. 1997. *Cooperation for health development: The World Health Organization's support to programmes at the country level: Synthesis report*. London: London School of Hygiene and Tropical Medicine.

Lucas, R., and O. Stark. 1985. Motivations to remit: Evidence from Botswana. *Journal of Political Economy* 93 (5): 901–18.

Luke, D. F. 2000. OAU/AEC member states, the Seattle preparatory process and Seattle: A personal reflection. *Journal of World Trade* 34 (3): 39–46.

Mach, A. 1998. The new WHO commit to making a difference. *British Medical Journal* 317 (7154): 302.

Macpherson, C. B. 1973. *Democratic theory: Essays in retrieval*. Oxford: Clarendon Press.

Maddison, A. 2001. *The world economy: A millennial perspective*. Paris: OECD Development Centre.

Maggi, G. 1999. The role of multilateral institutions in international trade cooperation. *American Economic Review* 89 (1): 190–214.

Malthus, T. R. 1992. *An essay on the principle of population*, 5th ed. London: J. Murray (reprint of original 1817 publication).

Maredia, M., and D. K. Byerlee. 2000. Efficiency of research investments in the presence of international spillovers: Wheat research in developing countries. *Agricultural Economics* 22 (1): 1–16.

Marra, M. 2001. Agricultural biotechnology: A critical review of the impact evidence to date. In *The future of food: Biotechnology markets and policies in an international setting*, ed. P.G. Pardey. Washington, D.C.: International Food Policy Research Institute.

Marshall, E. 1998. Private help for a public database? *Science* 280 (5364): 667–68.

Martindale, D., and P. H. Gleick. 2001. How we can do it. Special edition on safeguarding our water. *Scientific American* (February): 38–55.

Maxwell, G., and R. Ames. 1981. Economists free ride, does anyone else? Experiments in the provision of public goods IV. *Journal of Public Economics* 15 (3): 295–310.

Maxwell, S. 1996. Food security: A post-modern perspective. *Food Policy* 21 (2): 155–70.

Mazur, J. 2000. Labor's new internationalism. *Foreign Affairs* 79 (1): 79–93.

McCalla, A. F., and C. L. Revoredo. 2001. Prospects for global food security: A critical appraisal of past projections and predictions. 2020 Food, Agriculture, and

Environment Discussion Paper No. 35. Washington, D.C.: International Food Policy Research Institute.

Measham, A. R., and M. Chatterjee. 1999. *Wasting away: The crisis in malnutrition in India*. Washington, D.C.: World Bank.

Meinzen-Dick, R., and S. M. Sullins. 1994. Water markets in Pakistan: Participation and productivity. Environment and Production Technology Division Discussion Paper No. 4. Washington, D.C.: International Food Policy Research Institute.

Mellor, J. W. 1999. Faster more equitable growth: The relation between growth in agriculture and poverty reduction. Consulting Assistance on Economic Reform II, Conference on Development Assistance in the Twenty-First Century: Challenging the Conventional Wisdom on Assistance and Development, at Harvard Institute for International Development, Cambridge, Mass., U.S.A., September 30–October 1.

Meltzer, A. H., and A. Lerrick. 2000. What the World Bank ought to be doing. *Washington Post,* April 11.

Mena, J., and R. Sanders. 1998. Swiss pharmaceutical company Novartis commits $25 million to support biotechnology research at U.C. Berkeley. University of California, Berkeley, Public Affairs News Release (November 23).

Mendelsohn, R., W. D. Nordhaus, and D. Shaw. 1994. The impact of global warming on agriculture: A Ricardian analysis. *American Economic Review* 84 (4): 753–71.

Messina, W. A., Jr., and J. L. Seale, Jr. 1990. U.S. sugar policy: A welfare analysis of policy options under pending Caribbean Basin Expansion Act Legislation. Staff Paper 382. Gainesville, Fla., U.S.A.: University of Florida, Food and Resource Economics Department, March.

Michalopoulos, C. 1999. Developing country strategies for the Millennium Round. *Journal of World Trade* 33 (5): 1–30.

Migdal, J. S. 1988. *Strong societies and weak states: State-society relations and state capabilities in the Third World.* Princeton, N.J., U.S.A.: Princeton University Press.

Milanovic, B. 2002. True world income distribution 1988 and 1993: First calculation based on household surveys alone. *Economic Journal* 112 (476): 51–92.

Millimet, R. M. 1995. The impact of the Uruguay Round and the new agreement on sanitary and phytosanitary measures. *Transnational Law and Contemporary Problems* 5: 449–92.

Morris, M., J-M. Ribaut, M. Khairallah, and K. Dreher. 2001. Potential impacts of biotechnology-assisted selection on plant breeding programs in developing countries. In *The future of food: Biotechnology markets and policy in an international setting,* ed. P. G. Pardey. Washington, D.C.: International Food Policy Research Institute.

NAS (National Academy of Sciences). 2000. *Transgenic plants and world agriculture.* Washington, D.C.: National Academy Press.

New York Times. 1999. Globalization vs. nature. November 22.

New York Times. 2002. The specter of starvation. June 15.

Newberry, D. M. G., and J. E. Stiglitz. 1981. *The theory of commodity price stabilization: A study in the economics of risk.* Oxford: Clarendon Press.

Nickum, J.E. 1994. Beijing's maturing socialist water economy. In *Metropolitan water use conflicts in Asia and the Pacific,* ed. J. E. Nickum and K. W. Easter. East-West Center and United Nations Centre for Regional Development. Oxford: Westview Press.

Nottenburg, C., P. G. Pardey, and B. D. Wright. 2002. Accessing other peoples' technologies for non-profit research. *Australian Journal of Agricultural and Resource Economics* 46 (3): 389–416.

NRC (National Research Council). 2000. *Genetically modified pest-protected plants: Science and regulation.* Washington, D.C.: National Academy Press. <http://www.nap.edu/books/0309069300/html/index.html >.

NRC (National Research Council), Board on Agriculture and Natural Resources. 1999. *Our common journey: A transition toward sustainability.* Washington, D.C.: National Academy Press.

———. 2000. *Genetically modified pest-protected plants: Science and regulation.* Washington, D.C.: National Academy Press.

NRC (National Research Council), Committee on Genetic Vulnerability of Major Crops. 1972. *Genetic vulnerability of major crops.* Washington, D.C.: National Academy of Sciences.

Odell, J. S. 2000. The Seattle impasse and its implications for the World Trade Organization. Paper presented at the conference The Political Economy of International Trade, University of Minnesota, St. Paul, Minn., U.S.A., September 15–16.

OECD (Organisation of Economic Co-Operation and Development), Development Assistance Committee. n.d. <http://www.oecd.org/dac/htm/online.htm#dac/o> accessed July 2001.

Ostry, S. 2000. The Uruguay Round as a grand bargain between "North" and "South." Paper presented at the conference The Political Economy of International Trade, University of Minnesota, St. Paul, Minn., U.S.A., September 15–16. Mimeo.

Oweis, T., A. Hachum, and J. Kijne. 1999. *Water harvesting and supplementary irrigation for improved water use efficiency in dry areas.* SWIM Paper 7. Colombo, Sri Lanka: International Water Management Institute.

Paarlberg, R. 1999. The weak link between world food markets and world food security. In *Policy reform, market stability and food security,* ed. R. Paarlberg and T. Roe. St. Paul, Minn., U.S.A.: International Agricultural Trade Research Consortium, Department of Applied Economics, University of Minnesota.

———. 2002. Governance and food security in an age of globalization. 2020 Food, Agriculture and the Environment. Discussion Paper No. 36. Washington, D.C.: International Food Policy Research Institute.

Pardey, P. G. 2001. Biotechnology markets and policies—Overview. Chapter 1 in *The future of food: Biotechnology markets and policies in an international setting,* ed. P. G. Pardey. Washington, D.C.: International Food Policy Research Institute.

Pardey, P. G., and N. M. Beintema. 2001. *Slow magic: Agricultural R&D a century after Mendel.* Food Policy Report. Washington, D.C.: International Food Policy Research Institute.

Pardey, P. G., J. Roseboom, and N. Beintema. 1997. Investments in African agricultural research. *World Development* 25 (3): 409–23.

Pardey, P. G., J. Roseboom, and B. J. Craig. 1992. A yardstick for international comparisons: An application to national agricultural research expenditures. *Economic Development and Cultural Change* 40 (2): 333–49.

Pardey, P. G., J. M. Alston, C. Chan-Kang, E. C. Magalhães, and S. A. Vosti. 2002. Assessing and attributing the benefits from varietal improvement research: Evidence from Embrapa, Brazil. Environment and Production Technology Division Discussion Paper No. 95. Washington, D.C.: International Food Policy Research Institute.

Patterson, O. 2002. Beyond compassion: Selfish reasons for being unselfish. *Daedalus: Journal of the American Academy of Arts and Sciences* 131 (1): 26–38.

Peabody, J. W. 1995. An organizational analysis of the World Health Organization: Narrowing the gap between promise and performance. *Social Science and Medicine* 40 (6): 731–43.

Pearson, C. S. 2000. *Economics and the global environment.* Cambridge, U.K.: Cambridge University Press.

Pehu, E. 2002. *Investing in science for agriculture and rural development in the 21st century: Challenges, issues and options.* Task Force on Science & Technology in Securing Food in the 21st Century, Agriculture and Rural Development Working Paper. Washington, D.C.: World Bank.

Perlez, J. 2001. U.N. chief calls on U.S. companies to donate to AIDS Fund. *New York Times.* June 2

Piddington, K. 1992. The role of the World Bank. In *The institutional politics of the environment: Actors, interests and institutions,* ed. A. Hurrell and B. Kingsbury. Oxford: Clarendon Press.

Pielke, R. A. Jr. 2001. Room for doubt. *Nature* 410: 151.

Pingali, P. L., and P. W. Heisey. 2001. Cereal-crop productivity in developing countries: Past trends and future prospects. Chapter 5 in *Agricultural science policy: Changing global agendas,* ed. J. M. Alston, P. G. Pardey, and M. J. Taylor. Baltimore: Johns Hopkins University Press for the International Food Policy Research Institute.

Pinstrup-Andersen, P., and R. Pandya-Lorch. 1995. *Agricultural growth is the key to poverty alleviation in low-income countries.* 2020 Brief No. 15. Washington, D.C.: International Food Policy Research Institute.

Pinstrup-Andersen, P., D. Nygaard, and A. Ratta. 1995. *The right to food: Widely accepted and poorly protected.* 2020 Brief 22. Washington, D.C.: International Food Policy Research Institute.

Pinstrup-Andersen, P., R. Pandya-Lorch, and M. W. Rosegrant. 1997. *The world food situation: Recent developments, emerging issues, and long-term prospects.* Food Policy Report. Washington, D.C.: International Food Policy Research Institute.

———. 1999. *World food prospects: Critical issues for the early twenty-first century.* Food Policy Report. Washington, D.C.: International Food Policy Research Institute.

Pistorius, R. 1997. *Scientists, plants and politics: A history of the plant genetic resources movement.* Rome: International Plant Genetic Resources Institute.

Plucknett, D. L., N. J. H. Smith, and S. Ozgediz. 1990. *Networking in international agricultural research.* Ithaca, N.Y., U.S.A.: Cornell University Press.

Pollack, A. 2001. No altered corn found in allergy samples. *New York Times.* July 11.

Posnett, J., and T. Sandler. 1986. Joint supply and the finance of charitable activity. *Public Finance Quarterly* 14 (2): 209–22.

Postel, S. 1992. *Last oasis: Facing water scarcity.* The World Watch Environmental Alert Series. New York: W. W. Norton.

———. 1999. *Pillar of sand. Can the irrigation miracle last?* New York: W. W. Norton.

Pray, C. E., J. Huang, D. Ma, and F. Qiao. 2001. Impact of Bt cotton in China. *World Development* 29 (5): 813–25.

Princen, T., and M. Finger. 1994. *Environmental NGOs in world politics: Linking the local and the global.* London: Rutledge.

Program on International Policy Attitudes. 2001. Americans on foreign aid and world hunger: A study of U.S. public attitudes. Center for the Study of Policy Attitudes and the Center for International and Security Studies. University of Maryland, College Park, Md., U.S.A.

Qaim, M. 1998. *Transgenic virus resistant potatoes in Mexico: Potential socioeconomic implications of north-south biotechnology transfer.* Brief No. 7. Ithaca, N.Y., U.S.A.: International Service for the Acquisition of Agri-Biotech Applications.

Quisumbing, A. R., and J. A. Maluccio. 2000. Intrahousehold allocation and gender relations: New empirical evidence from four developing countries. Food Consumption and Nutrition Division Discussion Paper No. 84. Washington, D.C.: International Food Policy Research Institute.

Quisumbing, A. R., L. R. Brown, H. S. Feldstein, L. Haddad, and C. Peña. 1995. *Women: The key to food security.* Food Policy Report. Washington, D.C.: International Food Policy Research Institute.

Rausser, G. 1999. Public/private alliances. *AgBioForum* 2 (1): 5–10.

Rawls, J. 1971. *A theory of justice.* Oxford: Clarendon Press.

Raymond, S. 1997. *Global public health collaboration: Organizing for a time of renewal.* New York: New York Academy of Sciences.

Reilly, J. 1999a. What does climate change mean for agriculture in developing countries? A comment on Mendelsohn and Dinar. *World Bank Research Observer* 14 (2): 295–305.

———. 1999b. Climate change: Can agriculture adapt? *Choices* 14 (1): 4–8.

Roberts, A. 2001. NGOs: New gods overseas. In *The World in 2001.* London: The Economist Publications.

Rosegrant, M. W., and X. Cai. 2001. Water scarcity and food security: Alternative futures for the 21st century. *Journal of Water Science and Technology* 43 (4): 61–70.

Rosegrant, M. W., and P. B. R. Hazell. 2000. *Transforming the rural Asian economy: The unfinished revolution.* Oxford: Oxford University Press.

Rosegrant, M. W., and C. Ringler. 1997. World food markets into the 21st century: Environmental and resource constraints and policies. *Australian Journal of Agricultural and Resource Economics* 41 (3): 401–28.

———. 2000. Asian economic crisis and the long-term global food situation. *Food Policy* 25 (3): 243–54.

Rosegrant, M. W., M. Agcaoili-Sombilla, and N. D. Perez. 1995. *Global food projec-*

tions to 2020: Implications for investment. 2020 Discussion Paper No. 5. Washington, D.C.: International Food Policy Research Institute.

Rosegrant, M. W., N. Leach, and R. V. Gerpacio. 1999. Alternative futures for world cereal and meat consumption. *Proceedings of the Nutrition Society* 58 (2): 219–34.

Rosegrant, M. W., M. S. Paisner, S. Meijer, and J. Witcover. 2001. Investment requirements: What will the costs be? In *Global food projections to 2020: Evaluating trends and alternative futures,* ed. M. W. Rosegrant, M. S. Paisner, S. Meijer, and J. Witcover. Washington, D.C.: International Food Policy Research Institute.

Rosen, B. N. 1995. Environmental product standards, trade and European consumer goods marketing: Processes, threats and opportunities. *Columbia Journal of World Business* 30: 74–86.

Rosenau, J. N. 1990. *Turbulence in world politics: A theory of change and continuity.* Princeton, N.J., U.S.A.: Princeton University Press.

Rosenberg, T. 2001. How to solve the world's AIDS crisis. *New York Times Magazine.* January 28.

Rosenzweig, M. R. 1988a. Risk, implicit contracts and the family in rural areas of low-income countries. *Economic Journal* 98 (393): 1148–70.

———. 1998b. Social learning and economic growth: Empirical evidence. Background paper for the World Development Report 1998/99. World Bank, Washington, D.C.

Rothchild, D., and N. Chazan. 1988. *The precarious balance: State and society in Africa.* Boulder, Colo.: Westview Press.

Ruggiero, R. 1999. Opening remarks to the high level symposium on trade and the environment. New York, March 15, 1999.

Runge, C. F. 1977. American agricultural assistance and the new international economic order. *World Development* 5 (8): 725–46.

———. 1981. Institutions and common property externalities: The assurance problem in economic development. Ph.D. diss. University of Wisconsin, Madison, Wisc., U.S.A.

———. 1984. Institutions and the free rider: The assurance problem in collective action. *Journal of Politics* 46 (1): 154–81.

———. 1997. Environmental protection from farm to market. Chapter 13 in *Thinking ecologically: The next generation of environmental policy,* ed. M. R. Chertow and D. C. Esty. New Haven, Conn., U.S.A.: Yale University Press.

———. 2001. A global environment organization (GEO) and the world trading system. *Journal of World Trade* 35 (4): 399–426.

Runge, C. F., and G. Fox. 1999. Issue Study 2. Feedlot production of cattle in the United States and Canada: Some environmental implications of the North American Free Trade Agreement (NAFTA). In *Assessing environmental effects of the North American Free Trade Agreement (NAFTA): An analytic framework (Phase II) and issue studies.* Montreal, Canada: Commission for Environmental Cooperation, Communications and Public Outreach Department.

Runge, C. F., and L. Jackson. 2000. Labeling, trade, and genetically modified organisms: A proposed solution. *Journal of World Trade* 33 (6): 111–22.

Runge, C. F., and B. Senauer. 2000. A removable feast. *Foreign Affairs* 79 (3): 39–51.

Runge, C. F., G.-L. Bagnara, and L. Jackson. 2001. Differing U.S. and European perspectives on GMOs: Political, economic and cultural issues. *The Estey Centre Journal of International Law and Trade Policy* 2 (2): 221–34.

Runge, C. F, F. Ortalo-Magne, and P. Vande Kamp. 1994. *Freer trade, protected environment: Balancing trade liberalization and environmental interests.* New York: Council on Foreign Relations.

Runge, C. F., E. Cap, P. Faeth, P. McGinnis, D. Papegeorgiou, J. Tobey, and R. Housman. 1997. *Sustainable trade expansion in Latin America and the Caribbean: Analysis and assessment.* Washington, D.C.: World Resources Institute.

Ruttan, V. W. 1989. Why foreign economic assistance? *Economic Development and Cultural Change* 37 (January): 411–24.

———, ed. 1993. *Why food aid?* Baltimore: Johns Hopkins University Press.

Salamon, L. M. 1994. The rise of the nonprofit sector. *Foreign Affairs* 73 (4): 109–22.

Salamon, L. M., R. List, S. W. Sokolowski, and Assoc., S. Toepler, H. K. Anheir, eds. 1999. *Global civil society: Dimensions of the nonprofit sector.* Baltimore: Johns Hopkins Comparative Nonprofit Sector Project.

Salazar-Xirinachs, J. M. 2000. The trade-labor nexus: Developing countries' perspectives. *Journal of International Economic Law* 3 (2): 377–85.

Sampson, G. P. 2000. *Trade, environment, and the WTO: The post Seattle agenda.* Policy Essay No. 27. London: Overseas Development Institute.

Sandler, T. 1997. *Global challenges: An approach to environmental, political and economic problems.* New York: Cambridge University Press.

———. 2002. Financing international public goods. In *International public goods: Incentives, measurement, and financing,* ed. M. Ferroni, and A. Mody. Norwell, Mass.: Kluwer Academic Publishers.

Schelling, T. A. 1978. *Micromotives and macrobehavior.* New York: Norton.

Schiff, S. 1999. FAO to boost third world role at WTO talks. *Feedstuffs* 71 (48): 1.

Schimmelpfennig, D., J. Lewandrowski, J. Reilly, M. Tsigas, and I. Parry. 1996. Agricultural adaptation to climate change: Issues of long run sustainability. Agricultural Economic Report Number 740. Washington, D.C.: U.S. Department of Agriculture.

Schmemann, S. 2002. Annan cautions business as forum ends. *New York Times.* February 5.

Schuh, G. E. 2000a. Developing country interests in WTO agricultural policies. Paper presented at the conference The Political Economy of International Trade, University of Minnesota, St. Paul, Minn., U.S.A., September 15–16.

———. 2000b. The household: The neglected link in research and programs for poverty alleviation. *Food Policy* 25: 233–41.

Schultz, T. P. 1994. Human capital, family planning, and their effects on population growth. *American Economic Review* 84 (2): 255–60.

Schultz, T. W. 1961. Investing in human capital. *American Economic Review* 51 (1): 1–17.

———. 1982. *Investing in people: The economics of population quality.* Berkeley, Calif.: University of California Press.

———. 1993. *The economics of being poor.* Oxford: Blackwell.

Scitovsky, T. 1992. *The joyless economy: The psychology of human satisfaction.* New York: Oxford University Press.

Seckler, D., U. Amarasinghe, D. Molden, R. de Silva, and R. Barker. 1998. World water demand and supply, 1990–2025: Scenario's and issues. Research Report 19. Colombo, Sri Lanka: International Waste Management Institute.

Sen, A. K. 1981. *Poverty and famines: An essay on entitlement and deprivation.* Oxford: Clarendon Press.

———. 1999. *Development as freedom.* New York: Alfred A. Knopf.

Sen, B. 1997. *Health and poverty in the context of country development strategy: A case study on Bangladesh.* Macroeconomics, Health and Development Series Paper No. 26. Geneva: World Health Organization.

Senauer, B., and M. Garcia. 1991. Determinants of the nutrition and health status of preschool children: An analysis with longitudinal data. *Economic Development and Cultural Change* 39 (2): 371–90.

Senauer, B., and M. Sur. 2001. Ending global hunger in the 21st century: Projections of the number of food insecure people. *Review of Agricultural Economics* 25 (Spring/Summer): 68–81.

Senauer, B., M. Garcia, and E. Jacinto. 1988. Determinants of the intrahousehold allocation of food in the rural Philippines. *American Journal of Agricultural Economics* 70 (1): 170–80.

Serageldin, I. 2001. Changing agendas for agricultural research. Chapter 2 in *Agricultural science policy: Changing global agendas,* ed. J. M. Alston, P. G. Pardey, and M. J. Taylor. Baltimore: Johns Hopkins University Press for the International Food Policy Research Institute.

Shaffer, G. C. 2001. The World Trade Organization under challenge: Democracy and the law and politics of the WTO: Treatment of trade and environment matters. *Harvard Environmental Law Review* 25 (1): 1–50.

Shane, M., L. Teigen, M. Gehlhar, and T. Roe. 2000. Economic growth and world food insecurity: A parametric approach. *Food Policy* 25 (June): 297–315.

Shapouri, S., and S. Rosen. 1999. *Food security assessment: Why countries are at risk.* Agriculture Information Bulletin No. 754. Washington D.C.: U.S. Department of Agriculture, Economic Research Service.

Shapouri, S., and M. Trueblood. 2001. Impacts of agricultural policy reforms on low-income countries. Chapter 6 in *Agricultural policy reform and the WTO: The road ahead,* ed. M. E. Burfisher. Agricultural Economic Report 802. Washington, D.C.: U.S. Department of Agriculture, Economic Research Service.

Sikkink, K. 1993. Human rights, principled issue networks, and sovereignty in Latin America. *International Organization* 47 (3): 411–31.

Simmons, P. J. 1998. Learning to live with NGOs. *Foreign Policy* (Fall): 82–95.

Skidelsky, R. 2001. *John Maynard Keynes: Fighting for Britain, 1937–1946.* New York: Viking Press.

Smil, V. 2000. *Feeding the world: A challenge for the twenty-first century.* Cambridge, Mass., U.S.A.: The MIT Press.

Smith, B. D. 1995. *The emergence of agriculture.* New York: Scientific American Library.

Smith, L. 1999. Can FAO's measures of chronic undernourishment be strengthened? Food Consumption and Nutrition Division Discussion Paper No. 44. Washington, D.C.: International Food Policy Research Institute.

Smith, L. C., and L. Haddad. 2000. Overcoming child malnutrition in developing countries: Past achievements and future choices. Food, Agriculture and the Environment Discussion Paper 30. Washington, D.C.: International Food Policy Research Institute.

Smith, N. J. H., J. T. Williams, D. L. Plucknett, and J. Talbot. 1992. *Tropical forests and their crops*. Ithaca, N.Y., U.S.A.: Comstock Publishing.

Smith, P. J. 1998. Patent rights and bilateral exchange: A cross-country analysis of U.S. exports, FDI, and licensing. Paper presented at NBER Summer Institute on International Trade and Investment, Cambridge, Mass., U.S.A., August 3–6.

Smith, V. H., M. R. Kehoe, and M. E. Cremer. 1995. The private provision of public goods: Altruism and voluntary giving. *Journal of Public Economics* 58 (1): 107–26.

Stanley, A. 1999. Charges fly in race at U.N. hunger agency. *New York Times.* November 13.

Stoufias, E., and B. McClafferty. 2001. Is Progresa working? A summary of the results of an evaluation by IFPRI. Food Consumption and Nutrition Division Discussion Paper No. 118. Washington, D.C.: International Food Policy Research Institute.

Strutt, A., and K. Anderson. 2000. Will trade liberalization harm the environment? The case of Indonesia to 2020. *Environment and Resource Economics* 17 (November): 203–32.

Svedberg, P. 1998. 841 million undernourished? On the tyranny of deriving a number. Seminar Paper No. 656. Stockholm: Institute of International Economic Studies.

Thomas, D. 1997. Incomes, expenditures, and health outcomes: Evidence on intrahousehold resource allocation. Chapter 9 in *Intrahousehold resource allocation in developing countries: Models, methods, and policy,* ed. L. Haddad, J. Hoddinott, and H. Alderman. Baltimore: Johns Hopkins University Press for the International Food Policy Research Institute.

Tilman, D., J. Fargione, B. Wolff, C. D'Antonio, A. Dobson, R. Howarth, D. Schindler, W. H. Schlesinger, D. Simberloff, D. Swackhamer. 2001. Forecasting agriculturally driven global environmental change. *Science* 292 (5515): 281–84.

Timmer, C. P. 1997. How well do the poor connect to the growth process? Consulting Assistance on Economic Reform Discussion Paper No. 178. Harvard Institute for International Development, Cambridge, Mass., U.S.A.

Traxler, G., S. Godoy-Avila, J. Falck-Zepeda, and J. de Jesús Espinoza-Arellano. 2001. Transgenic cotton in Mexico: Economic and environmental impacts. Paper presented at a consultation on Biotechnology and Rural Livelihood—Enhancing the Benefits at the International Service for National Agricultural Research, the Hague, the Netherlands.

Trebilcock, M., and J. Soloway, 2000. International trade policy and domestic food safety regulations: The case for substantial deference by the WTO dispute settlement body under the SPS Agreement. Paper presented at the conference

The Political Economy of International Trade, University of Minnesota, St. Paul, Minn., U.S.A., September 15–16.

Tribe, D. E. 1991. *Doing well by doing good.* London: Pluto Press.

UNAIDS (Joint United Nations Program on HIV/AIDS). 2000. *Report on the global HIV/AIDS epidemic.* Geneva: World Health Organization.

UN (United Nations). 2000. *2000—A better world for all: Progress towards the international development goals.* New York: United Nations.

UN, ACC/SCN (Administrative Committee on Coordination, Subcommittee on Nutrition). 1991. *Some options for improving nutrition in the 1990s, Supplement to SCN News No. 7* (mid-1991). Geneva: United Nations.

———. 2000. *Fourth report on the world nutrition situation: Nutrition through the life cycle.* Geneva: UN ACC/SCN in collaboration with the International Food Policy Research Institute and the World Health Organization.

UNDP (United Nations Development Programme). 1999a. *Human development report 1999.* Oxford: Oxford University Press.

———. 1999b. *Reinventing global governance for humanity and equity.* New York: Oxford University Press.

UNFPA (United Nations Population Fund). 2001. *The state of world population 2001.* New York: United Nations.

UN, Population Division. 1998. *World population growth from year 0 to 2050.* New York: United Nations.

UN, Population Division, Department of Economic and Social Affairs. 1998. World population nearing 6 billion: Projected close to 9 billion by 2050. <http://www.un.org> accessed October 20, 1999.

———. 1999a. Long-range population projections: Based on the 1998 revision. <http://www.un.org> accessed October 20, 1999.

———. 1999b. *The world at six billion.* New York: United Nations.

———. 2000. Long-range population projections: Based on the 1998 revision. New York: United Nations. <http://www.un.org> accessed October 20, 1999.

———. 2001. *World population projections—The 2000 revision: Highlights.* New York: United Nations.

USAID (U.S. Agency for International Development). 2000. USAID's global development alliance. <http://www.usaid.gov> accessed July 3, 2001.

———. 2001. International affairs budget authority tracker: FY 1999–2002. <http://www.usaid.gov> accessed October 22, 2001.

———. 2003. Initiative to cut hunger in Africa. <http://www.usaid.gov> accessed February 3, 2003.

U.S. Bureau of Census. 2001. *Statistical abstract of the United States: 121st edition.* Washington D.C.: U.S. Government Printing Office.

USDA (U.S. Department of Agriculture). 1947. Miscellaneous Publication No. 630. Washington, D.C.

USDA, ERS (U. S. Department of Agriculture, Economic Research Service). 1999. *Food security assessment,* GFA 11. Washington, D.C.: ERS.

USDA, FAS (U.S. Department of Agriculture, Foreign Agricultural Service). 2002. Programmed U.S. food aid for FY2001: Region by country summary. <http//:www.fas.usda.gov/excredits/quarterly/2001/2001-aid.pdf> accessed July 2002.

USDA, NASS (U.S. Department of Agriculture, National Agricultural Statistical

Service). 2000. *Milk production, disposition and Income: 1999 Summary.* Washington, D.C.: NASS.

———. 2001. *Trends in U.S. agriculture: A walk through the past and a step into the new millennium.* Washington, D.C.: NASS. <http://www.usda.gov/nass/pubs/trends/index.htm> accessed June 2001 and December 2001.

U.S. House of Representatives Subcommittee on Basic Research. 2000. Seeds of opportunity: An assessment of the benefits, safety, and oversight of plant genomics and agricultural biotechnology. Report prepared by Chairman Nick Smith, April 13. <http://www.house.gov/science/smithreport_041300.pdf>.

Victor, D. G., and C. F. Runge. 2002a. Farming the genetic frontier. *Foreign Affairs* 81(3): 107–21.

———. 2002b. *Sustaining a revolution: A policy strategy for crop engineering.* New York: Council on Foreign Relations.

von Braun, J., T. Teklu, and P. Webb. 1998. *Famine in Africa: Causes, responses, and prevention.* Baltimore: Johns Hopkins University Press for the International Food Policy Research Institute.

von Braun, J., H. Bouis, S. Kumar, and R. Pandya-Lorch. 1992. *Improving food security of the poor: Concept, policy, and programs.* Washington, D.C.: International Food Policy Research Institute.

von Hayek, F. A. 1991. *Economic freedom.* Oxford: Basil Blackwell.

Wackernagel, M., N. B. Schulz, D. Deumling, A. C. Linares, M. Jenkins, V. Kapos, C. Monfreda, J. Loh, N. Myers, R. Norgaard, and J. Randers. 2002. Tracking the ecological overshoot of the human economy. *Proceedings of the National Academy of Sciences* 99 (14): 9266–71.

Wade, R. 2001. Global inequality: Winners and losers. *The Economist.* April 28: 72–74.

Wahid, A. 1999. The Grameen Bank and women in Bangladesh. *Challenge* (September-October): 94–101.

Walt, G. 1998. Globalization of international health. *Lancet* 351 (February 7): 434–38.

Wasow, B. 2000. New world, bum deal? *Foreign Affairs* (Letters to the Editor) 79 (4): 168–69.

Waterfield, C. 1985. Disaggregating food consumption parameters: Designing targeted nutrition interventions. *Food Policy* 10 (November): 337–51.

WCD (World Commission on Dams) 2000. *Dams and development: A new framework for decision-making.* London: Earthscan Publications.

White, P. 1999. The role of UN specialized agencies in complex emergencies: A case study of FAO. *Third World Quarterly* 20 (1): 223–38.

WHO (World Health Organization). 1999. *World health report 1999: Making a difference.* Geneva: WHO.

———. 2002. *Report of the commission on macroeconomics and health.* Geneva: WHO.

Wolfe, D. 1996. Potential impact of climate change on agriculture and food supply. In *Sustainable development and global climate change: Conflicts and connections,* ed. J. White, W. R. Wagner, and W. H. Petry. Proceedings of a conference sponsored by the Center for Environmental Information, Washington, D.C., December 4–5, 1995. Washington, D.C.: Published with the assistance of the U.S. Global Change Research Program.

Wood, S., K. Sebastian, and S. J. Scherr. 2000. Pilot analysis of global ecosystems: Agroecosystems. Washington D.C.: International Food Policy Research Institute and World Resources Institute. <http://www.ifpri.org> and <http://www.wri.org/wr2000>.

World Bank. 1986. *Poverty and hunger: Issues and options for food security in developing countries.* Washington, D.C.: World Bank.

———. 1990. *World development report 1990: Poverty.* New York: Oxford University Press.

———. 1993. *World development report 1993: Investing in health.* Washington, D.C.: Oxford University Press.

———. 1997. *World development report 1997: The state in a changing world.* Washington, D.C.: World Bank.

———. 1999. Poverty Web site: <http://www.worldbank.org/poverty>.

———. 2000a. *Annual report 2000.* Washington, D.C.: World Bank. <http://www.worldbank.org>.

———. 2000b. *A better world for all: Progress towards the international development goals.* Washington, D.C.: World Bank.

———. 2000c. *Global commodity markets: A comprehensive review and price forecast.* Development prospects group, commodities team. Washington, D.C.: World Bank.

———. 2000d. *World development indicators 2000.* Washington, D.C.: Oxford University Press.

———. 2001a. *Engendering development through gender equality in rights, resource, and voice.* World Bank Policy Research Report. Washington, D.C.: World Bank.

———. 2001b. *Global economic prospects and the developing countries.* World Bank Policy Study. Washington, D.C.: World Bank.

———. 2001c. *Statistical information management analysis database.* Washington, D.C.: World Bank.

———. 2001d. *World development report 2000/2001: Attacking poverty.* Washington, D.C.: Oxford University Press.

———. 2002a. *Draft rural strategy: Reaching the rural poor.* Washington, D.C.: World Bank. <http://lnweb18.worldbank.org/ESSD/essdext.nsf/11ByDocName/Strategy>.

———. 2002b. Reaching the MDG's to cost $40–60 billion annually in additional aid, says bank. <http://www.worldbank.org> accessed February 2002.

———. 2002c. *World development indicators 2002.* Washington, D.C.: World Bank, subscribers version.

Wright, B. D. 1997. Crop genetic resource policy: The role of ex situ genebanks. *Australian Journal of Agricultural and Resource Economics* 14 (1): 81–115.

Yusuf, S. 2001. Globalization and the challenge for developing countries. Policy Research Working Paper No. 2618. Washington, D.C.: World Bank.

Zeller, M., M. Sharma, A. U. Ahmed, and S. Rashid. 2001. *Group-based financial institutions for the rural poor in Bangladesh: An Institutional and household level analysis.* Research Report No. 120. Washington, D.C.: International Food Policy Research Institute.

Zimmerman, R. 2001. A shot in the arm: How Bill Gates brings his business tactics to vaccinating the poor. *Wall Street Journal.* December 3.

INDEX

Page numbers for entries occurring in figures are followed by an *f;* those for entries occurring in notes, by an *n;* and those for entries occurring in tables, by a *t.*